THE CLEMSON TIGERS

From 1896 To Glory

BY LOU SAHADI

WILLIAM MORROW AND COMPANY, INC.

New York   1983

Library of Congress Catalog Card Number: 83-61792

ISBN: 0-688-02164-6

Printed in the United States of America

First Edition

1 2 3 4 5 6 7 8 9 10

To Frank Howard who started it;
Danny Ford who kept it going;
B. C. Inabinet, who is what Clemson is all about;
And to Bob Bradley, who knows all about hush puppies and fried chicken;
Most of all to the most loyal followers of all, the Clemson fans.

The author wishes to thank the following for their invaluable assistance in the voluminous research required in compiling this book, namely, Bob Bradley, Tim Bourret, Kim Kelly, Al Bynum, Jeff Rhodes, Jill Mixon, Cricket Yates, and Sam Blackman. Finally, to Bruce Lee and Elizabeth Terhune, two dedicated editors who labored tirelessly to make certain the printed word was perfectly constructed, and especially to Gerry Repp who designed the material day and night against a tight deadline a few months after Lila Karpf came up with the idea of this book in the first place.

Photo Credits: Color and black and white photographs courtesy of Clemson Sports Publicity Department; Charles C. Hucks, Jr. Pages 170, 172, 174, 175, 176, 179, 180, 181, 183, 184, 188.

CONTENTS

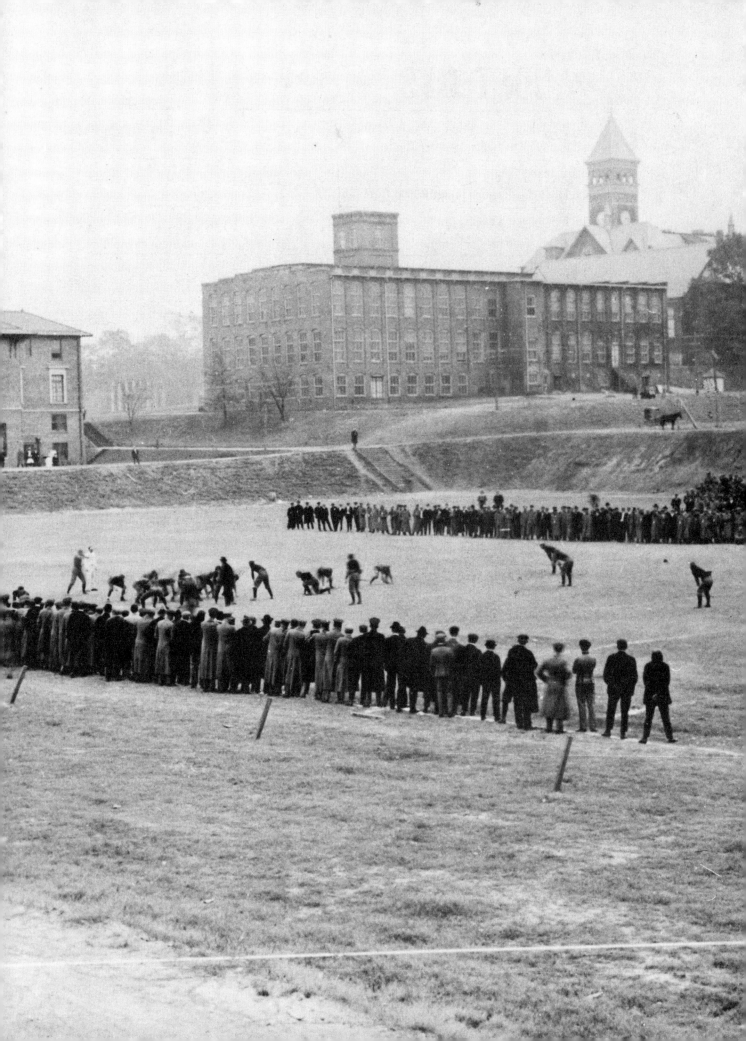

THE EARLY YEARS

"Horny-Handed Sons of Toil"

Life seems to have a slower pace at Clemson, a sleepy town located in the lush hills of Western South Carolina with its large man-made lake called Hartwell Reservoir. During most of the year there are more students than townspeople; and when school is out, no one in the town appears to hurry in this idyllic, rustic setting. It hasn't been too many years since Highway 93 was carved out of the red clay Carolina soil, the paving laid, and Clemson linked to the outside world by a four-lane highway. Even then, travelers have had a hard time finding it on the map. The Holiday Inn, Pixie & Bill's, two filling stations, and a small shopping center, plus a traffic light, represented the approach to the town in its entirety. Only recently has the town's skyline changed with the addition of a Ramada Inn. Why then is the reason the name of Clemson is known far and wide across our great nation? The answer: football.

For nearly a century the Clemson Tigers have been a team to reckon with. Today the town boasts 8,000 residents. The University enrolls 11,000 students, but it is the Tigers who are number one.

Clemson first opened its doors in 1893 as a small, land-grant college. Two strong-willed individuals were responsible for its start. One was Ben Tillman, who was governor of the state throughout most of the 1890's. A colorful, suspenders-wearing individual, Tillman was more popularly known as "Pitchfork Ben" because of his deep sentiments for the country and farm people of the state. He looked upon South Carolina University in Columbia, which was then nearly one hundred years old, as a center of vanity and snobbery, and he made his feelings known around the state. His spirited speeches attracted the support of Tom Clemson, the son-in-law of John C. Calhoun, who had been Vice President of the United States for eight years, 1825-1832, under President Andrew Jackson. Originally from Abbeville, South Carolina, Calhoun had an 800-acre plantation called Fort Hill. After Calhoun's death in 1850, Tom Clemson acquired the plantation and used it to create the college campus. Spurred by Tillman's criticism of South Carolina University, Clemson generously offered not only to provide land but money as well for a new state school for agricultural and military education. Clemson was granted military status by the federal government. Students completing their military

Riggs Field at the turn of the century. It was named after professor W. M. Riggs who coached Clemson's first football team in 1896.

Clemson's first football team in 1896. Front row, from left: Frank Tompkins; A. M. Chreitzburg; J. D. Maxwell; R. G. Hamilton (Captain); and C. W. Gentry. Middle row, from left: J. M. Blaine; J. T. Hanvey; W. K. Howze; G. H. Swygert; L. L. Hendricks; A. S. Shealy; and George Hanvey. Top row, from left: C. K. Chreitzburg; Jim White; Jack Mathis; Coach W. M. Riggs; J. A. Stone; Theo Vogel; W. M. Brock.

requirements would receive a lieutenant's rank and could join the army as a regular or maintain a reserve commission should they decide to remain in civilian life. Those pursuing the military curriculum would be required to attend class in uniform. It was all that Tillman needed. With the legislature's approval, he removed Carolina's agricultural and mechanical schools and reestablished them at Clemson. He practically reduced South Carolina University to a shell, and it was then reorganized as South Carolina College. When Clemson opened its doors in 1893, 466 students enrolled while South Carolina's student body dwindled to 72 the same year. Thus, the bitter seed of the Clemson-South Carolina rivalry was sown and never forgotten by supporters of South Carolina. The almost century-old rivalry is vividly portrayed today by the chant of Carolina football fans: "Agriculture, horticulture, A. B. Law, Clemson, Clemson, Sow, Cow, Sow."

Clemson fielded its first football team in 1896. That September, a group of 30 students met in the Barracks to organize the Football Association. An early supporter of their efforts was Professor W. M. Riggs, who had played the sport as an undergraduate at Auburn College in Alabama. Riggs coached the football team that year; surprisingly, Clemson won two of the three games they played. They opened with a 14-6 victory over Furman; lost to South Carolina, 12-6; and then ended the season with a 16-0 triumph over Wofford. Riggs was assisted by another professor, R. V. T. Bowman, in whose honor Bowman Field was named several years later.

Although 30 students had tried out for the team, only 21 made it. They were J. M. Blain, W. T. Brock, A. M. Chreitzberg, C. K. Chreitzberg, C. W. Gentry, R. G. Hamilton, J. T. Harvey. L. I. Hendrick, W. K. Howze, G. G. Legare, A. J. Mathis, J. D. Maxwell, J. A. Parks, E. S. Pegues, A. S. Shealy, J. A. Stone, J. F. Sullivan, G. H. Swygert, F. G. Thompkins, R. T. Vogel, and J. D. White.

The next year though, in 1897, the students felt that Riggs, who had coached without any remuneration, should devote his entire time to academics. It was also agreed that a full-time football coach should be hired. M. W. Wil-

7

Statue of Thomas Green Clemson.

The old Agriculture Building in 1910.

liams coached Clemson that year and finished with a 2-2 record. In 1898, J. A. Payton, an assistant coach at Auburn, was hired as coach. After an opening defeat to Georgia, Clemson finished with three straight victories.

However, due to a lack of funds, Riggs was back coaching in 1899. There was no lack of victories. Clemson won its first four games before losing to Georgia and Auburn. In only four years while football was still in its infancy on the peaceful, rolling campus, Clemson had done well. Tillman was proud of them. He referred to the students as "horny-handed sons of toil." Most of the student body had labored as farmers before entering college. They were rugged individuals, playing without headgear and only a little padding at the elbows and knees. Few had nose or shin guards. The uni-

forms were tightly fitted and made of a canvas fabric. Since they didn't have helmets and wore their hair long, the players could have been called Lions. However, the orange and purple striped jerseys and stockings that they wore resembled Tigers, which they were nicknamed.

Riggs, however, was still primarily needed for his ability as an administrator and faculty member. He was, in fact, in later years to become president of Clemson. So after the 1899 season, a large meeting was held on December 7 which resulted in the creation of the Football Aid Society. The Society was the forerunner to the Clemson College Athletic Association. Its sole purpose was to aid the football program, and its primary objective was to secure a coach for the 1900 season. B. H. Rawl

8

was elected the Society's first president and W. G. Hill, secretary-treasurer. When the Society met a second time, it generated its first monies. A total of 132 people pledged $372.50 within an hour. A ways and means committee was also appointed with the objective of raising additional funds.. The Society had the full support of Riggs. He spoke at the meeting:

"So long as the game of football helps to make better men of our students, stronger in body, more active in mind—men full of energy, enthusiasm, and an indomitable personal courage; men not easily daunted by obstacles or opposition; who control their tempers and restrain their appetites, who can deal honorably with a vanquished adversary and can take victory moderately and defeat without bitterness.

"And so long as football properly controlled and regulated helps the student in his college duties, instead of hindering him; gives zest and pleasure to college life, makes name and fame for the college on account of victories won, not only by skill and prowess of the team on the gridiron but by their gentlemanly conduct in the streets of the town they play, in the hotels where they quarter, and on the trains.

"So long as it helps to bring about a closer bond of sympathy between students and members of the faculty by creating a common interest apart from the routine duties—so long as in all these ways the best interests of this and other colleges are advanced, and in the course of education aided in its highest mission, which is to make the best men out of the ma-

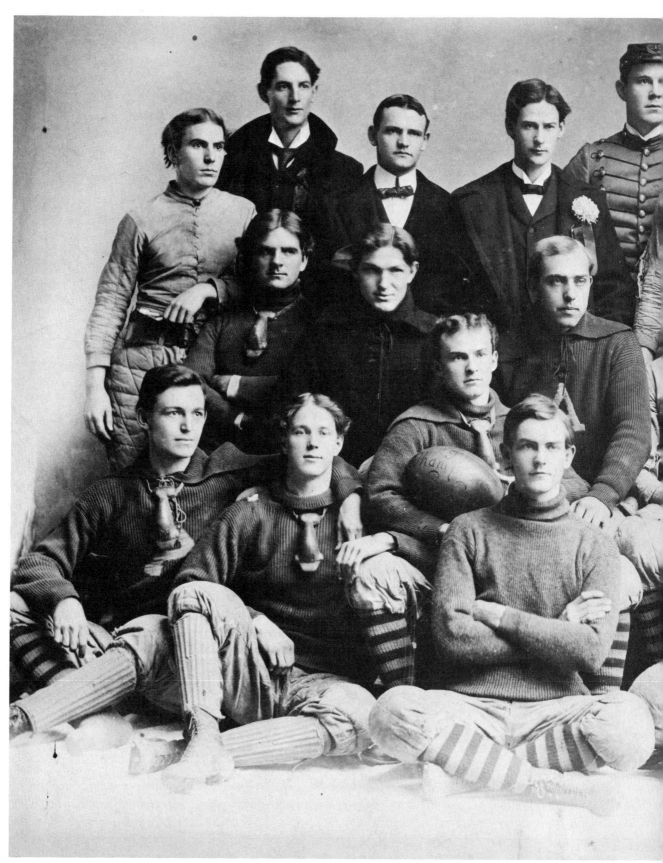

The 1897 Clemson football team. Front row from left: Sullivan; Maxwell; Brock; Vogel; Gentry and Shealy. Middle row, from left: Hendrix; Walker; Swygert; G. Hanvey and J. Hanvey. Top row, from left: Ansel; Bowman (referee); Williams (coach); Riggs (coach); Chreitzberg (manager); Garland; LaBoon and Duckworth.

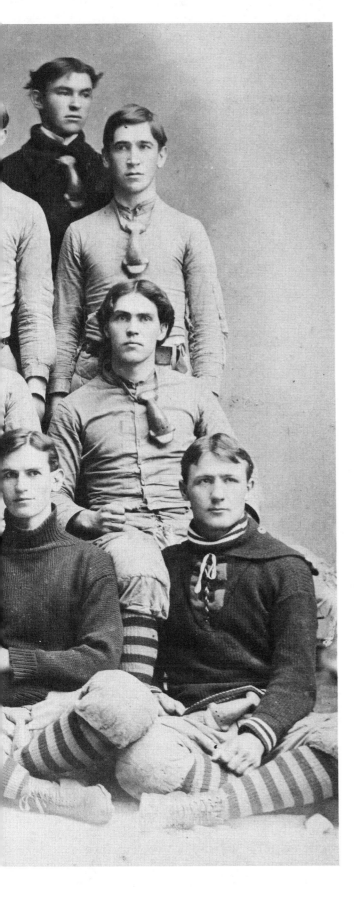

terial at hand, so long we will say for the game of football, long may it live and prosper."

Riggs then went on and looked to Auburn again for a coach. For the third consecutive time he got one. He succeeded in bringing a budding genius, John Heisman, to Clemson. In the four years that Heisman coached there, Clemson became a football power in the south.

Heisman was a northerner, born of German parents in Pennsylvania. His real given name was Johann Wilhelm, but he changed that to John William when he attended Brown and later the University of Pennsylvania before the turn of the 20th century. A new game called football was beginning to become popular on the campuses of colleges in the east and north. It interested Heisman immensely. After playing at both Brown and Pennsylvania, Heisman was so obsessed with the game that he started coaching at Oberlin College in 1892. In his first season there, Heisman produced an undefeated team. He coached at Akron University in 1893 and the following year returned to Oberlin. However, in 1895 he was lured south to Auburn.

It was that same year that Heisman became infatuated with the possibilities of a forward pass, which was an illegal play during the formative years of the game. He saw it used for the first time while scouting a game between North Carolina and Georgia. While getting ready to punt, the North Carolina kicker was surrounded by Georgia linemen and couldn't get his kick off. Instead, he inadvertently threw the ball towards a teammate who caught it and ran 70 yards for the game's only touchdown. The Georgia players screamed in protest but to no avail. The referee admitted that he hadn't seen the ball thrown and allowed the touchdown. In the years ahead, Heisman championed for the legalization of the forward pass by the Football Rules Committee. In the meantime, he improvised by making use of a lateral. It was the second innovation that Heisman had developed. Years before, he had instituted the center snap a year before Amos Alonzo Stagg of the University of Chicago introduced it. Heisman produced strong teams at Auburn in the five years he was there.

The arrival of Heisman at Clemson in 1900

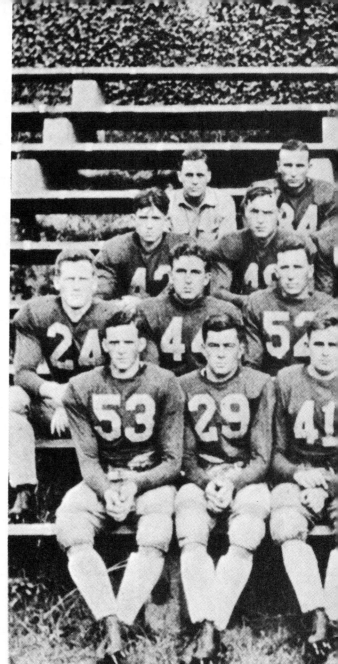

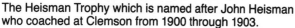
The Heisman Trophy which is named after John Heisman who coached at Clemson from 1900 through 1903.

began what was called the "Golden Age" of football. In its very first game under Heisman, Clemson routed Davidson, 64-0. The Tigers didn't stop there and went on to defeat Wofford, 21-0; South Carolina, 51-0; Georgia, 39-5; V.P.I., 12-5; and Alabama, 35-0. In winning all six of its games, Clemson recorded its first undefeated season, thoroughly outscoring its opponents, 222-10.

Heisman was a perfectionist. One of his ingenious characteristics was in originating plays. Only rarely did he ever use the same play twice. He didn't have any patience with players who were not bright and couldn't

quickly learn his signal system or intricate tactics. For that reason, he barely substituted during games, making use of only three or four reserves at most. Heisman demanded that his players remain in excellent physical shape to play the expected 70 minutes of football required back then.

The following year, in 1901, Clemson finished with a 3-1-1 record. After opening with a 6-6 tie against Tennessee, Clemson stampeded Guilford, 122-0, which remains today as the most points ever scored by a Tiger football team. The Tigers went on to beat Georgia, 29-5; lost to V.P.I., 17-11; and closed out the

12

The 1930 team finished with an 8-2 record, the best since 1906.
It also marked Josh Cody's final season as coach after four years.

season with a 22-10 victory over North Carolina. The next year Clemson was 6-1, with its only loss occurring in the middle of the season, 12-6, to South Carolina. In between Clemson defeated North Carolina State, 11-5; Georgia Tech, 44-5; Furman, 28-0; Georgia, 36-0; Auburn, 16-0; and Tennessee, 11-0.

The 1902 team was considered the best that Heisman produced. The ploy he used that season before the Georgia Tech game was perhaps the cleverest ruse in the school's history. A day before the game, Heisman dispatched a group of cadets into Atlanta, masquerading as the Clemson football team. He gave them in-

structions to live it up around town and make certain that they were visible to Georgia Tech officials. They carried out their mission unfailingly. Not only were they seen, but they were entertained by the partisan local citizens. Since the supposed Clemson football players partied until the late hours, Tech was confident of an easy win the next day.

However, on game day, Heisman arrived with his team. They had spent the night in Lula, Georgia, a small railroad stop north of Atlanta. Clemson easily disposed of the stunned Tech eleven, 44-5.

The following season was to be Heisman's

Quarterback Don King (1952-'55) led Clemson in passing, rushing, punting and punt returns in 1953.

last at Clemson. In 1903, the Tigers went 4-1-1, defeating Georgia, 29-0; Georgia Tech, 73-0; North Carolina State 24-0; and Davidson, 24-0. They lost to North Carolina, 11-6, and were tied by Cumberland in Heisman's final game as coach, 6-6.

Once again Georgia Tech was victimized by Heisman's cunning. Vet Sitton, Clemson's left end who had played so brilliantly against Tech the year before, was nursing an injury. When word reached Atlanta that he would not be able to play, Tech officials displayed guarded optimism. They felt that Heisman was trying to fool them a second time. What they didn't know was that Heisman had an extremely capable substitute in Gil Ellison. Although Ellison wasn't as fast as Sitton, he was bigger and stronger; and his play against Tech helped

fashion the easy 73-0 victory. The win brought an extra reward to Clemson. The University of Georgia team had made a deal with the Clemson players, offering them a bushel of apples for every point they would defeat Tech above the score Clemson made against them, which was 29. The Tigers ended up with 44 bushels of apples that fall.

They also lost Heisman. Georgia Tech was determined to get him as coach. They lured him with an offer of $2,250 a year, plus 30% of the gate receipts after expenses. The financial possibilities far exceeded the $1,800 Heisman was making at Clemson. But Heisman had stamped an indelible mark on Clemson football. He compiled a 19-3-2 record, winning 85% of his games. It still ranks as the highest winning percentage in Clemson

14

history.

Before he left to begin a long career at Georgia Tech, Heisman was asked to name his All-Heisman Team, along with his philosophy of coaching. The depth of his genius can be easily recognized in the story he submitted for publication in the 1903 annual of The Oconeean, the Clemson yearbook. Heisman wrote:

"It is hardly an exaggeration to say that the possibilities in the scientific development of the game of football are only beginning to be realized. Perfection was supposed to have been attained a dozen years ago; but each successive season since has witnessed the invention of new plays and improved systems of offense and defense, until now the game is as far ahead of what it was a decade ago as the elec-

tric car is ahead of the old time stage coach. Each college now aims to have a style of play of its own, and so many and various have these systems—particularly of offensive play—become, that no one defensive formation will suffice to meet the attack of all the teams on a season's schedule, as was formerly the case.

"This state of affairs has created a greater demand than ever before for scientific and original coaches—coaches who can devise plays that will gain ground in spite of the best and most up-to-date knowledge of the principles of defense, and who, when confronted by the exigency, can invent defensive combinations to stop the most powerful and puzzling attack, when that attack is known and understood; yet, at the same time, leaving no weak or unguarded spots for unexpected or surprise assaults. Naturally enough, then, not all good players make good coaches. To play one position well under competent instruction is one thing; but to understand all positions and combine them in effective formations is quite a difficult thing. Beyond this still remains the necessity on the part of the coach for an ability to impart his own knowledge, to inspire his men, to keep them in good physical condition, to adjust the development of his team to the varying demands of schedules oft changed; and, finally, to study his men individually and know of what each is personally capable. In the light of these required qualifications, it is small wonder that successful coaches—i.e., those who can consistently turn out winning teams year after year no matter what the obstacles and conditions—are few and far between, and when found it is equally small wonder that they command salaries practically without limit.

"At Clemson we have a style of football play radically different from any other on earth. Its notoriety and the fear and admiration of it have spread throughout the length and breadth of the entire Southern world of football and even further. There is not a single offensive play used that was ever learned from any other college, nor are the defensive formations any less different than those of other teams. Three wonderfully successful seasons of 'Heisman Football' have served to establish

Jess Neely, who coached from 1931-'39, talks with some of his players, from left, Don Willis; Red Pearson; Bob Bailey and Dan Coleman.

16

the system as Clemson's traditional policy of play. All colleges should have fixed athletic traditions and should be loyal to them as to the institution itself; and to the complete unity and harmony of athletic opinion and sentiment existing at Clemson is due no small share of the credit of her glorious athletic record.

"I have often been asked to select from all the teams that I have coached an All-Heisman Eleven, and I will here endeavor to make such a selection. The task will be no easy one, for in the course of eleven years of coaching many more than eleven times eleven players have come under my instruction, and of this great number it may perhaps be said that none were poor (else they came in for little or no instruction), few were ordinary, nearly all were good, and some were great.

"The teams I coached and, therefore, have to select from, are the Oberlin College (Ohio) teams of '92 and '94; the Bucknell College (Ohio) team of '93; the Auburn (Ala.) teams of '95, '96, '97, '98, and '99; and the Clemson (S. Car.) teams of '00, '01, and '02. No two of these teams were coached in exactly similar systems. The changes of play from year to year were frequently startlingly marked, and players who did exceptionally good work under one system might not have been so fortunate under the system of a different season; but as I invariably make my plays conform to the needs and abilities of the players I have on hand (not the players to the plays), I would anticipate no difficulty in evolving a system to suit the eleven best men. Such a team would be as follows:

John Heisman was the most successful coach in Clemson history, compiling a four year record of 19-3-2.

SECOND ELEVEN

Position	Player	Team
Right End	Merriam	Oberlin '92
Right Tackle	Walker	Clemson '00
Right Guard	Forsythe	Clemson '02
Center	Culver	Auburn '95
Left Guard	Harvey	Auburn '96
Left Tackle	Wise	Bucknell '93
Left End	Fauver	Oberlin '94
Quarterback	Huguley	Auburn '99
Right Half	Stokes	Auburn '97
Left Half	Pearman	Clemson '01
Fullback	Shafer	Auburn '95"

The Golden Age that had begun with Heisman lasted until 1907, and Clemson became a gridiron force. In seven years the Tigers won 33, lost only 12, and tied seven games while outscoring their opponents, 967 to 249. Shack Shealy followed Heisman in 1904, and in the one year he coached had a 3-3-1 record. E. B. Cochems took over; and he, too, lasted only a year and produced a 3-2-1 mark. Bob Williams coached in 1906 and turned in a 4-0-3 record. In 1907, young Frank Shaughnessy, who later went on to become one of the nation's most respected coaches, had a 4-4 record. After that season, Clemson's football fortunes sank into what has been described as the

ALL HEISMAN ELEVEN

Position	Player	Team
Right End	Sitton	Clemson '02
Right Tackle	Pierce	Auburn '97
Right Guard	Vann	Auburn '97
Center	Mitcham	Auburn '98
Left Guard	Glenn	Auburn '95
Left Tackle	Teeters	Oberlin '92
Left End	Johnson	Oberlin '92
Quarterback (Capt.)	Williams	Oberlin '92
Right Half	Hunter	Clemson '01
Left Half	Williams	Auburn '96
Fullback	Penton	Auburn '97

Dark Ages. During a span of almost two decades, Clemson had a 69-82-10 record.

The downfall began in 1908 with the Pendleton Escapade. On April 1 of that year, 306 cadets were expelled for a prank they took part in. What the free spirited cadets had done was to remove a Civil War cannon from the town square of Pendleton, which was four miles up the road, and bring the relic back to Clemson. It was considered to be conduct unbecoming of future officers. Many of the football stars as well as future star players were among those who were expelled.

Yet, it was during the so-called Dark Ages of Clemson football that the school's anthem was created. It resulted from adversity, or perhaps better yet, embarrassment, during the final months of World War I when Clemson's cadets, who were part of a Reserve Officers Training Corps during the war, were on maneuvers with other college officers in Plattsburg, New York, in 1918. During an assembly of the young trainees, each college was asked to sing its alma mater. At the time, Clemson didn't have one. Instead, they reverted to a number of cheers that were used during foot-

McFADDEN STAR AS TIGERS TAKE TRACK EVENT

CLEMSON WINS STATE CONTEST

Bonnie Banks Sets Three New Records—Little Of U. S. C. Second

CAROLINA SECOND

CLINTON, May 4.—(P)—Banks McFadden of Clemson shattered three records here high scoring honors with 24 1-4 points and led his team to the championship of the state track meet today. The Tigers amassed 54 points.

LITTLE ALSO STARS

McFadden was forced to share the limelight, though, for Little of the University of South Carolina won the century and 220 dashes and took seconds in the low hurdles and broad jump to score 16 points. Davis of Presbyterian pulled the "iron man" stunt by winning the ball mile and two-mile runs. Presnell of Clemson claimed a share of the glory by setting a new record in the pole vault.

Second to Clemson in team standings was the University of South Carolina with 29 points. Citadel was third with 25. Presbyterian and Furman tied for fourth with 19 1-2. Newberry was sixth with 14 and Wofford seventh with 2.

McFadden set a new broad jump record in the preliminary trials when he jumped 23 feet 3 7-8 inches to erase the record which Little set in 1936 at 22 feet 11 1-2 inches. He galloped the 220-yard low hurdles in 25.9 seconds to better the mark Fuger of Clemson set at 24.1 on 1936. McFadden tied two the 120-yard high hurdles in 14.6, bettering the mark which Fuger set in 15 seconds in 1936.

PRESNELL SETS MARK

Presnell of Clemson vaulted 12 feet 6 5-8 inches bettering the mark Fuger of Clemson set at 12 feet 4 inches in 1932.

In amassing his high score McFadden won both the high and low hurdles and broad jump, placed third in the shot put and ran on the winning relay team.

LITTLE, Carolina

McFADDEN, Clemson

McFadden not only excelled on the gridiron, but he also starred in basketball and track. He was the school's first All-American in both football and basketball.

Banks McFadden starred for Clemson in 1937-'39 and led the Tigers to their first bowl game, the 1940 Cotton Bowl.

19

Jess Neely, top left, coached Clemson for nine years, 1931-'39.
Standing next to him is Frank Howard, who took over as head coach in 1940.

20

ball games. Albert C. Corcoran, a junior from Charleston, was humiliated and never forgot that moment. After returning to Clemson, he worked for several months compiling appropriate words for an alma mater. In 1919, during his senior year, he revealed his words to The Tiger, Clemson's student newspaper, which published them. They are:

"Where the Blue Ridge yawns its
    greatness
  Where the Tigers play,
Here the sons of dear old Clemson
  Reign supreme always.
Dear old Clemson we will tiumph,
  And with all our might,
That the Tiger's roar may echo
  O'er the mountain height.
We will dream of greater conquests
  For our past is grand
And her sons have fought and
    conquered
  Every foreign land.
When the mountains smile in
    grandeur
  O'er the hill and dale,
Here the Tiger lair is nestling
  Swept by storm and gale.
We are brothers strong in manhood
  For we work and strive
And old Alma Mater reigneth
  Ever in our lives."

There was only one problem. There wasn't any music to sing with the words. School officials decided the best remedy would be to utilize the music of Cornell's Alma Mater, "Above Cayuga's Waters." It was sung to that melody for some 35 years until Dr. John Butler, who became head of the Clemson music department, composed the melody that is used today.

When Josh Cody became coach in 1927, Clemson began to become a positive force in football once again. Although he had been a star tackle at Vanderbilt University, and a second team All-American there his final year in 1919, Cody never had been a head coach until he arrived at Clemson. Yet, in his very first season, Cody brought an end to three straight losing years by leading Clemson to a 5-3-1 record. It was only the beginning. In the next three years, Clemson was 8-3, 8-3, and 8-2 and

Captain Frank Jervey has been involved with Clemson athletics since before World War I.

appeared well on the way towards a winning program with a 24-8 record. Cody had defeated South Carolina all four years; and many historians felt that his 1930 team, which lost only to Tennessee and Florida, was the best in the school's history.

However, the success on the football field did not carry over into the athletic department. During his final two years, Cody became involved in a power struggle with athletic director J. G. Mutt Gee, who had been a center on the 1914-17 Clemson teams. The bad blood was the result of an awkward situation. As athletic director, Gee received $3,000 a year and was Cody's boss. However, Gee also worked as a line coach on the football staff. Gee not only received an additional $3,000 but in that capacity had to answer to Cody. Cody emerged as the power and took over both the head coaching and athletic director's positions.

Just before the start of the 1931 season, Cody returned to Vanderbilt as coach of his alma mater. The Clemson football program was in shambles. The equipment was poor,

Clemson Memorial Stadium in 1951.

and the athletic department was in debt. Yet, before he left, Cody had developed such Clemson stars as Henry W. Asbill, J. Craig, A. D. Fordham, R. M. "Fattso" Hall, L. C. Harvin, Bob Jones, Johnny Justus, Goat McMillan, O. D. Padgett, O. K. Pressley, D. F. Sowell, Bob Swofford, Maxey Welch, Foggy Woodruff, and Mike Yarborough.

When Jess Neely arrived for the 1931 season, he began by shaking his head. Like Cody, Neely was also from Vanderbilt. However, after his graduation, he had coached at Southwestern of Memphis for four years before joining coach Wallace Wade's staff at Alabama. When Wade left to take over at Duke, Neely came to Clemson, probably wishing he had made use of his law degree instead. Not only was the debt and inferior football equipment obviously a glaring fact, but Neely didn't have much of a team. Graduation claimed many of the players, and it was far too late to even attempt any form of recruiting. The players who were left from Cody's final season were subjected to shabby locker rooms and

poor coaching facilities. The alumni didn't appear the least bit concerned. They were satisfied that Cody had defeated South Carolina four straight times and Furman in three of the four years.

It took only one season for the alumni to realize the poor condition of the football program. Neely could only manage a 1-6-2 in 1931. The weak record was further magnified by the realization that Clemson had scored only three touchdowns the entire season. Undismayed, Neely told Captain Frank Jervey that if he could get about ten thousand dollars, he could field a competitive football team. It took seven years for Neely to upgrade Clemson's football program. The breakthrough came in 1938 when Clemson went 7-1-1. In Neely's last season the following year, Clemson was 9-1, losing only to Tulane by a single point, 7-6. More important, Clemson received the first post-season bowl invitation in its history when it was invited to play Boston in the Cotton Bowl. Banks McFadden, the team's star running back who later played professional football with the Brooklyn Dodgers, remembered the team's long trip to Dallas. It was the longest trip any football team had ever made in the history of Clemson. McFadden smiled at the memories one day at the Intramural Building where he directs Clemson's intramural sports program. He sat back on a sofa in his office and recalled Clemson's first bowl game.

"We were happy that we were selected to play," McFadden said. "Of course, nobody knew anything about Clemson then and Boston College was well known in the east. We had to make the trip by train which would take two days. We had a very humorous guy on the team named Goon Miller. He was always looking for a way to make money. On some of our other trips, he'd slip over to the grocery store and buy about three dozen apples. Then, he'd shine them up and after the train got going, he'd walk up and down the aisle and we'd all get hungry looking at him. He'd charge us 10¢ each when back then you could buy three or four apples for a nickel, but we didn't mind.

"However, on the trip to Dallas, we were scheduled to eat in the dining car. This was a whole new experience for the team. Captain Holcombe, who was in charge of the dining hall at the college, loaded about three bushels of apples on the train. Goon didn't know a thing about it. He did his usual number and went to the grocery store before we boarded the train, only this time he bought three big bags for the long trip. About halfway to Atlanta, Goon starts walking up and down the aisle doing his apple routine. This time nobody paid attention to him. He couldn't figure out why. Slowly, we all started to the dining car and each one of us came back eating an apple. Goon got upset and wondered where all the apples came from. He was stuck with about five dozen of them. Near the end of the trip he reduced the price to a nickel, and by then our supply of apples was gone.

"It was quite a trip for a bunch of country boys. The train stopped about 30 miles outside of Dallas, and a group of cowboys got on and passed out real cowboy hats to everyone. The people in Texas were real hospitable to us. They had something for us to do every night in Dallas. We socialized with the Boston College players a lot because everywhere we were invited, they were invited, too. We noticed that they were bigger than us and they outnumbered us by a large margin. We knew we'd be in for a tough game. The game was hard fought but clean and we beat the Eagles, 6-3."

McFadden was Clemson's first bonafide All-American and was the biggest star to play under Neely, but there were other standouts during his nine years as coach. They included Bob Bailey, Net Berry, Carl Black, M. P. Black, Bill Bryant, Lowell Bryant, J. F. Deitz, Mac Folger, Gus Goins, W. H. Hall, John Heinemann, Streak Lawton, Tom Moorer, Ace Parker, Jackie Payne, Red Pearson, Charlie Timmons, Monk Willis, Henry Woodard, and Charlie Woods.

"Jess Neely is the coach who put Clemson back on the right track," McFadden said. "When Frank Howard took over when Neely left to go to Rice, he moved it forward another notch."

Clemson football was about to enter another era under Frank Howard who shaped the Tigers' gridiron fortunes for the next 30 years.

Captain Frank Jervey receives an award for his long service to Clemson athletics.

2

IPTAY

"I Could Get A Yankee To Love Clemson"

When Josh Cody retired in 1930 after four highly successful years as head coach, Clemson's football fortunes crashed along with the stock market. Cody had compiled a 29-11-1 record before he left, and Jess Neely took over for the 1931 season. Although Neely later went on to become a successful coach at Rice University, his seasons at Clemson were referred to as the "Seven Lean Years." It took him five years to produce a winning season. His record was 27-33-7. There was some consternation among some influential alumni after Neely's first season in which Clemson finished 1-6-2.

After the 1931 Citadel game in Florence in which Clemson was beaten, 6-0, Captain Frank Jervey, Neely, assistant coach Joe Davis, and Captain Pete Heffner were sitting in a car outside the stadium talking quietly. Jervey was working in Washington as a liaison between the military and the school; and Heffner, who was a member of the military staff at Clemson, had a strong interest in athletics and assisted with the coaching in his spare moments.

"What we ought to do," he said, "is get the alumni to give Jess some backing by helping him finance the football team."

"How much do you think we should ask from each person?" Jervey asked Neely.

"How about $50 each?" Neely answered. "That way we can form a '50 Club.' If I could get $10,000 a year to build the football program, I could give Clemson fans a winning team."

During the drive back to Clemson, the four men continued their conversation and decided that Jervey would begin writing letters to the more influential Clemson alumni when he returned to Washington. (One of his first letters was to Rupert H. (Rube) Fike, M.D., a cancer specialist in Atlanta who had fallen in love with the Tigers in 1900 when he watched the Clemson-Wofford game through a knothole in a fence. He later graduated in the class of 1908.) After a year of correspondence, a dozen alumni gathered on October 19, 1932, in the Jefferson Hotel in Columbia, immediately following the game against South Carolina. From the outset, Fike believed the $50 figure was a bit too high for people to pay during the Depression years. Nevertheless, he agreed to start the 50

Coach Frank Howard kicks off IPTAY's 1961 spring membership drive. Left is Dr. Glenn Lawhon.

Club; but he still believed after returning to his practice in Atlanta that if a smaller amount was requested, it would attract a bigger list of people. The idea excited him. He decided to ask for $10 instead of $50. In Atlanta, he presented his idea to two other Clemson graduates, J. E. M. Mitchell, Class of 1912, and Milton Berry, Class of 1913.

Though it took another year, progress was made toward implementing Fike's plan to solicit $10 from Clemson alumni under the slogan, "I Pay Ten A Year." On August 21, 1934, Fike wrote Neely:

"Last night we had a little meeting out at my house and organized the IPTAY Club. Those attending the meeting were George Suggs, Gene Cox, E. L. Hutchins, Bill Dukes, J. R. Pennell, George Klugh, Milton Berry, and Jack Mitchell."

According to Fike, a constitution was formulated and IPTAY was to be a secret organization. It stated that "anyone who has matriculated at Clemson, has been employed by the college, or is a friend of the college, who can and will subscribe to the purpose of the order by taking the oath of secrecy and paying initiation and yearly fees, when invited for membership is eligible."

It further stated that the purpose of the Clemson Order of IPTAY "shall be to provide annual financial support to the athletic department at Clemson and to assist in every other way possible to regain for Clemson the high athletic standing which rightfully belongs to her."

The Bengal Tiger, Persia Tiger, and Sumatra Tiger would be the president, vice president, and secretary, respectively. The Exalted Iryaas would be the head coach at Clemson, with "Iryaas" meaning, "I receive yours and acknowledge same." A "lair" would mean a unit body of the order; and "region" designated a state, province, or foreign country.

Neely's initiation into the order took place at Clemson as scheduled on September 22, 1934, in the office of J. H. "Uncle Jake" Woodward. In addition to Fike, Berry, and Mitchell, who came from Atlanta, others present were Leonard R. Booker and J. C. Littlejohn. The seven were the vanguard of IPTAY. When the season was over, they began a state-

The 1962 IPTAY Jamboree, presentation of awards to athletes by R. R. "Red" Ritchie behind microphone.

Coach Frank Howard breaks out with a smile during 1961 drive.

E. P. "Gene" Willimon, left, executive secretary of IPTAY
from 1950-'77, presents an IPTAY Award Blanket to W. G. DesChamps at the 1961 IPTAY Jamboree.

wide campaign soliciting memberships to the organization. By the end of 1935, they had succeeded in signing up 185 members. The following were members of IPTAY when it was formed its first year:

M. A. Abbott, Joe E. Auld, R. W. Bailey, J. H. Baker, W. Louis Balentine, C. P. Ballenger, A. F. Ballentine, G. R. Barksdale, W. D. Barnett, W. A. Barnette, J. W. Barnwell, Jr., C. B. Barre, J. M. Bates, David L. Batson, John P. Batson, M. D. Berry, Lewis Black, J. F. Blackmon, John C. Boesch, L. R. Booker, T. L. Bradley, Goode Bryan, W. V. Byers, Norman Byrd, S. W. Cannon, C. J. Cates. E. P. Caughman, and J. B. Caughman.

Also, J. B. Chambers, R. J. Cheatham, W. R. Clardy, J. Roy Clark, Ed Clements, F. H. Clinkscales, Edward Cothran, F. H. Cothran, A. H. Cottingham, M. E. Cox, M. C. Crain, P. C. Crayton, W. C. Dargan, George H. Davis, Joe W. Davis, J. B. Douthit, W. D. Drew, D. T. Duncan, G. H. Dunlap, A. G. Ellison, Rudolph Farmer, R. F. Fike, R. F. Fraser, C. B. Free, Ed J. Freeman, W. E. Freeman, Henry L. Fulmer, and Gaston Gage.

Also, H. I. Gaines, J. M. Gilfillin, Wilburn N. Ginn, H. Earle Graves, R. G. Hamilton, George Hanvey, Claude Harmon, George A. Harrison, P. B. Harrison, L. C. Haskell, M. W. Heiss, W. C. Herron, T. C. Heyward, V. B. Higgins, Frank Hodges, H. M. Hodges, Joe Holland, P. H. Hollingsworth, F. J. Howard, W. K. Howze, Herman A. Hunter, E. L. Hutchins, W. D. Hutchins, B. F. Hutto, Frank J. Jervey, and A. McC. Johnstone.

Also, John D. Jones, M. Haynesworth Jones, R. M. Jones, J. A. Jordan, H. S. Kennerly, J. M. Killian, A. M. Klugh, George F. Klugh, F. B. Lietsey, Ben T. Leppard, D. S. Lewis, C. H. Linegerger, C. E. Littlejohn, J. C. Littlejohn, J. P. Littlejohn, W. K. Livingstone, P. S. McCollum, L. C. McCraw, R. M. McGregor, W. S. McKemie, S. J. McKenney, J. B. McKerley, William G. McLeod, F. R. McMeekin, and S. C. McMeekin.

Also, T. R. McMeekin, W. K. Magill, Harold Major, E. R. Manning, A. F. Martin, Jr., Bryan Marvin, L. A. May, Vernon E. Merchant, J. C. Metts, Lee W. Milford, J. E. M. Mitchell, T. S. Moorman, Edgar Morris, J. R. Moss, Jess Neely, J. C. Neville, W. P. Nicholson, A. D. Park, E.

G. Parker, F. L. Parks, S. D. Parler, John Pearson, S. M. Pennell, W. G. Perry, W. L. Perry, Hugh E. Phillips, H. R. Pollitzer, and J. Warren Quinn.

Also, W. H. Ramsey, W. S. Ray, T. B. Reeves, Cecil Reid, W. D. Robertson, Cecil P. Roper, T. H. Roper, J. E. Rosemond, F. M. Routh, H. E. Russell, Fred S. Sadler, W. Schirmer, W. H. Scott, Joe H. Seal, Henry Selter, Joe Sherman, E. W. Sikes, T. D. Simmons, Hoke Sloan, John Smeltzer, Joe J. Smith, A. G. Stanford, R. A. Stevenson, J. C. Stribling, R. S. Stribling, L. P. Thackston, and Frank R. Thompson.

Also, William A. Thompson, J. Strom Thurmond, B. J. Truesdale, George M. Truluck, H. R. Turner, R. H. Tuttle, J. P. Voight, H. C. Walter, T. M. Walsh, H. C. Wannamaker, J. S. Watkins, David J. Watson, J. W. Welborn, David White, E. B. White, E. C. Wiggins, Jack S. Williams, Leon Williams, J. S. Williamson, Lenair Wolfe, J. H. Woodward, L. R. Young, and D. F. Youngblood.

Wealthy IPTAY members were informed that the "T" didn't necessarily have to represent $10 but could be for $20, $200, or $2,000. Some, like Earl Glassock, a farmer in Harmony, South Carolina, couldn't even afford $10. Instead, he traded $10 worth of sweet milk for his membership card. In the early years of the organization, other legal tender included such items as sweet potatoes and turnip greens. Neely, as the Exalted Iryaas, had to acknowledge everything that came in through IPTAY. Not only did the $10 fee entitle the donor to a membership card, but it also included such benefits as a subscription to the school's weekly newspaper; a weekly letter from the head coach; a windshield sticker which was dated every year; and finally, first right on the purchase of tickets. Even a local bookmaker joined IPTAY, but only because he picked up some tips from the coach's weekly letter.

Fired up by a new wave of spirit from the countryside, Clemson finished the 1935 season with a 6-3 record. After two break-even years, the 1938 team produced a 7-1-1 mark. In Neely's last season, in 1939, Clemson was 8-1 and defeated Boston College in the 1940 Cotton Bowl, 6-3.

"When we came to Clemson in 1931," said

Joe Turner, executive director of IPTAY since 1979.

son. "Aw, cheer up, boys. You'll be on the outside next fall, and you can start sending me that ten a year."

By 1954, IPTAY began to change with the times. Although the secret ritual was abandoned after its first five years, the most significant change was when Dr. Fike retired as president, after serving as its only one for 20 years. IPTAY's purpose (to finance Clemson athletics) remained the same but its leadership was revamped to include a board of directors composed of nine people. Three of these would be appointed by the chairman of the Clemson Athletic Council. The remaining six would be elected officials representing the six districts in which the State of South Carolina is divided. IPTAY wanted to grow through geographic representation. The objective for the directors was to generate more interest for IPTAY and Clemson within their respective districts.

The redesign worked. Today, there are over 17,000 card-carrying IPTAY members. The doctrine of IPTAY is spread throughout all of South Carolina's counties and even in the larger cities in Georgia and North Carolina. It is the largest fund raising organization of any college in the country and presents a model for other colleges to follow.

Penn State's Kay Kustanbauter, director of the Nittany Lion Club, states: "I visited IPTAY, and they are the standard that most schools follow. They were doing it first, and they've been doing it for 47 years."

Joe Turner, the current executive secretary of IPTAY, had a simple explanation for the organization's success.

"We utilize a massive marketing campaign, TV shows, billboards, bumper stickers. We're like McDonald's."

He also pointed out that the "T" in IPTAY has ballooned to $30. "Some," Turner adds, "give more than $2,000."

The organization raised over $1 million in 1978; and in 1981, IPTAY collected $3.1 million from its followers, ninety percent of whom live in South Carolina, Georgia, and North Carolina, almost defying the imagination in regard to fund raising. Member privileges include parking permits and priorities to purchase tickets. Larger donators have an ex-

Neely, "there wasn't 20 cents in the treasury; and when I left, there was over $20,000."

Indeed, IPTAY was beginning to grow. Just prior to World War II, its membership had risen to 1,620. However, during the war years IPTAY's members numbered only 297. Clemson's gridiron accomplishments also dwindled. Frank Howard, who had succeeded Neely as head coach in 1940, went through the pains of three losing seasons in 1942-44 and heard the cries of fans for his scalp. Howard had a sympathetic ear in IPTAY.

"Now, you fellows get me some boys who can run and throw and kick and block, and I 'spect I'll be a pretty good coach myself," said Howard.

They did, too. By 1948, Clemson finished with its first unbeaten, untied record since 1900, 11-0. They earned a trip to the Gator Bowl and won that, too, beating Missouri, 24-23. There were many teary-eyed seniors that Howard consoled after the final game that sea-

The first time IPTAY raised $500,000 was in 1962. Marking the occasion are from University President Dr. R. C. Edwards; athletic director Bill McLellan and T. C. Atkinson

tra incentive, an opportunity to buy tickets to the ACC basketball tournament or any bowl games the football team plays in.

Although the football program requires the largest budget, a total of 410 athletic scholarships in all sports are allocated through the monies raised through IPTAY. Once an IPTAY scholarship has been awarded to an athlete, it can never be withdrawn. However, there are two requirements that an athlete must maintain—one is good scholastic standing; and the other is his obligation to conduct himself like a gentleman at all times, which in reality is demanded of all Clemson students.

B. C. Inabinet, chairman of the board of Defender Industries, was a former football star in the early 1950's who benefitted from an IPTAY scholarship. Today, not only is his corporation recognized as a leader in its field of textile plant maintenance, but Inabinet himself is acknowledged as the top contributor to IPTAY. So valued is Inabinet's support, that Clemson president Bill Atchley bestowed the honorary title of Ambassador of Clemson on the jovial Inabinet early in the spring of 1982. Not only that, but the former lineman was the only non-player to receive a diamond Orange Bowl ring after Clemson defeated Nebraska in the 1982 bowl game. Besides being a generous contributor to IPTAY, Inabinet also owns one of the luxury private boxes in Memorial Stadium that costs him some $26,000 when he's through entertaining after a season of Clemson football. He is unabashed when expressing his love for Clemson.

"I never, never miss a game," said Inabinet. "Something like Clemson gets into your blood. In the early years, it was just like the spirit at West Point, and The Citadel. Clemson spirit is one of the real identifiable things in this country. The people go way back. It's real family, and that's the most beautiful thing about it. That's why I do a lot of entertaining for my company and friends. I want them to experience the Clemson spirit. There isn't anything like it. Why, I could get a Yankee to love Clemson."

Since he contributed $35,000 at the beginning, Inabinet is a lifetime member of IPTAY. Although he has lost track of the exact amount, he has donated to Clemson's athletic program an additional $60,000 to $80,000 over and beyond his initial contribution. He's the type of Clemson lover that would write a check at the drop of a pen.

Inabinet was a much sought-after prospect when he graduated from Dreher High School in Columbia. He could have gone to any one of 50 colleges who tried to recruit him. One would have imagined that he would have enrolled at South Carolina, which was in his own hometown.

"Senator Strom Thurmond recruited me to Clemson, and the people in South Carolina wanted me to stay in the state," said Inabinet. "Columbia was my home, but I loved Clemson. It was no hard decision."

There is also no mistaking George Alley's love for Clemson, either. Like Inabinet, he, too, is from Columbia; and Alley's law offices are rampant with tiger designs on rugs, ashtrays, and desks. On the wall close to his desk is a photograph of Clemson wide receiver Jerry Butler's game-winning catch that defeated South Carolina in 1977. It is autographed. Alley is also a lifetime donor of IPTAY and has given some $50,000 over the years. He left Clemson in 1948 and earned his law degree from the University of Virginia several years later. He's never forgotten Clemson.

"I just love Clemson," Alley said simply. "I wish I had lots of money; I mean lots and lots of money. I'd give it all to Clemson. I go up there every chance I get. My wife graduated from Clemson. My son's wife did; her dad did, too. My daughter graduated from Clemson; her son did also. My daughter's husband graduated from Clemson, as did his father. My three grandchildren joined IPTAY as gold card ($500) members the day they were born."

Alley is recognized as the first scholarship donor at Clemson. At the time, he donated a sum of $2,000 to the school. He figures that he has given about $2,000 a year to IPTAY for the last 10 to 12 years.

"Anything that benefits Clemson, I want to get it before the public," said Alley. "I always wanted to go there. I've felt that way since I was a small boy. I remember seeing the cadets coming down to Columbia for football games. I just love the place."

B. C. Inabinet, chairman of the board of Defender Industries in Colum
is one of IPTAY's biggest contributors. He played tackle for Clemson from 1953-

3

FAN-MANIA

"A Different Breed"

The cars arrive early on football Saturday. At Clemson, it is a way of life. To a stranger, it is a phenomenon. On any one of six Saturdays during the football season, more than 63,000 Clemson fans pack Memorial Stadium to cheer their beloved Tigers. They come from all parts of the state, driving campers, panel trucks, station wagons, pick-up trucks, and just plain automobiles. Yet, the genuine love of these fans for Clemson reaches far beyond the boundaries of South Carolina. The cheering section arrives from the neighboring states of North Carolina and Georgia and some even from as far as Virginia and Florida.

Their day begins early. They flock to any one of the downtown land-marks on Main Street, such as *Mr. Knickerbocker, Ibrahim's Tiger Shop,* and a bit later, to *Bob Higby's Esso Club. Mr. Knickerbocker* is the biggest novelty store in town. It boasts that it sells more Clemson souvenirs than anybody in South Carolina. It probably does. The proprietor, James Spearman, is a long-time resident. Surprisingly enough, he was the town barber for more than 20 years. However, when the post-war fad of crew cuts went out of style, he realized it was time to change professions. He then opened a clothing store but had enough vision to change to the novelty business when he saw the fanaticism of Clemson fans continue to grow over the years.

"Clemson people are a different breed," claimed Spearman one day in front of his attractive store. "We know that some of them will come out of the woodwork when the Tigers have a good season, but most are going to be there when their team plays. I think that the faithful Clemson foot-ball fans know football. They know Clemson had a super team in 1981 and lost some players the following year. They knew Danny Ford had to rebuild, and they had a good feeling about him.

"I was talking to my banker just this morning. He was already asking me what bowl the boys were going to. Of course, they don't know that; but everybody, it seems, wants to know so they can get their reservations in. One fellow, in fact, was by here not so long ago and said that he had a chance to buy 100 tickets to the Cotton Bowl. He wanted to know if it was a good buy. There are some people who have already made reservations at three or four different places where the big bowls are."

A capacity crowd in Memorial Stadium in 1978,
the first year of the newly erected upper deck.

Painting the Tiger paw on Highway 93.

The Paw has been symbolic with
Clemson football the last several years.

36

Besides the store in Clemson, Spearman has another one in Greenville. He also has a warehouse for the 500 or so items he sells. The list of orange and white merchandise with a tiger paw on them defies the imagination: sweat shirts, T-shirts, lamps, Raggedy Ann dolls, golf club covers, golf balls, tote stools, bath towels, stamp pads, baby booties, salt and pepper shakers, telephones, gift wrapping, napkins, bib overalls, Frisbees, bikini panties, and birth announcements with the inscription of "We're proud to introduce our new Cub." There's even a wristwatch that sells for $44.95 that plays "Tiger Rag" at the pressing of a button.

Down the road, Bob Higby is the well-known owner of the Esso Club, a filling station that anyone in Clemson will tell you isn't all that well known for pumping gas. Instead,

Higby rings up mostly beer sales on his cash register, starting as early as 9 o'clock in the morning.

"People have said that we sell more beer than gas here, and I think that we do on Saturdays," said Higby. "The place is so crowded that you can't get a car in here for gas, anyway, In the old days people would come by after the game and stay for a little while. Now I have trouble running them off at midnight. They all want to talk. What I don't like seeing are the types who were talking bad about the coaching staff and all in 1980. It infuriated me because the same ones were bragging when we were No. 1 in 1981. That's a real sore spot with me. I get awfully mad when people come in here in orange and if it doesn't go well, they start criticizing. None of them could do the job

The Orange Paw adds an interesting touch on a pretty face.

Mr. Tiger waves to the crowd.

that the coaching staff does. They ought to stick with them through thick and thin."

It is obvious Higby has a deep love for Clemson. His old gas station is truly a spa. A great many out-of-towners use it as a meeting place the night before a game. That's another event entirely. Often, when Clemson plays a fierce rival such as Georgia, Higby's place becomes the home of the Clemson Honky Tonk Sympathy Orchestra—a group that specializes in strictly country-bluegrass and square dance music.

"We just get them out there on the lot, and they promenade around the pumps," said Higby.

There seems to be some sort of happening for every Clemson home game. But the best one is the annual First Friday parade that takes place before the first home game of the season. Its aim is to get the student body and

Ricky Capps doing pushups after a Tiger touchdown.

Capps, "Mr. Tiger," takes a well deserved break.

39

The serenity that is Clemson on a warm autumn evening.

the town to be aware that the football season has arrived. In 1981, they really didn't need any extra stimulants to herald the season, not with Georgia scheduled for the opening game. The Clemson-Georgia rivalry has intensified in recent years, almost to the point of matching the South Carolina one.

"I hate Georgia," remarked Jack Harmon, the owner of Jack's Barbeque, which is right next door to Higby's place. "South Carolina is not really a legitimate educational institution. It's horsefeathers, but Georgia…"

Chris Patterson, who was a senior at Clemson that year, was chairman of the First Friday parade. The march began on Main Street under a huge banner that bore the message, "Curb The Dawgs." The parade finished at the campus amphitheatre where a giant pep rally took place.

"'First Friday is more of a big party," said Patterson. "You know, 'Let's get behind the team and beat hell out of everybody we play.' It gets everybody's blood running orange. The parade we had before the Georgia game was the biggest one in eight years. We had about 40,000 for the parade and pep rally. The year

before, we had 25-30,000 for Rice. Who the hell is Rice?"

Patterson tried to get Woody Hayes, the former coach of Ohio State, as grand marshal of the parade. There was no telling what the reaction would have been. Hayes had resigned after the 1978 Gator Bowl in which Ohio State lost to Clemson, 17-15, in Danny Ford's very first game as head coach. (Ford had been the Clemson coach less than two weeks, replacing Charlie Pell who quit before the game.) That game attracted more national attention than any other bowl game that year when Hayes lost his temper and hit Clemson middle guard Charlie Bauman near the game's end.

"Woody Hayes called on Tuesday to turn us down," said Patterson. "He was really nice. He asked me if the rivalry was as big as Ohio State-Michigan. I told him it was bigger because we're so close together."

Frank Howard, the retired Clemson coach, didn't think so. He's been around Clemson longer than most people, having coached the Tigers from 1940 to 1969. No one has come close to that in all the years of Clemson football. Howard is such a symbol of Clemson that

Tillman Hall was erected in 1

Clemson graduate Shawn Weatherly was the 1980 Miss Universe.

The 1981 Tiger Tailgate Show team, from left, former cheerleader Joe Erwin; WFBC disc jockey Russ Cassell and Clemson promotion director Allison Dalton.

Clemson radio announcers Tim Bourret and Jim Phillips.

he is referred to in the school's press guide as "The Legend."

"The Georgia rivalry isn't any bigger than Tech was, and it isn't as big as South Carolina," said Howard. "The fans just like to beat Georgia. It's not exactly a passing thing. This particular rivalry came on because there's such a rebirth of football fans at Clemson. South Carolina is do or die. You win that one, you can stay around here a long time. They come to you and tell you, 'Coach, remember, we got to live down here. Don't lose it.'"

Although he had been at Clemson only three years at the time, Ford looked at the Georgia rivalry a bit differently. He, too, was part of the rebirth of Clemson football fanaticism, having led the Tigers to the Peach Bowl in 1979 in his first full year as coach.

"I think it has grown because, one, their fans are similar to our fans—both like football," said Ford. "Two, they are side-by-side, and they brag on each other and fuss with each other in a sportsman-like way. Three, both schools are willing to have first-class athletic programs. One is always trying to outdo the other. They feel they can recruit players in South Carolina, and we feel we can go into Georgia and do the same. The don't like us coming down there, and we don't like them coming up here."

Yet, there is no way to explain what makes Clemson fans so loyal, so intense. Howard, for all the years he's been at Clemson, couldn't offer an answer. He pondered the thought one day and shook his head. "I'll tell you the truth, I've never seen anything like it," Howard said. "No other school comes close."

It was a spirit that Clemson needed since it had always been known as "the other school in the state."

Although Clemson's curriculum has been expanded through the years to offer more courses of study than ever before, it is still regarded as an agricultural college despite the fact that almost half of the students are enrolled in the school of engineering. Many non-Clemson lovers callously look down at the institution as a farmer's school or, even more unflattering, a redneck's school. Being a perpetual underdog has probably done more than anything else to unite fans under an us-against-them stigma that prevails all year long.

"Some institutions do look down at us," said Jimmy Howard, Frank's son, who attended Clemson and played on the football team in the early 1960's. "Carolina probably looks down on Clemson because we're from a small-town, small-college atmosphere; but I think they really envy us. Hell, I'd hate to go to South Carolina. It's so big, what with 26,000 students."

The spirit is perpetuated by the school's Central Spirit Committee. Jane Robelot, a pretty, perky disc jockey on WFBC radio in Clemson, was a member of the 35-person committee when she attended Clemson a few years back. She doesn't hide the fact the committee cleverly capitalizes on the redneck image.

"We play the role," she smiled. "We wear the orange overalls and play the farmer role. We laugh about it, too."

Yet, some of the fans even accept it. One in particular who did was Punk Bodiford.

"South Carolina put out a bumper sticker that said, 'Rednecks Turn Orange In The Fall,'" said Bodiford. "For two weeks, I thought the Clemson athletic department had put that out. You couldn't find it around here. Yet, that's no insult."

Instead, on the roads leading into Clemson a driver can't help but discover orange-painted paws. The paw has become the one symbol most easily identifiable with Clemson. They begin on Highway 93 outside of Easley and all other highways leading into Pickens County. The Tiger Paw was first seen in 1970, when Clemson's president at the time, R. C. Edwards, wanted to cultivate a new image for the school. He was so determined to do so that he hired the Henderson Advertising Agency for the job. They decided they should start the project by writing to every college in America who were nicknamed Tigers and requesting their logos. The agency quickly discovered that the logos were all pretty much alike. Several weeks later, the agency came up with the idea of a Tiger Paw, not just any paw but an orange one. The agency then contacted the Museum of Natural History in Chicago to obtain a plaster of paris mold of a tiger's paw. Today, the paw is a part of the city of Clemson. It is now emblazoned on all the major streets and the ones around the universtiy. The paw doesn't stop there. It has tracked its way to everything that is Clemson—the helmets, uniforms, a bank building, billboards, office desks, every souvenir imaginable, napkins, stationery, clothing, political ads, and even on toilet seats. The Tiger Paw is perhaps the hottest merchandising item among the nation's colleges.

"Clemson considered registering the Tiger Paw and owning exclusive rights to it," said Allison Dalton, the school's promotion director, "but we figure the more that we use it and other people use it, the better. We get more dollars worth of free exposure and advertising letting anyone who wants to use it than we would off the royalties. People identify the paw with Clemson."

Dalton spends long hours maintaining fan interest. He works closely with IPTAY ("I Pay Thirty A Year"), the school's fund raising organization, and also co-hosts the Tiger Tailgate Show on Saturday mornings over WFBC Radio with Russ Cassell and Kim Kelly, Clemson's assistant sports information director. The talk show, a popular one, is on for two hours before a game and attracts a live audience of hundreds of Clemson fans.

The Clemson crowd is a wholesome group. Although they are fiercely loyal to the Tigers, they are not raucous or rowdy. Rather, the congregation of cars and people sometimes resembles a church outing. It is a family oriented group that arrives hours before game time to participate in the hundreds of tailgate parties and the opportunity to visit with friends and family from around the state. The attendance of children appears to be encouraged by parents, which in the years ahead will promulgate the doctrine of loyal Clemson followers. The refreshing part of all this picnic atmosphere is that it is an orderly throng that conscientiously avoids the ugly aftermath of other outdoor barbecues, namely, the refuse and debris. The fans tidily clean up before and after each game in appreciation for being allowed to park all over the rolling campus.

What it all means is that the Clemson people have got it all down to a science. School officials have generously allowed the 9,000 or so cars that arrive on a Saturday morning to park on the grassy knolls surrounding Memorial Stadium. The vehicles are expertly directed by a cordon of state troopers without any semblance of a traffic jam and guided into neat rows by parking attendants furnished by the school. The traffic exercise is conducted in precise one, two, three order.

Before he died in 1982, J. Garner Bagnal, class of 1934, almost did it blindfolded. Bagnal, who was 70 at the time, had never missed a home game and only occasionally missed one on the road. To avoid the early Saturday crush of traffic on Interstate 85, Bagnal would arrive in Clemson on Friday from his home in Statesville, N.C. He set his cruise control at 55 mph, and some three hours and fifteen minutes later he arrived at his beloved alma mater. There are thousands like him.

Then there are those like Bobby Watts of Columbia, who never attended Clemson. One could not find a more loyal fan than the 44-year-old Watts, who is an insurance agent for Prudential, is married, and has two sons, Michael, 18, and Gregg, 11, who will probably enroll at Clemson. Watts has been attending Clemson games since 1972 and has listened to every Tiger game on radio since 1948. However, on September 3, 1980, Watts was severely burned in a fire, suffering second and third degree burns over his body. He was flown in a paramedic helicopter to Charleston and remained in intensive care for 45 days. His complete hospital stay lasted 99 days. While he was there, he gave strict orders to attendants that he would take all the burn treatments required as long as they didn't interfere with his listening to Clemson games on Saturdays. A schedule was worked out, and Watts was a happy person. The following year he was back at Clemson, attending every one of the 1981 home games.

Attending a game in Memorial Stadium is a vibrant experience. One leaves the tranquil serenity of the tailgate scene and enters Memorial Stadium, more widely known as Death Valley, where the chemistry is like no other in any college stadium across America. The quiet, family picnic set transforms itself into an incessant roar of controlled crowd exuberance. So vociferous, so intense is Clemson fan

Delta Delta Delta Sorority strut their stuff at a Homecoming pep rally.

behavior that opposing coaches hate to bring their teams into Death Valley. The Clemson crowd has been referred to as Clemson's 12th man. It was because of the thunder of the crowd in Death Valley that the NCAA rules committee passed a new amendment in 1982 to its 1978 rule governing crowd noise. Instead of two warnings per snap, the rule was changed to two warnings per game with a violation resulting in a penalty on the home team. In the Atlantic Coast Conference, the rule is known as the "Clemson Rule." Other coaches look upon the rule with joy. Too often they had to organize practices with loudspeakers blaring out crowd noises as a backdrop to acquaint their players with the incredible decibel level of Memorial Stadium. Ford had some reservations about the new dictate.

"Everybody will have to adjust," said Ford. "There's no way around it. We've all got to understand. We're talking about five yards or even fifteen yards for unsportsmanlike conduct, plus delay of game. Our crowd is a very good crowd, noisy sometimes, but good. We aren't any worse about the rule, but certain people mention us all the time as an example. There are some people who have played here and said it wasn't any worse than other places. It's going to put a lot more responsibility on the officials as to calling the time out. They'll be the judges, and they've got to do what they think is right. If there's any doubt, they've got

to go with the offensive team. It's a lot of responsibility, and they've got a tough job having to handle that and do everything else they have to do.

"Maybe some people aren't used to playing before noise, and maybe it's an unfair advantage; but we've played at places where the fans can really make noise. We played at Notre Dame, and they had crowd noise. It was loud, but it was fun to play in that atmosphere."

No matter what the NCAA says, however, the crowd in Memorial Stadium is going to grow. In the past four years, 13,855 seats have been added to the concrete and steel structure, bringing the total seating capacity to 57,307. Not included, naturally, are the 6,500 additional fans seated on the grassy hill inside the stadium behind the east end zone. Furthermore, there are plans to double deck the north stands, which will add another 15,000 seats. This is monumental testimony to Clemson's fan support since 1958 when the stadium only held 38,000. It is entirely conceivable that when the new construction is completed, crowds of close to 80,000 will not be uncommon.

One thing is certain, however; the grassy bank at the east end will remain. It's part of the tradition that is Clemson. It is a sea of orange and white that almost mesmerizes a visiting team in their approach to the end zone.

45

4

FRANK HOWARD

"I'll Spend An Eterntiy
Listening To The Cheers Of My Tigers"

Frank Howard doesn't look like he belongs sitting behind a desk. Even now, 15 years since he retired as Clemson's legendary football coach, Howard looks like he still belongs on the field where he spent 30 years. On the walls of his office in the Frank Jervey Athletic Center are vestiges of the past, neatly framed old photographs and citations from governors and award committees recognizing his accomplishments during the past four decades. When the phone rings, as it often does, Howard has to sort through letters, files, and mementos cluttering his desk to find it. The phone, incidentally, is orange. During his years at Clemson, Howard has seen 52 other Atlantic Coach Conference head coaches come and go. The office is Howard's for life, and he is looked upon as the athletic department's good will ambassador.

At 74, Frank Howard is as sturdy as ever, chewing a wad of tobacco that makes him expectorate into a paper cup during pauses of a conversation. Tobacco chewing has always been one of his diversions.

"I ain't got a drop of liquor to offer you, but I can offer you a good chew of tobacco," he drawls in his best country twang. "This here is Reynolds natural leaf. I'd chewed Penn's Thin since 1924, but they quit making it in 1981. Tell you what, though. I missed coaching for a while; but after being out as long as I've been out, I don't miss it much now."

Essentially, he has no real complaints. Most colleges would give a coach a gold watch at a testimonial dinner and wish him well in the years of his retirement, but Clemson made a place for Howard, and deservingly so. Howard and Clemson have been synonymous through the years when the school was struggling to gain an identity. He, more than any other coach, created the mania that is Clemson football. Certainly, no other coach has been at Clemson longer; and it is reasonable to assume that no other ever will.

"If there wasn't a Frank Howard, Clemson would have had to create one," remarked Dick Ensley, the manager at the town's Holiday Inn. "That's how much he's meant to the school. He just loves to sit around and tell stories. I've heard some of them many times, but I don't mind hearing them again because most of them are so funny."

The Holiday Inn is just a three-minute ride from Clemson. Howard

Frank Howard, who coached Clemson longer than anyone else, works his players on the sled. Howard coached 30 years, 1940-'69, and is known as "The Legend."

Howard's 1947 staff, top row, from left, Bob Jones; Banks McFadden; Rock Norman and Randy Hinson. Bottom row, from left, Goat McMillan; Walter Cox; Howard and Russ Cohen.

stops there regularly for his morning coffee before driving to his office at Jervey Athletic Center. It is his way of keeping in touch with the local gentry, which he enjoys doing so much. One morning he has his coffee with a couple of state troopers. Another time he sits with several local businessmen. Even early in the morning, Howard is awake enough to crack a few jokes, which is his style.

"Bob Hope came here a few years back and asked me to give him the grand tour," Howard tells a visitor who stopped by his table. "Well, I picked him up, and we drove down to the first stop light. Then, we went on down to the other one. Ol' Bob turned to me and said, 'Frank, I thought you were going to show me around town?' Well, I just looked at him and told him, 'Good Lord, Bob. If you want me to, we'll back up and I'll show you again.'"

There isn't a better storyteller either than Howard. Told with pure country charm, he has repeated some of Clemson's football lore hundreds of times, and people still like to hear them. He is still referred to as coach; he will sit

and talk about Clemson with anyone who asks him, including people he's met for the first time. That's how much Clemson has meant to Howard all these years. He has a genuine love affair with the school and the town itself.

Born in 1909 in the country town of Barlow Bend, Alabama, which he identifies as being "three wagon greasings from Mobile," Howard spent his childhood on a farm and played what he describes as "cow pasture baseball" because there weren't enough kids around to play football. He entered Alabama in 1927 on an academic scholarship from the Birmingham News. As a 178-pound sophomore, he was a reserve guard playing on the same team with Bear Bryant. In his last two years, Howard was a starter. He completed a fine career at Alabama by playing in the 1931 Rose Bowl rout of Washington State, 24-0.

"I made sure that I was good enough to play on the first team my final two years," said Howard, "just to keep from playing against them in practice. The first team had some big ones. They had a couple of boys who were

Howard is presented with a gigantic rug his players used to run down the hill on the east end when entering the stadium.

about 240 pounds. That would be big now, and it was really big then. The most I ever weighed was 178 pounds. I didn't want to have to hit those big boys in practice. I'd rather hit the small ones."

Howard earned extra money at Alabama by working as a bouncer on weekends at campus dances. He remembered one particular student who always came to the dances inebriated. Naturally, Howard would have to ask the student to leave. After throwing him out so often, Howard had him blacklisted. He was restricted from attending any of the dances held on campus. Some ten years later, Howard met the former student, who was now a bank executive, at a racetrack in New Orleans.

"'You got me restricted, you son of a bitch,'" Howard remembers the executive's opening remark. "'Here, give me two dollars.' He went and made a show bet on the worst horse in the race, a horse named, believe it or not, Re-

stricted. Well, the race started; and Restricted was right out in front. The farther they ran, the farther ahead he got. Ol' Restricted must have won that race by twelve lengths. He paid $97 on a show bet, and that old boy thought he was throwing my two dollars away."

After his graduation from Alabama, Howard actually had an offer to coach high school football in Hopkinsville, Kentucky. He was planning to leave for Kentucky until he received a letter from Clemson coach Jeff Neely offering him a job on his staff for the 1931 season. Although the high school position would pay $200 more, Howard accepted the job at Clemson.

"In 1931, you didn't ask much about a job," said Howard. "You took anything that was available. You were lucky to have any job. Going to Clemson was the best decision I ever made. Neely offered me a job as line coach, and I also had to coach the track team. At that

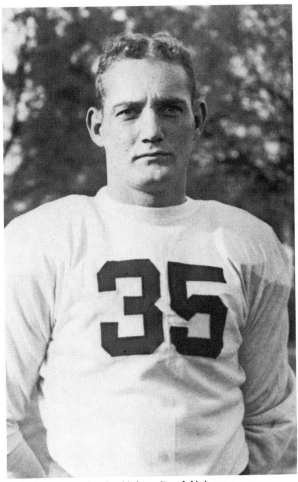

Howard played for the University of Alabama.

Under Howard, Clemson gained national recognition.

time, I'd never seen a track meet. I went to track school for a week, and I got all the track books I could find. I got to where I liked it. I coached the team for nine years; and after a while, I was considered a pretty good track coach. That wasn't all. I was the ticket manager, recruited players, and had charge of the football equipment. In my spare time I cut grass, lined tennis courts, and operated the canteen while the regular man was out to lunch."

Howard came to love Clemson. In 1933 he married Anna Tribble of Anderson, South Carolina, and he stayed as an assistant on Neely's staff for nine years. When Neely left to become head coach of Rice Institute in Houston, Texas, in 1940, Howard was named as his successor. His appointment was unique. Howard's name was placed in nomination by Professor S. R. "Slim" Rhodes at an athletic council meeting that had been scheduled to hire a

replacement for Neely. Howard, who was seated in the back of the room, supposedly waiting to be interviewed as a prospective candidate, seconded the nomination. The other council members took it from there and voted for Howard as Clemson's 17th head football coach. Howard received a four-year contract, which he ultimately misplaced several years later on a business trip. It was the only contract he received during his 30 years at Clemson. Every year after that his acceptance to an offer to continue as coach was formalized by a handshake.

"I never asked for another contract, and they never offered me one," remarked Howard after breakfast one morning. "I guess I'm the only coach who ever wore out three college presidents. I never will forget that first one, Dr. Sykes. When he hired me he said, 'Coach, there's only one request I want to make.'

51

Howard and his staff prepare to leave for Armed Forces clinics in Germany in 1958. From left, Bob Jones; Banks McFadden; Howard and Charlie Waller.

In Nuremberg, Germany, Howard and his coaching staff met with three former Clemson alumni. From left, Lt. Col. Claude "Randy" Hinson; Bob Jones; Charlie Waller; Lt. William Polhemus; Howard; Lt. Edward Huggins and Banks McFadden.

"I said, 'Doc, what's that?'"

"He replied, 'I don't want you to go round telling people what I pay you.'"

"I said, 'Heck, you don't need to worry none cause I'm ashamed of it as you are.'"

"Then I worked for a fellow named Dr. Poole. I went to see him about a pay raise. He told me, 'Coach, I can't raise your pay; but I can give you some titles and degrees.'"

"I said, 'Doc, you know those titles and degrees are fine; but they don't educate kids, and they don't put groceries on the table.' Still, I didn't get the raise.

"So, then one of my ex-managers, Bob Edwards, got to be president. Before that he was president of IPTAY one time. However, he was superintendent of a cotton mill down in Abbeville, South Carolina, at the time I called him. I needed his help. Some efficiency expert had come down here and made a report on athletics that I didn't agree with. I told Bob that we had to convince the board of trustees that this stuff was wrong. So, I got up all this information about what other schools were doing and all that kind of stuff. Then I told Bob, 'Let's don't ask to keep what we got, let's ask for more. Let's ask for the book concessions and a $50,000 appropriation to run the intramural program.'

"When we met with the board, Bob made a good impression. We got the concessions, got $25,000, and kept everything we had. The board ended up offering Bob a job as vice president of the school. After Dr. Poole died, Bob was made president. The next time he met with the board, he recommended a sizeable pay raise for me. The board informed him that they couldn't pay a football coach more than a college president. He said, 'Well, I'll tell you, he's worth every cent I'm recommending; and I want you to comply with my request.' With that, they raised his pay $15,000 a year. So, he wasn't no dummy, was he?"

During his long years as coach, Howard developed a friendly rivalry with Douglas "Peahead" Walker, who was the head coach at Wake Forest. Howard would never hesitate to make Walker a victim of one of his pranks. One such time occurred when Wake Forest played a game at Clemson. The moment Howard saw Walker, he shouted, "There he is. He's

a fugitive." A state policeman who had accompanied Howard immediately handcuffed Walker to a telephone pole as Howard drove away laughing. Walker eventually proved who he was and rejoined his team later that evening.

However, the next day Walker experienced even further unpleasantries. It happened just as his team had arrived at the stadium. After his players had gone through the gate, Walker tried to do the same thing. A security guard stopped him and refused to allow Walker to enter. He didn't have a sideline pass, and the guard was adamant in forbidding him entry. Walker was exasperated. Finally, Walker yelled to his team captain, Pat Preston, to identify him. "I've never seen that man in my life," declared Preston, who had been rung in on the incident by Howard. Finally, a thoroughly furious Walker made it into the stadium.

"Peahead was so cheap he had sold his sideline pass for two dollars," Howard laughed as he recalled the incident.

But it didn't turn out to be so funny for Preston, who suffered Walker's wrath for a week. "I ran him until he knew who I was," snapped Walker, while Howard was still laughing.

In the summer of 1958, Howard and three of his coaches were asked by the State Department to conduct a series of football clinics in Europe for the U.S. Armed Services. When the news broke, Walker, who was now coaching Montreal in the Canadian Football League, couldn't resist the temptation to write Howard a letter. Naturally, it contained numerous jibes:

Dear Frank:
I see by the paper that you are going to Europe this summer to conduct some football clinics. I knew they were having a rough time over there, but I never dreamed it would come to this.

In an effort to make your trip smoother, I'm passing on some tips from my vast storehouse of international savoir faire:

In France there will be occasions when an introduction calls for you to kiss the lady's hand. Try not to be

Howard exchanges some thoughts with Boston College coach Mike Holovak before 1958 game.

chewing tobacco at this time for the juice could be embarrassing.

In Italy, don't call the Italians dagos, like you do some of your recruits from Pennsylvania. They're sensitive.

Tip well, despite your reputation.

Don't ask for grits and red gravy at French restaurants. Stay out of the Folies Bergere.

Don't talk politics. They're having enough trouble in western Germany without getting involved with someone from South Carolina.

Wear a beret at all times. With your bald head, they might shoot you down thinking Krushchev is out spying.

Should you go to the restaurant, "Tour D'Argent," in Paris, and they serve snails or escargots, enjoy them—don't shove them aside and say, "I ain't gonna eat them worms."

Don't try to converse in French or German. What could be worse than an Alabaman with a South Carolina ac-

cent trying to speak a foreign language while wearing a dental plate?

Dress the part. Buy some new clothes and wear coats that match the pants. Egg on the tie is not in style.

If a Frenchman kisses you on the cheek (and I don't think one would dare), don't report him to the gendarmes. It's just a custom over there. Like everybody getting drunk on Big Thursday.

Don't carry that sandbox on the airlines for use as a spittoon. They'll think you have a cat and hold you at customs.

If you should have occasion to eat with royalty or high officials and you should unexpectedly belch, say, "Excuse me, your highness" and not "dawg but them taters wuz good."

I hope this will help you, Howard. I thought the age of miracles had come when they started talking of a man going to the moon. This isn't near as

ridiculous as turning you loose in Paris.
Sincerely yours,
Peahead

Suffice to say, Howard didn't let the letter go unanswered. Besides, he always tries to get in the last word, no matter what or where. So in all his sarcastic splendor, Howard replied:

Dear Doug or Peahead
or Whatever Your Name Is:
I see you are spending a busy off-season composing trashy letters—counterfeited as tips on etiquette for my trip abroad. Walker, let's face it—we've known each other too long for that sort of attack. You, the Maxwell Bodenheim of the coaching business, offering advice.

Why, I remember you in Alabama as a boy. You talk about your vast knowledge of savoir faire, whatever that is. You didn't have an underwear change back then and two-tone shoes to you were a pair of black brogans with red clay on the soles.

You've come a long way since then, Walker, but you went too far when you tried to desecrate your old (former) buddy, Coach Howard. Peahead, you want the facts and here they are:

I'm off on a tour of Europe as an exchange professor. I think they call what I got a Fulbright Scholarship. Just a few people like me and the late Albert Einstein have been accorded this honor.

As a common professional coach, you're lucky I'm taking time to belittle myself to write you.

If the truth were really known, the press would realize you wrote those filthy lies out of envy for me being picked as an international lecturer and expert on football, which I am. The government is paying my way clear to Germany to conduct a clinic.

Looking back on your dismal career, I recall the only clinic you ever conducted was the Greater Wake County Clinic (where Wake Forest was former-

Howard considers Fred Cone the finest player he ever coached.

ly located) and the only ones who showed up were your assistants at Wake Forest. None of them are coaching now, so that's a pretty good indication of your ability in that field.

When the Baptists kicked you out at Wake Forest for being a heathen, Herman Hickman felt sorry for you and hired you as his assistant at Yale. He had hoped to get a few laughs—but the only guffaws came from the rest of the Ivy League. They laughed you clean out of the place and I understand a wealthy alumnus paid your first year's salary at Montreal to be sure you'd never come back.

In New Haven today they have two unusual hotels. One is where George Washington slept and it's doing a landslide business. The other is where you slept and it's still padlocked by the health department. The Yale history department calls the two most socially

Howard's friendly adversary, Peahead Walker, makes a point to Bill McLellan, and Howard.

significant movements in modern history the chasing of Pancho Villa into Mexico and the running of you into the north woods.

I can think of a couple of incidents which reveal your true character. One took place at Greenville, S.C., last winter at the Touchdown Club meeting. Several of our coaches, including yourself, were invited out to a fine old Southern mansion for a social hour. I overheard what you said to the host—to show how much you've been around. You said, "I sure enjoyed it but when I first came in I thought I was going to an Elks Club."

Then there was the time you invited me to Montreal and we ate out at one of those fancy restaurants. They brought out some snails (or escargots, as you call 'em) and you never had seen any before. But trying to impress me, you tried to eat them. You picked one up, shell and all, put it in your mouth and cracked it like a chestnut. And you're worried about my manners.

The picture some of the papers car-

ried of you—it must have been made years ago. The last time I saw you I remember an old, haggard, wrinkled face—a map of disaster from what that Edmonton coach does to you in the Canadian League every year.

Peahead, you old reprobate, you only did one smart thing in your life—and that was selling Jim Tatum for a tie and a turkey gobbler when you managed him in the old Coastal Plains League. And speaking of ties, I recall that those loud neckpieces you once wore with delight caused you to originate the sack look—the Sad Sack.

In past years, you've been a member of the Clemson IPTAY Club, naturally giving the minimum of $10. I'm cancelling your membership as of today. Some of my $500 members give me a little guff I have to take. But for a cheap $10, I don't have to listen to you at all.

The only regret I have about your misleading letter (that somehow got into the papers all over the country) is that it embarrassed some of my good

comedian in his own right, Howard serves some prime ribs to Bob Hope.

Ever the fun lover, Howard sports a wig for ACC commissioner Bob James.

alumni. They didn't have any idea I knew anybody as uncouth as you.

I have talked to my lawyer about bringing suit against you, but he advised against it and told me just to consider the source. I hope you freeze to death in Canada next fall—or that the French population in Montreal burns you at the stake, like Jo Ann of Ark, when you lose the Grey Cup again.

Yours irreverently,
Frank Howard,
Professor and
Fulbright Scholar

P.S. I've just received an offer from a Paris film company to play the leading (masculine) role in the next Brigitte Bardot movie. If I accept, I'll try to get you a bit part, something like my grandfather, who dies in the first reel.

When he returned from Europe, Howard and his staff assembled a strong team. The 1958 Clemson Tigers finished 8-3. It was the most victories since the 1950 team which won nine games. Clemson was invited to play in the 1959 Sugar Bowl and lost to heavily favored LSU. Howard's 1959 team was even better, finishing with a 9-2 record. That season the Tigers appeared in the Bluebonnet Bowl and whipped Rice 23-7. The next three years were only average, as Clemson compiled a 17-13 record.

Yet, in 1963, Clemson opened its season against the University of Oklahoma at Norman, Oklahoma. It was an ambitious opener. The year before, Clemson had finished with a 6-4 record, which hardly qualified the Tigers to meet a strong, national power like Oklahoma. Howard couldn't let the occasion pass without expressing his thoughts. He wrote an open letter to The Norman Transcript practically pleading his case:

"I have been making football schedules out for Clemson since 1940. For the first 18 years we opened each season with Presbyterian College, a small school about 75 miles from us. During that time, it was usually a question of how to hold the score down. They only beat us one time (13 to 12 in 1943) and most of the time the score was in the 50s on up. One year we won 76-0, another time 68-7 and there were several times we scored 50 points or better.

"In 1957 we defeated Presbyterian 66-0 and the following weekend we went up to play Coach Jim Tatum's team at North Carolina. Our boys hadn't felt much hitting the week before and those Tar Heels really bounced us around to the tune of 26-0. I decided right then and there that in the era of big time football, the day was gone for the easy opener. The following year we opened against Virginia and had to come from behind twice to win 20-15.

"The next weekend we played Tatum again and three times we had to come back to win 26-21. That was also my 100th coaching victory and my first one over Tatum. He had beaten me four times while at Maryland and once at North Carolina. I never got to play Jim again because of his untimely death just prior to the 1959 season.

"Since that '57 season when we had an easy opener and then nearly got run out of Chapel Hill the next weekend, I've changed my scheduling tactics. Since then we've opened with teams like Virginia, North Carolina, Florida, Wake Forest, and Georgia Tech. And this year there's no doubt that I bit off the biggest chew so far when I scheduled Oklahoma.

"We've been wanting to play Oklahoma for a long time but Bud Wilkinson stays so busy all the time recruiting those good Texas and Oklahoma boys and going around rubbing the President's back that it's kinda hard to catch him at home.

"We finally got him over here in Greenville several years ago to speak at the Touchdown Jamboree and while he was in town a couple of days speaking and packing up all that loot they gave him, I had a chance to button-hole him and agree on a date. That was four years ago and, of course, neither of us knew what kind of team we were going to have in 1963. But it just seems my luck that we are going to catch Oklahoma when they are coming back to a national power.

"Everybody kept asking me a couple of years ago 'Why can't we have a team like Oklahoma and Notre Dame?' And in 1961, we did. All three of us were 5-5.

"But Coach Charlie Waller, my offensive coach, and I came out to watch the Oklahoma spring game this past season and Bud and I have also agreed to trade last year's films as a scouting aid for our opening game at Norman September 21st.

"I noticed Bud is already saying that he'll probably have his best team this season since coming to Oklahoma. And I'll have to agree with him, but I kinda hate for my team to be the one to get the acid test.

"My boys are nothing but some po' little country fellas trying to get a college education and playing a little football on the side. When the Oklahoma Branch of the Society of Cruelty to

Animals sees that little scrawny bunch of mine step off that plane, they might have the game called off.

"Or it might be that I'll have to do my team like I did when we went out to play TCU in the Bluebonnet Bowl of 1959. We had heard so much about Abe Martin's fine team that my boys really had the jitters. I had to blindfold them all and lead 'em into the stadium.

"Bud must help on the track recruiting also and then picks the fastest ones for his football team. I've never seen such a fast bunch of boys as he has. Just so those Oklahoma backs wouldn't look so fast I went down to Daytona this year to watch the Firecracker 400. I don't believe Bud has any quite as fast as Fireball went that day, but maybe they don't use Pure gas. Even though it will be September and probably hot as blue blazes, believe I might have my boys wear an extra sweat shirt out there at Norman. If those Okies run as fast as they have in the past, I'm afraid some of my boys might catch pneumonia.

"Seriously though, we are really looking forward to playing Oklahoma. Bud and I have been good friends down through the years and we consult with each other a lot during the season exchanging ideas. I hope he doesn't beat me too bad though because I'd hate to be in a bad humor when we sit down across the table from each other after the game counting out the split in the gate."

Several years later, in 1966, Clemson marked another milestone. For the first time in 30 years, they had a game scheduled against Alabama. Like Oklahoma, Alabama also was a national power under head coach Paul "Bear" Bryant. The game was a homecoming for Howard, who had played at Alabama with Bryant in the late 20's. Once again Howard expressed his sentiments in an open letter to the local newspaper in Tuscaloosa:

"In 1927 I reported for freshman football at the University of Alabama along with approximately 250 other freshman football players. Believe it or not, I received a Birmingham News scholarship for one year and had I not been a fairly decent football player, I probably would have had one year and one year only. Of these 250 boys who reported in 1927, there were 11 of us left who played in the January 1, 1931 Rose Bowl football game. The coach at Alabama at that time was Coach Wallace Wade and he had a lot of similarity with Coach Bear Bryant.

"I have heard that when Coach Bryant became the coach at Texas A & M he took 135 boys to Junction City, Texas for his pre-season workout. After this pre-season workout there were 27 left and the saying in Texas was not "Remember the Alamo," but "Remember Junction City." I am only trying to say that Coach Wade was just as tough a taskmaster as Bear Bryant and his disciples are today.

"I have recently heard that Coach Jordan at Auburn was going into the ministry. The saying is that 'He would rather bear the cross than cross the Bear.' Coach Jordan might feel that way as he has been playing Alabama and Bryant's team for several years, but this is my first year of facing The Bear and while the people of Alabama may think he can walk on the Black Warrior River, he has got to prove these feats to me.

"I will forever be grateful to the University of Alabama, Coach Wallace Wade and the Birmingham News for giving me an opportunity to get an education which would have been impossible for me had it not been for football. While I have not done as well as Joe Namath, my education at Alabama has been very kind to me and for the last 36 years I have been coaching at the finest school in the country that is located in South Carolina, and have also come in contact on our campus with some of the finest people I have

Clemson president Dr. Franklin Poole wishes Howard luck before 1957 Orange Bowl game.

Bob Bradley, Howard and Bill McLellan are all smiles after Clemson defeated Furman, 36-19, to earn 1959 Sugar Bowl bid.

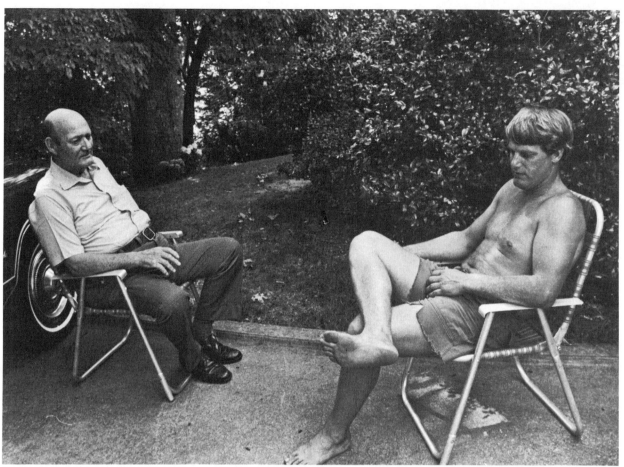

Howard spends a quiet moment with son, Jimmy.

ever known.

"While at Alabama it was my good fortune to be associated with a fine coaching staff such as Coach Wallace Wade, Coach Hank Crisp (God bless him), and Coach Jess Neely. Coach Neely broke me into coaching and also into chewing tobacco. In addition to having a fine coaching staff, we also had a fine group of football players. I will never forget the likes of Jess Eberdt, John Miller, Fred Singleton, Boots Clemente, Jimmy Moore, Bo Dotherow, Newt Godfree, Monk Campbell, John Cain, Ralph McRight, and John Henry Suther. All of these boys were fine football players and I can truthfully say while football today is much better than it was at that time, all of these fellows were such fierce competitors that they would play on any college team today.

"Back in the late '20's we didn't have all the conveniences that exist at Alabama today. All of the football players ate at Claude Stallworth's Bullpen and while the food was good and wholesome at times, it was not too plentiful. We had one helping and that was it unless someone had something on his plate that he did not like. I recall very vividly some of the players taking dead birds and putting them on the table so that some player with a weak stomach would get up and leave and the rest of us could share his meal.

"We also did not have air conditioned living quarters and most of us stayed in either the gymnasium, the B. O. House or Gorgars' Hall. Our favorite pastime during those years was sitting out in front of the gym on Sunday afternoon and watching all of the pretty girls go by with some fraternity boy who had an automobile. The fortunate ones could rent a U-Drive-It for Sunday night for $.05 a mile and $.05 an hour. You can bet your bottom dollar that the hour charge ran more than the mileage charge in those days.

"I also recall a few of the pranks that we used to play on each other. One time we were in Atlanta and someone looked up the telephone number of the zoo. They left this number and also the name of Miss Lions for Ralph McRight to call. When he got the number and asked to speak to Miss Lions they told him there were quite a few lions out there, but none of them could talk very well. When J. B. Whitworth kicked a field goal in the Rose Bowl, the first thing he said when the ball went through the uprights was 'he wondered if his Dad back in Arkansas was listening.'

"I could go on and on with experiences at Alabama, but feel that my 300 words are about up and I would like to take this opportunity to wish Coach Bear Bryant and his national champions all the luck in the world except when they play those Clemson Tigers from Clemson, South Carolina."

Howard likes to tell of the time he visited Bryant in his office. He saw a red phone and asked Bryant what it was for. Bryant told him it was direct to God.

"You mean I can call God?" asked Howard.

"Sure can," answered Bryant.

"How much would it cost?" wondered Howard.

"Only about $20," replied Bryant.

The next year Bryant returned the visit to Howard at Clemson. He spotted an orange phone on Howard's desk.

"What's that for?" inquired Bryant.

"That's a special phone to God," remarked Howard.

"How much would it cost to call from here?" asked Bryant.

"Doesn't cost a thing," exclaimed Howard. "Around here that's a local call."

Howard claims he had a chance to hire Bryant as an assistant in 1941 but decided against it.

"Smartest thing I ever did in not hiring Bryant," Howard says. "Why, in three months he would have cut my throat, drunk my blood, had my job, and had us on probation; but that Bear, he had him all those good players at Alabama. Like Joe Namath, for one. One day he was telling his boys how he wants them to have short hair and a crease in their pants and to be good in studies. He said, 'I don't want no dumbbells on my squad. If there are any dumbbells in this room, stand up.' So, Namath, he stands up. Bryant looks at him and said, 'Joe, you ain't no dumbbell. Why are you standing?' Namath replied, 'I hate to see you standing there all by yourself, coach.'

"Then one time Texas called me and wanted to know the best backfield coach in the country. I said, 'I don't know his name, but there's that backfield coach at Auburn.' Well, they called and hired Charlie Waller. So in about two years, he got fired. The whole bunch did. Charlie called me and asked me for a job. So I

The popular coach walks off the field with an added prize.

63

told him, I said, 'Charlie, you come over here and I'll talk to you.' In the meantime, I called Auburn. I said, 'Look, what kind of backfield coach is this Charlie Waller?' Fellow said, "Well, hell, you recommended him to Texas.' I said, 'Yeah, I sure did,' but I said, 'You know, there's a helluva lot of difference between recommendin' a fellow and hirin' him yourself.'" Howard did hire Waller, and he coached on Howard's staff from 1957-1965.

Howard always enjoyed a good rapport with the press. Basically, he always made time to accommodate the writers and radio announcers who covered the team. One of his favorite writers in the early 1940's was Carter "Scoop" Latimer, who worked for the Atlanta *American*. If there was one thing that Latimer liked besides writing, it was drinking. Sometimes he

Victory number 150 came in 1966.

mixed the two, which didn't always work out too well. Yet, Scoop had enough friends to bail him out of trouble. Once, when he was covering a Clemson game, he got so drunk he couldn't finish writing his story and passed out in the press box. His cronies bailed him out. Several kept filing stories over the Western Union wire. After they had sent six of them, the newspaper sent back a message to stop, it didn't need any more Clemson stories.

"Ol' Scoop could drink some," said Howard. "After he left Atlanta, he began working for the paper in Greenville. Now, Scoop would call me at home every night. He'd say. 'Coach, I have to get a story,' So, I'd give him one. Then one day our sports publicity man asks me, 'Where in the hell is Latimer getting all those stories? He knows more about what's going on at Clemson than I do.'

"I liked ol' Scoop. He was a good fellow 'cept he drank too much. One time I had me this suite in a hotel in Atlanta. There was two bedrooms and this here big living room in between with all this liquor on the table. One of my assistants who was with us saw all those bottles and got worried. I told him, not to worry none, 'cause I'd sleep in the same room with Scoop. So, we all got to bed around midnight. At about 3 o'clock, I hear all this noise in the other room. I get up, and here's ol' Scoop drunk to the world. He looks up at me and says, 'You think I don't know nobody. I'm going to show you.' He picks up the phone and calls Ty Cobb in Detroit. Then in calls Jack Dempsey from Montana. Finally, he calls Jack Welborn in California. He talked for hours before he finally passed out. Later in the day when we checked out, I had a bill for $265. That was just for one day.

"'Nother time Scoop flew with us up to Boston to cover our game. I knew from the moment we got back on the plane that it was going to be a rough trip home. Ol' Scoop got to drinking; and by the time we landed in South Carolina, he was out cold, drunk to the world. It took four people to carry him off the plane like a dead man. Never saw anyone that could drink so much, but he was a good writer."

Under Howard, along with his humor, Clemson began to generate national exposure.

Howard in a playful moment with Coach Bear Bryant after Alabama defeated Clemson, 26-0 in 1966.

Mostly, it was through the bowl appearances that the Tigers made. Before Howard took over as head coach for the 1940 season, Clemson had appeared in only one major bowl game, the 1940 Cotton Bowl, which was Jess Neely's final game as coach before he went to Rice. Beginning with the 1949 Gator Bowl, Howard led the Tigers to six post-season bowl games—the 1951 Orange Bowl, 1952 Gator Bowl, 1957 Orange Bowl, 1959 Sugar Bowl, and the 1959 Bluebonnet Bowl which was played in December of that year. His teams won six Atlantic Coast Conference championships, more than any other school.

Howard's 1948 team went 11-0 and led to its first bowl appearance under him. Yet, Howard doesn't consider that team the best he ever coached. "That was the best record one of my teams ever had," said Howard, "but that wasn't my best team. The best I ever had was either in 1958 or '59."

In 1958, Clemson finished with an 8-3 record. The following season they improved to 9-2. Following the '58 campaign, Clemson was matched against LSU in the Sugar Bowl on New Year's Day. Clemson lost in a thrilling game, 7-0, when Heisman Trophy winner Billy Cannon threw a touchdown pass in the third quarter and then proceeded to kick the extra point before 82,000 fans.

"Cannon was a good player, but they didn't hurt us the rest of the time," recalled Howard. "We hurt ourselves with fumbles and other mistakes. I remember we ran a screen pass that coulda won the game, but it was dropped. That's the kind of day it was."

When his 1959 team went 9-2, Clemson was invited to play TCU in the Bluebonnet Bowl that December. Clemson became the first college to appear in two post-season bowl games the same year. They took advantage of the opportunity to defeat a good TCU team, 23-7, overcoming a 7-3 deficit in the process.

"That TCU bunch had one heckuva team," remembered Howard. "I remember Bob Lilly was one of their players, and he was big; but he wasn't the only one. I think there were eight tackles out there that day, and the smallest went about 260. I'm telling you, there was some good hitting out there that day.

"We had this one pass play that scored every time we threw it. I finally told my team not to run it any more. We were beating old Abe Martin (TCU's coach and a friend of Howard) pretty bad. It was the best bowl game a team of mine ever played.

"My undefeated 1948 team had some pretty fair players. Bobby Gage, Fred Cone, and Ray Matthews were all standout players. What made that season so satisfying was that the year before the team had gone 4-5. The team was quick and fast and liked to play, but it was one-platoon football then. I only had about 16 good players, and some of them had to play all 60 minutes. We beat Missouri, 24-23, in the Gator Bowl; and folks have since said that it was the best Gator Bowl ever played.

"Two years later we played Miami in the Orange Bowl and beat them 15-14. We were trailing 14-13 with about four minutes left when Sterling Smith, one of my guards, broke through and tackled a Miami runner, Frank Smith, in his own end zone for a safety that won the game."

Howard tosses the ball to Hootie Ingram who took over when Howard finally retired following the 1969 season after 30 years as Clemson's coach.

Howard's teams weren't fancy. They played hard-nosed football. Howard was a strong exponent of the single wing, which had always been described as "three yards and a cloud of dust." However, the evolution of the T-formation made the single wing obsolete. After Clemson was blanked, 14-0, by Miami in the 1952 Gator Bowl, Howard had to yield to the changing trends of college football and install the T-formation. It wasn't all that easy.

"We were one of the last teams to change from the single wing," said Howard. "That was the only offense I knew anything about, and that's the way I recruited my players. I had to go out and learn the T-formation; so I went to Bud Wilkinson, one of the best teachers I knew of. That, plus talking to other coaches and watching films was all I did.

"The T was a lot easier to coach. Only the quarterback is a specialist. The other backs were interchangeable. But in the single wing, every position is a specialist. I can tell you, we got more long gains from the single wing than we did with the T. I never did figure out why. I reckon it was because you had more men leading on wide plays. But because so many men led the play and because the play usually went wherever the blocking back went, defenses learned to shoot people through the gaps and run down plays from behind. That meant the end of the single wing.

"Shucks, today's supposedly modern offenses and defenses are often updated versions of old systems. The Wishbone is the same damned thing as the T. Take a T, split one end, move the fullback up a couple of yards and you have the Wishbone. The 3-4 defense, which is considered a daring new idea in pro football, is the same thing as the 5-2 or 'Oklahoma' defense colleges have been using for years. The only difference is that the two outside men on the front line, called linebackers by the pros, are called ends in college. We were using the 3-4 defense in the '50's, and we didn't know it. Some of these young coaches today don't remember what was done in the past. They ain't done a damn thing new. Coaches frequently get credit they don't deserve for inventions. They see a high school team do something, so they try it. If it works, they say they invented it. Hell, they didn't in-

The rock that was presented to Howard by S. C. Jones, Class of 1919. Jones brought the rock back to Clemson from Death Valley, California.

vent it. Some poor little high school coach did."

Howard is reluctant to name the finest player he ever coached, but when pressed, he invariably lists Fred Cone as the best player he had during his 30 years as coach. Cone was a running back from 1948-50, and how Howard ever recruited him for Clemson was something out of the ordinary. He actually recruited Cone as a favor to his sister.

"Back then, about 1946 or '47, when all them boys was getting out of the army, they was having trouble getting in school," recalls Howard. "What I mean by that was that all the schools were crowded. Now, I had a sister in Biloxi, Mississippi. We used to go down and play Tulane all the time, and I'd send my sister two tickets. She'd come to watch us play because she was just about 80 or 90 miles from New Orleans.

"One year, I believe it was 1946, she wrote back and asked for four tickets. Cone was visiting his sister, who lived next door to my sis-

A gifted speaker, Howard creates a laugh at the 1974 ceremonies dedicating the field in his honor.

ter, and she wanted to bring them to the game. At the time, I was allowed to bring 40 football players a year into college, and I had 39 on my list. I didn't know anything about Cone at the time except that he never played high school football none. He was from a little biddy town in Alabama called Pineapple, which I don't believe is even on the map. He'd played six-man football some and had been in the army. He wanted to go to Auburn or Alabama, but they were filled up.

"Since I had one open spot, I added Cone's name to it. After he came to school and I saw how good he was, I called my sister. I asked her how did she know that Fred was gonna be such a great player? She said, 'Well, I saw him diving off a diving board one time.' That boy had quickness and power. If you had him cornered, he'd run over you. He was just a good team man and a good humor man. He had a lot of wit about him."

Recruiting wasn't all that easy. At times, Howard had to use his own wit to help him overcome obstacles he encountered while recruiting players. One such time occurred in 1933, when Howard was the line coach on Neely's staff. Neely sent him to Charleston to look at a prospect, a tackle who weighed about 240 pounds, which was big back then.

"Somebody wrote coach Neely about this big ol' boy Jesse Jones who weighed 240 or 250 pounds," said Howard. "Well, that was a good size boy back then, not like they are today when tackles weigh about 280 pounds. Coach Neely told me to get in the car and go see this here boy. Well, back then the road to Charleston wasn't paved none. It took me all day to get there from Clemson, and I got red mud all over me. The cars didn't have no air conditioning and I was wringing wet. I finally

68

came to a house in the country where Jones lived. I knocked on the door; and a little fella, looked like he weighed about 150 pounds, answered. I asked for Jesse Jones. 'That's me,' he replied. 'Well, Jesse. I'll tell you what, son. I'm selling Saturday Evening Post, and I wonder if you'd be interested in a subscription?'

"Another time I remember I got this here letter from this fella up in Virginia. He was telling me about this tackle he had, said that he only weighed 155 pounds but he'd grow and fill out, that this boy's great-great-grandfather came over on the Mayflower, one of his uncles was the governor of Virginia and another one of his uncles was a Supreme Court judge, and felt that I should give him a scholarship. I wrote him back real quick and told him that I was looking for a boy to play football; I don't want one for breeding purposes.

"Another time I went to Lakeland, Georgia, to look at another big boy. Well, we used to travel on $4.50 a day back then; and that was your hotel, your eats, and everything. When I got there, I pulled into a gas station. I never will forget it. All these old fellas were sitting around playing checkers. I looked at them and asked if anyone could tell me where Johnny Davis lives. Didn't a one of them look up and say anything. So, I ate my supper, since there was nothing else to do. Got me a Coca-Cola and a package of peanut butter crackers. I was a pretty good checker player, so I sat down and watched these fellas play for about an hour. Finally, I asked them to let me play a game. They obliged me, and I proceeded to give them that country store move. That's one of those moves where you block all of 'em and they can't move so you win. I got friendly with those fellas, and they felt I was a decent kind of fella. I said I wish somebody would tell me where I can find that boy 'cause I might want to give him a scholarship to college. So, one of those fellas told me, he says, 'Mister, get in the car and I'll take you there. I live next door to him.' Well, on the way around I ask him, I said, 'You know, you caused me to lose about three, four hours here. I could be on into Jacksonville by now. Why didn't you tell me where that boy lived, where I could go see him and talk to him?' He said, 'Mister, that boy's daddy is the biggest bootlegger in this part of the

country; and we thought you was one of them there revenue men.'

"After so many years, recruiting got to be a chore. It got so you couldn't hardly recruit, what with the ACC making the academic requirements so much higher than they were in other conferences. I got tired of fighting it. Besides, all the mamas and papas thought their boys were All-Americans; but I know only one out of three was worth a damn, and I didn't know which one."

It was during Howard's long coaching tenure that Memorial Stadium became more familiarly known as Death Valley. Howard devised a ritual for his players at every home game. They would leave the dressing room high behind the east end of the stadium and run down the hill through the goal posts and onto the field as the enthusiastic Clemson fans stood and applauded. Psychologically, the scene created a feeling of invincibility. Through the years, Clemson has dominated games played in Death Valley. Back in the early '50's, S. C. Jones, a 1919 Clemson graduate, was traveling through Death Valley, California. He stopped his car long enough to pick up a rock that weighed about ten pounds and placed it in the trunk of the car. He brought it back to Clemson and presented it to Howard, saying that since Memorial Stadium was known as Death Valley it was only appropriate that he should have a rock from the real Death Valley. The rock lay around Howard's office for several years. Finally, Howard got tired of looking at it. He told Gene Willimon, who had played for Clemson in 1932-33, to take the rock and put it on the field somewhere. Willimon had a better idea. He had the rock mounted on a cement pedestal and had it placed on the top of the hill at the east end of the stadium. From that day on, the players would touch the rock as they ran down the field.

"On the first Friday we had it," said Howard, "I turned to my team and said, 'Lookie here, boys. If any of you boys are gonna go out and give me 120 percent, I'll let you rub my rock; and it'll give you supernatural powers.' Well, the rock story got in the papers. Then I got a letter from a woman. She said no wonder I didn't win more games. I believed in rocks in-

An aerial view of the 1974 Georgia game that attracted a capacity crowd of 43,000.

stead of God. She said if I'd've believed in God instead of rocks, I would've been a lot better coach."

The fierce South Carolina-Clemson rivalry flourished in Howard's time. The game was played on Thursdays to commemorate State Fair Week. The Thursday meeting finally ended in 1959 when the game was moved back to Saturday and played in subsequent years as a home game by the respective schools. Howard never appreciated the treatment Clemson received during the Thursday games at the Columbia Fairgrounds.

"They treated us like stepchildren," said Howard. "We had to carry our own bleachers down there, and our people had to pay twice. They had to pay to get into the Fairgrounds, and then they had to pay to get into the game.

I remember back in 1946 when there were 5,000 counterfeit tickets around, and they wouldn't let the people in. Pretty soon the crowd knocked the gates down. There were people everywhere. They were selling beer from the inbounds markers. Whenever the play would move, people just surged around. There were so many people in front of me I couldn't see. I remember one boy from South Carolina was returning a punt, and they wouldn't let him get out of bounds. He tried to, but they kept pushing him back in. One ol' drunk behind me kept yelling some nasty things at me. I started to take a swing at him, but one of my coaches grabbed my arm and stopped me. It was a good thing that he did. There probably would have been a riot if he hadn't grabbed my arm."

70

The 1969 season was Howard's final one as coach. When he stepped down, he had recorded 165 victories, which was 19th on the list of active or retired coaches. Even on his retirement, Howard managed to express his humor.

"I retired for health reasons," said Howard. "The alumni got sick of me. Seriously, I was in it long enough. I felt these people deserved to see another kind of football. They looked at me long enough."

President Robert C. Edwards released the following statement regarding Howard's retirement on December 10, 1969:

"As he announces his own decision, reached on his own initiative, to retire as head football coach and devote his full time to the responsibilities of the athletic directorship, I salute Frank Howard for all he is and all he has meant to Clemson.

"No one anywhere is in a better position than I am to appreciate Frank Howard. I have known him intimately since he came to the Clemson campus while I was a student in 1931. I have worked with him closely and admiringly both before and after I came into the Administration of this University.

"He is big time in every way. He has brought national recognition to Clemson, to the State of South Carolina, and to the Atlantic Coast Conference. He has been a stimulating force among the alumni and friends of Clemson. His lifetime record as a coach speaks for itself.

"As athletic director he will continue, with my full support, to foster the strengthening of Clemson's program in all sports.

"In football and in our total athletic program we will continue to maintain the highest standards. Intercollegiate football is a vital part of our total educational program. We are determined that Clemson shall continue to compete effectively with the finest teams in the nation.

"A successor to Frank Howard as head football coach will be announced as soon as possible after one is selected. We are confident that the successor, whoever he may be, will have the character, ability and experience to keep Clemson football in the big time, and to build effectively on the foundations Frank has laid."

Following Howard's retirement in 1969, Clemson fell on some lean years. The football program, which was beginning to develop some national stature, began to flounder. Hootie Ingram took over from Howard and lasted only three years. As in most cases, replacing a legend like Howard was difficult. Ingram's teams were 12-21. He resigned after the 1972 season. Red Parker became Clemson's 19th football coach in 1973. After a 5-6 record his first year, Parker appeared to have the Tigers back on the winning track when his 1974 team finished 7-4. However, after two losing seasons, Parker was fired following the 1976 campaign. In the seven years since Howard left, Clemson had only one winning season and was 29-46-2 over that period of time.

"Those were very sad times for us here," said Howard.

Howard remained on as athletic director for two years. In 1971, Bill McLellan was named as athletic director. It allowed Howard more time for banquet speeches and public appearances, which he always loves to do, anyway. Even now, he often looks back at his coaching experiences that seem endless. After all, 30 years in one spot is a long time. He doesn't intend to leave, either. Howard purchased a cemetery plot on Cemetery Hill which is on a hill overlooking Memorial Stadium.

"That's where I'll spend all eternity, listening to the cheers for my Tigers," Howard says. "I had a lot of offers to leave and go to other schools, but I always liked it around here. I knew the students, the professors, and the townspeople. If I went somewhere else, I don't know if the people would approve of my stories or chewing tobacco. If we were losing, people said it was nasty and unbecoming. All I know is a lot of professors used to bum tobacco from me."

Maybe some of them still do.

5

SOUTH CAROLINA RIVALRY

"The Clemson-South Carolina Rivalry, They Don't Let Die"

There wasn't a team Howard enjoyed beating more, when he was coaching, than South Carolina. Since he coached longer than anyone else at Clemson, he faced the hated Gamecocks 30 times but came up a little short, beating South Carolina 13 times, losing 15, while two other games resulted in ties. Even today he doesn't mask his dislike for South Carolina, calling them "a bunch of chickens." The seeds of bitterness that became the roots of the age-old Clemson-South Carolina rivalry existed since even before the turn of the century. Benjamin T. "Pitchfork Ben" Tillman, a farmer from Edgefield, began the campaign for legislation several years earlier that established an agricultural college separate and apart from the main institution in Columbia. South Carolina was the first state institution and has always been recognized as the state university. Located in the capital, which is also the state's largest city, hasn't hurt its status, either. Clemson, then, has always been snubbed as the poor, country cousins. South Carolina fans never let Tiger followers forget that Clemson began as an agricultural school.

Thus, in 1896, Clemson's first year of football, South Carolina had already been playing football for five years. On November 13, 1896, Clemson and South Carolina met on the gridiron for the very first time as part of State Fair Week in Columbia. Although it rained at various intervals during the day, a crowd of close to 2,000 people paid a 25¢ admission charge to view the first of what became a long series of games which over the years were popularly referred to as Big Thursday. Not surprisingly, South Carolina won that first game, 12-6, in a contest The State newspaper called "A Superb Game." Today, Logan Elementary School on Elmwood Avenue rests on the portion of the State Fairgrounds where 200 Clemson student fans, who made that journey to Columbia, cheered their team in the game that was the beginning of what was to be their school's fiercest rivalry in the years ahead.

However, over the next four years, little Clemson defeated South Carolina every time. The 1901 game, unfortunately, was cancelled due to a dispute with Fair officials about gate receipts. The disagreement was short-lived. Clemson and South Carolina returned to the battlefield in 1902 with both sides feeling all the pent-up frustrations that had resulted from

Clemson's Coleman Glaze (80) brings South Carolina's
Billy Gambrell to a halt in 1961 game.

the previous year's cancellation. Although Clemson's team had been known as the "Tigers" since they first began playing football, the year marked the first time the nickname "Gamecocks" was applied to South Carolina after several futile years in which the Columbia school searched for an appropriate name. Clemson was heavily favored. However, South Carolina managed to upset the Tigers, 12-6, and another heated battle took place a few days after the game.

Some 400 Clemson cadets had attended the game and, as in past years, had been allowed to remain in Columbia for the remainder of the week to enjoy the State Fair. In the previous four years during which Clemson had triumphed, the cadets had paraded around town with garnet and black cloth, the South Carolina colors. Thus, savoring their victory, South Carolina students celebrated by carrying around the main streets of Columbia a large transparency they had removed from the window of a tobacco store of a Gamecock crowing over a sad-looking Tiger. The Clemson contingent felt that the gesture was in bad taste and demanded that the transparency should not be displayed in the Elks' parade on Friday night. They made their feelings known to the parade officials as well as the law enforcement officials. Both groups agreed with the Clemson students. However, the South Carolina students felt that city officials were wrong in yielding to the Clemson supporters and refused to acknowledge the request.

Indeed, the figure, then, did appear during the parade, held high in the air by the happy Carolina students. Tension increased when the Clemson cadets were dismissed near the steps of the Capitol building. The band of cadets marched, in military formation, to Sumter Street making their way through the main entrance of the South Carolina campus, determined to capture the display. A group of Carolina students in opposition quickly rallied around the trophy, determined not to see it destroyed. Clearly outnumbered by almost three-to-one, as well as out-armed, they were lucky that Christie Benet, a local businessman who was also an assistant coach, appeared on the scene, which threatened to turn into a small war. His intention was to mediate the

dispute, stalling long enough for the police to arrive. With both sides warning one another of the impending physical harm, Benet offered to fight one or, at the most, any two Clemson diehards. The challenge didn't satisfy the Clemson contingent. However, finally surrounded by police and faculty members, a joint committee of six students worked out a peaceful solution. The transparency was burned between the two warring groups as both sides cheered. Because of the seriousness of the 1902 incident, the Clemson-South Carolina series was then suspended for six years before being resumed in 1909. Ironically, Benet, years later, was made a trustee of Clemson after practicing law in Columbia.

Those six years worked wonders for Clemson. From 1909 and on for the next six meetings, the Tigers emerged victorious five of the six times. The losses understandably rankled Carolina. So, in 1915 the Gamecocks employed ringers and handily won their first three games that season. An investigation uncovered the ruse before the Clemson game, and the unauthorized players were banned from participating against Clemson or any other team. The game produced the first tie in the series, 0-0. Then, starting in 1916 Clemson won four consecutive times. This was the first time this had happened since the 1897-1900 period.

Coach Josh Cody in 1927-30 guided Clemson again through a streak of winning four consecutive games. Clemson established a winning edge over South Carolina at this time. Coach Jess Neely extended it even further. He led Clemson to seven consecutive victories from 1934 through 1940, the longest winning streak of the series. Unfortunately, in 1941, South Carolina edged Clemson, 18-14, to snap the Tigers' winning skein. This was the year Frank Howard began his long reign as Clemson's legendary coach, and the Carolina fans were so grateful for the victory that they presented coach Rex Enright with a Chrysler automobile and a silver service set. Clemson fans remember that the Tigers missed a first down by a foot, which could have led to the possible winning touchdown near the end of the game. Howard, especially, didn't appreciate losing to his arch rival his first year as

Tigers' Tom Duley moves out for a big gain in 1965 game which was won by South Carolina, 17-16.

coach, and he responded sharply:

"The only difference between an automobile and a coffin is about twelve inches of dirt."

Howard, however, went on to enjoy all the pageantry that surrounded Big Thursday. His wife, on the other hand, remembers it was the one game of the season he worried most about.

"I can always tell when Frank's worried," said Howard's wife, Anna. "He walks up and down and groans. Then he goes back to the kitchen and eats peanut butter with a spoon."

The game grew to be an important social and political event. It was always known as Big Thursday until 1958 when the game was switched to a Saturday after 61 years. Drinking and socializing was at a peak during State Fair Week, more so in fact than at any other time of the year, including Christmas. Women dressed in their most fashionable fall clothes, even if the weather was warm, which it often was; and each year the governor of the state always made it a point to attend the game, sitting during one half on the Clemson side and

then during the other half on the Carolina side.

One time during Prohibition, Governor John G. Richards, who was known as South Carolina's "Blue Sunday Governor," was upstaged by a drunk, delighting the fans attending the game. Somehow he got on the field during the halftime ceremonies and with a cane, which he used to improvise a rifle, fell in behind Clemson's snappy drill platoon. He playfully imitated the corps until the moment when the cadets did a countermarch and collided with the inebriated mimic. Unharmed, the drunk bouncily got up and walked toward midfield where the governor traditionally stood before switching sides for the second half. The drunk insisted on shaking hands with Governor Richards and with every honored guest who stood close by. As it turned out he was a Tiger fan. When the band began playing the Clemson Alma Mater, he stood at attention and took off his hat.

Big Thursday for a long time was a legal holiday in Richland County where the game was played. The entire state observed the day

Wayne Page closes in on South Carolina quarterback Mike Fair in 1965 contest.

as well, because of the zealousness of football fans throughout South Carolina. It was a day in which loyalties were reaffirmed, and you can be sure there were no neutral feelings from the Atlantic Ocean to Hog Back Mountain. For one family, Big Thursday meant that at Segars Mill, Henry Segars and his clan of eighteen would shut down the grist mill, close the general store, virtually bringing all work to a halt on the 1,000 acre spread Henry owned, and head for Columbia. The Segars were all Clemson supporters except for one son, Mac, who attended South Carolina before World War II. However, on Big Thursday, Mac joined the rest of the family on the Clemson side of the field.

One of the more memorable Big Thursday incidents took place in 1946. The game created a great deal of interest because South Carolina's popular coach, Enright, had returned to coaching for the first time since his tour of duty with the Navy. The game was completely sold out by August. Even professional scalpers had trouble securing tickets, which were as scarce as Republicans in the state capital. Then about a week before the game, tickets were mysteriously available for purchasing. Printer

C. Miles Morrison, who had printed the genuine tickets, discovered there was something wrong with the type that appeared on the new supply of tickets. He called the police, who then questioned the people selling the tickets. They finally admitted that they had brought in a batch of counterfeit tickets from an out-of-state printer.

It was only the beginning of the problem. On game day, an untold number of fans holding the counterfeits were denied admission to Carolina Stadium. Near game time, the angry crowd had swelled to thousands. Even Howard encountered trouble getting his players through the gates. He had to identify every player near the entrance. Finally, after he had gotten all his players safely through, Howard was stopped by a guard. He was taken aback for a moment.

"It doesn't matter if you let me in or not; but if you don't there isn't going to be a game," exclaimed Howard.

As soon as the kickoff took place, the frenzied mob stormed the gates, succeeded in crashing through, and headed straight for the sidelines. They ringed the entire field, five and six deep. They covered both benches and fans

76

who were sitting in the lower stands couldn't see the field. Clemson president Dr. Robert F. Poole was sitting with Secretary of State James F. Byrnes, and the only time they saw the ball was when it was punted. Fortunately, someone in their box had a portable radio, and they were able to keep abreast of the action that was taking place before them, even though they couldn't see anything.

At halftime, when Dr. Poole was leading Byrnes, Governor Williams, Governor-elect Strom Thurmond, and Senators Olin Johnston and Burnet Maybank to the South Carolina side of the field, their walk was interrupted when two Clemson fans ran on the field, one with a chicken in his hands. They stopped and began wringing the chicken's neck so feverishly that feathers were flying all over the place. Infuriated Carolina fans chased after them. Real trouble never developed. Quick-acting state policemen intervened and dispersed the combatants. Actually, Byrnes' presence on the field helped. A good portion of the crowd ran over to him just to shake his hand.

Bob Bradley, who for almost three decades has been Clemson's invaluable sports information director, and who is rightly considered a sports historian par excellence, was a student at the time.

"That '46 game was something," Bradley recalls. "Somebody had a live chicken in the Clemson student section. Well, they were throwing the poor thing up, and somebody would catch it. Then somebody else would throw it, and somebody else would catch it. Finally, at halftime a student took the chicken out to midfield and wrung its neck. As soon as the feathers started to fly, both student bodies met at midfield. I'll say one thing, though, the field was covered with feathers. I never knew a chicken had that many feathers."

Bradley saw his first Clemson-South Carolina game in 1941 when he was a freshman. "I had my little cadet uniform on back in '41, so everybody in Columbia knew I was from Clemson," said Bradley. "We were supposed to beat them good; but we lost, 18-14. I had to go into service after that, and I missed a few of the games, but I haven't missed one since 1953."

Until he died in 1964, leaving a void that no one would dare fill, Frank B. "Gator" Farr, a 1930 graduate of Clemson, returned to Clemson every year, the week before the South Carolina game, to preach the mock funeral of the Gamecock. It was no ordinary funeral, but a colorful ritual with enough pomp and ceremony as would be befitting a king's funeral. Farr would arrive at Clemson, having made the journey from his home in Paleteka, Florida, and perform his ceremony that same night dressed in split tails and top hat at a giant outdoor pep rally. An honor guard and pallbearers carried a coffin that had a stuffed chicken protruding at one end of the open box. The coffin itself dated back to 1940 when Clemson played in its first bowl game against Boston College. The Eagle students were so confident that they would devour the Tigers in the Cotton Bowl, they brought a coffin to Dallas all the way from Boston. After Clemson upset Boston College, 6-3, the Eagle fans gave the coffin to Clemson to take back.

Farr made good use of it. He would stand behind the coffin and read from a well-prepared text for some thirty minutes. His annual theme was, of course, that "no Gamecock shall strike a Tiger and be permitted to live." Then, he would recite from the ladies' ready-to-wear section of the fall edition of the Sears and Roebuck catalogue. And finally he would review Clemson's season, up until that point, and cleverly rhyme his text every two lines. Then the large student body would perform a snakedance through town before rallying around a large bonfire to conclude the night's festivities. "Gator" would pack up his outfit and keep it until next year when he would go through the routine again.

In 1948, Clemson enjoyed one of its greatest seasons, going unbeaten in eleven games before then going on to defeat Missouri in the Gator Bowl. The closest they came to losing was averted by a last minute touchdown that Clemson scored against Carolina for a 13-7 victory. The touchdown was set up on a great defensive play by tackle Phil Prince. Carolina quarterback Harold "Bo" Hagen was forced to punt from his own 28-yard line in the closing moments of the game. Prince broke through and blocked the punt. Oscar Thompson

Wide receiver Jerry Butler makes a fantastic catch of quarterback Steve Fuller's pass for a touchdown in last minute of play which gave Clemson a come-from-behind 31-27 victory in 1977.

scooped the ball and ran into the end zone with the winning touchdown.

"I just followed the coach's instructions and rushed to the outside," said Prince, now a senior vice-president with American Express in New York. "For some reason, Hagen was aiming toward my side of the field, and I got in and blocked the punt. Needless to say, Coach Howard was very pleased. Beating our arch rivals gave us a lift for the rest of the season. The win brought us together as a team."

It also brought a die-hard Clemson fan some quick money. Bradley remembers it.

"We were trailing 7-6, and this Clemson fan stood up in the stands and waved a $100 bill around, wanting to bet that Clemson would score on the next play. We didn't have the ball at the time, so he had a few takers. Well, Prince made the big play and blocked the punt; and we ran it in for the touchdown. So, this guy just went right to the people he had bets with and collected several hundred dollars.

"Most people don't realize it now," Bradley says, "but the rivalry with South Carolina didn't really peak until after World War II. Our biggest rival up until then had been Furman, but Furman dropped football during the

war, and their program went down a little bit because of that. South Carolina took over from that point, and it just grew from there. We always played on the third Thursday in October because they always had the State Fair in Columbia at the time; Big Thursday had been a tradition for 45 years before World War II and 16 afterwards. But that Thursday didn't work after a while because once the game was over, there was no football interest left in the state. There were still college and high school games to play, but the interest just wasn't the same."

The last Big Thursday game occurred on October 22, 1959. By that time, even the mild-mannered and jovial Howard was weary of the arrangement after having taken part in 30 of them, more than any other single coach.

"We always had to sit in the sun, and we got tired of going down there every year," said Howard. "We weren't getting half of the tickets, half of the program and concession sales, and it knocked one game out of our schedule because we couldn't play the Saturday before or the Saturday after the Thursday game."

The first Saturday meeting was scheduled for November 12, 1960. It was the first time Clemson was the home team in the long-running series. Sadly, the game didn't live up to the excitement of past ones, although Clemson won, 12-2. Bradley described it as "the worst game you'd ever want to see."

Perhaps the dullness created the tempo the following year when the game returned to Columbia. At least, it established the excellence for hijinks. Unfortunately, Clemson was the victim of a Carolina Caper that was cleverly schemed and executed. Two Sigma Nu Fraternity brothers, Dick Melton and Gordon Roman, devised a ruse that was shrouded with secrecy. Roman, a Yankee from New Jersey, spearheaded a plan to dress the members of the fraternity in Clemson uniforms and trot onto the field for pre-game warm-ups while the Tiger players were still getting ready in the dressing room. First, Roman had to convince Carolina coach Marvin Bass of the idea. Bass agreed to the antic and even provided a locker room for the Sigma Nus to dress in. Bass also supplied them with helmets which were white but had garnet and black stripes painted on

Tailback Cliff Austin breaks loose in 1982 game won by Clemson, 24-

them. It didn't present a problem to the anxious pranksters. They neatly covered the stripes with orange tape.

Uniforms, however, were another problem. There were no orange jerseys at all in the athletic department, so Melton and Roman made a check of high schools in the area and located some at, appropriately enough, Orangeburg High School. That wasn't all. The determined youngsters practiced for close to a month without their secret being uncovered. All that remained was perfect execution the day of the game. That required even more secrecy. The fraternity members who had dates for the game merely left their seats under the guise of going for a Coke and headed straight for the locker room instead.

A large crowd, as usual, had arrived early for the game. Some four sections of fans were filled by Clemson supporters, highlighted by the freshmen who had shaven heads and were wearing silly-looking orange beanies known as "rat hats," that were required until after the South Carolina game. When the imposters began running out of the visitor's tunnel, the Clemson band began to play the "Tiger Rag" as the entire Clemson section supported them with cheers. Right behind the team was a beefy person attired in a suit and fedora who resembled Howard.

The charade continued flawlessly. The jesters ran to the Clemson end of the field and lined up to begin their warm-up exercises. Nobody suspected anything. They then dispersed into specialty groups, offense and defense, and continued their drills. However, the crowd's suspicion was quickly aroused when the runners fumbled, the pass receivers dropped balls, and the kickers really couldn't kick. The last bit of nonsense resulted in the masqueraders doing the Chubby Checker version of "The Peppermint Twist." As soon as that happened, the stands of the Clemson section emptied onto the field. By now, it was each man for himself. Fortunately, there weren't any serious injuries, only bruised feelings.

"We thought we would fool them for a while," said Ronald Leitch, the prankster who impersonated Howard so well. "I wore an old

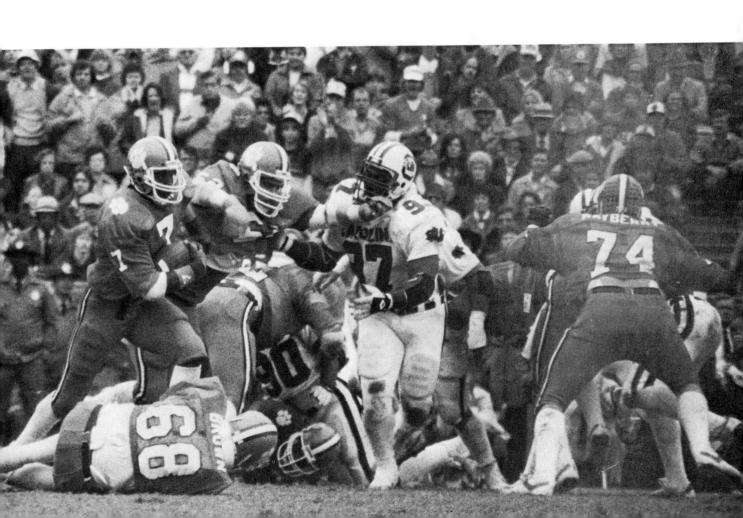

Clemson coach Frank Howard blows a kiss that marked the end of Big Thursday game in 1959.

brown suit my dad had, put on an old felt hat, and stuck five pieces of bubble gum in my cheeks. I met Frank Howard several years later at a civic club meeting. I went over and introduced myself and told him that I was the one who had played him. He was delighted and thought it was a great thing. He only wished Clemson had thought of it first."

The spoof is still talked about whenever Clemson and South Carolina get together. Cal McMeekin, a Clemson alumnus in Columbia, remembers the charade.

"It was a good trick, and I guess that's the kind of thing that makes a rivalry like this," says McMeekin, who claimed he wasn't entirely fooled by the shenanigans.

That same fraternity had another caper planned which would have certainly added to the excitement and brought the Clemson fans out of their seats and onto the field for a second time. However, it never took place.

"They had a scrawny-looking cow hidden under the stands," said Bradley, "and they were going to bring it out during the Homecoming ceremonies and present it as

Clemson's Homecoming Queen, but ole Bossy had a heart attack, and they never made it. I suppose that the cow got under there and heard all that commotion from those metal bleachers and just keeled over."

The game marked the last time the teams met during the middle part of the season. In 1962, the Clemson-South Carolina rivalry was officially ushered in as the last game on the schedule of both teams. Howard, who had been working toward that goal, liked it.

"It takes away from your season when you have to play your arch-rival in the middle of it," said Howard. "Playing it at the end of the year gives you something to look forward to."

The 1963 game was scheduled to be on regional television for the first time. However, the national tragedy created by the assassination of President John Kennedy forced the presidents of both institutions to postpone the game until the following Thursday, which happened to be Thanksgiving. The postponement, coupled with the holiday, resulted in the first non-capacity crowd to view the game since the days of World War II. It wasn't until

1977 that the series attracted regional television again. College football fans weren't disappointed at all. Clemson quarterback Steve Fuller drove the Tigers 67 yards in the final 50 seconds to pull out a last-second victory, 31-27. The dramatic play that Clemson fans remember was Fuller's 20-yard pass to wide receiver Jerry Butler, who made a leaping, twisting catch on the goal line for the winning touchdown.

Four years later, the series provided even more excitement. Clemson was driving toward its first undefeated season since 1948. Playing the game in Columbia only added to the tension. Not only was their unbeaten season on the line, but Clemson also had high hopes of finishing the 1981 season as the nation's number-one ranked team, which had never happened before. They entered the game as the country's number-two team, which was the highest rating they had ever achieved.

Mrs. Biddie Lee (Bill) Campbell, who lives in Anderson, and her friend, Mrs. Nettie Morgan of West Pulitzer, have been closely watching Clemson games for years, attending games together, and even making several post-season bowl trips. They were anxiously awaiting this one.

"This game means plenty, and it means we're going to win," said the 74-year-old Mrs. Campbell. "We're going down to the Orange Bowl, no question about it."

"I'm just anxious for it to be over with," said Mrs. Morgan. "It just has always been a fantastic rivalry. Of course, there are a lot of Gamecock fans around here; but we get along fine."

Even Abbey Richardson of New York, who was dating a Clemson graduate student at the time, was excited about the game, which Clemson won, 29-13.

"People down here just go crazy about these games," she said. "It almost scared me the first time I saw it. But when Rick took me to last year's South Carolina game, I kind of really got into it. Now I'm Clemson all the way."

Jim Phillips started broadcasting Tiger football games in 1968, and had no idea how intense the rivalry could become between Clemson and South Carolina. A native of Ohio, Phillips called the first Clemson-South Carolina game he ever saw. He had been exposed to such rivalries as Ohio State-Michigan and Purdue-Indiana, but never this one down south.

"I guess the first couple of years here I still thought the Ohio State-Michigan rivalry was it," said Phillips. "I thought that this series wasn't much to shout about. But Clemson finally won in '71 after three straight losses, and I saw the response then."

Phillips' broadcasts of Tiger football are aired over WFBC in Greenville and are carried by 70 stations throughout the state. In 1979, he made a friendly wager with Jim Forrest, a sports announcer in Columbia whom Phillips knew from Ohio. The bet was simple. One or the other would wear the jersey of the winning team. South Carolina won that year, and Phillips had to wear a Gamecock jersey on his television show.

"It actually turned into a big promotion," said Phillips. "I had a bigger audience that week. I wore it three days, then agreed to auction it for multiple sclerosis. A guy paid a hundred bucks for it, and we raised pretty close to $500. I wanted No. 38, the George Rogers jersey, but I couldn't get it. The one I got belonged to a nondescript player, a guy who never played. I don't even remember the number."

Clemson coach Danny Ford also learned how much the rivalry meant to Tiger fans. Ford had played at the University of Alabama, and was caught up in the deep-rooted rivalry with Auburn. After three years as Clemson's coach, he realized that this one was bigger.

"This is a game that's not always won by the best football team or by who's supposed to be the best football team," said Ford. "But on that Saturday, you prove who has the best football team. Now, Alabama-Auburn is a great, great rivalry, and they get after it. They have their land-grant jokes and their doctor and lawyer jokes; and there's books of 100 Alabama jokes and 100 Auburn jokes—just like it is here. But they let it die about the end of February.

"The Clemson-South Carolina rivalry, they don't let die. For 365 days a year there's somebody at every function you go to who's talking about Clemson or South Carolina against each other. It's simply the biggest and the best rivalry in football."

6

1940
COTTON BOWL

"That McFadden Put A Lot Of Gray Hairs On My Head"

The news that Clemson had been selected to play in the 1940 Cotton Bowl was received calmly, even though it was the first bowl bid the college had received. Daily life in the sleepy town was undisturbed. Pickens "Doc" McCollum still opened his campus drugstore before nine a.m. every day. Captain Frank Clinkscales, who was also the mayor, busied himself in his livery stable which was right in the middle of town. Hoke Sloan attended to his haberdashery in the same easygoing manner as always; and "Uncle Bill" Greenlea, who claimed he had worked as a houseboy on Thomas Clemson's plantation back in the 1880's, was busy raking the leaves that had fallen from the oak and elm trees that dotted the campus.

However, the mention of Clemson College created a shock in staid old Boston. The cosmopolitan city people had never even heard of Clemson. They wondered where it was located and who the upstarts might be who would play mighty Boston College. There was so much mystery regarding Clemson that the Boston Post dispatched one of its sportswriters, Gerry Hern, to the campus to whip up a series of articles about the school. It was an experience that the veteran correspondent never forgot.

Hern's odyssey began, of all places, in Knoxville, Tennessee. When Hern's newspaper was making his travel arrangements, they couldn't find an airport listing for Clemson. When he arrived, he claimed the first thing that happened to him was that he was almost run over by a mule. It was true. One of the mules in Clinkscales' stable had gotten loose and was running through the streets.

The quiet southern hamlet proved fascinating to Hern. He was intrigued by John Martin's General Store, Judge Kelleher's Emporium, Cliff Crawford's Dry Cleaners, and Mr. Newton's Shoe Parlor which advertised electrical shoe repairing. The only knowledge he had about the football team was that they had finished the season with an 8-1 record, were coached by Jess Neely, and had a triple threat All-American tailback named James "Bonnie Banks" McFadden who could run, throw, and kick with unrivaled skill.

Hern was also surprised to learn that Neely's office was on the second floor of the old fertilizer building. There was only a thin partition

Charlie Timmons ran for 115 yards against Boston College
and scored the game's only touchdown.

Banks McFadden was a triple threat
with his running, passing and kicking. He was
Clemson's first All-American in 1939.

separating Neely's office from the third grade of the campus grammar school for faculty children. The classroom was so close that Neely knew by heart all the words of the song the children sang every day, "Oats, peas, beans, and barley grow..."

Neely wasn't exactly a talkative person. He was deeply involved with the football team and spent most of his time on the field or in his office. In fact, whenever he dropped by one of the stores in town, he spoke so slowly that a local wag remarked, "You could roll a cigarette by the time Jess asks you how you're feeling." Meanwhile, Neely created an air of mystery by going to Atlanta for several days. Of course, he refused to comment on the reasons for the trip. The speculation around town was that he either went to see Clark Gable in "Gone With The Wind," or that he had held a secret meeting with Josh Cody, who had coached Clemson before Neely took over. Cody was now coaching Florida, which was the only team that had defeated Boston College that year, and there were suspicions that Neely was getting some scouting reports on the Eagles from the former Clemson coach.

Hern spent a week in Clemson. He seemed impressed with the town and its people whom he found to be friendly. The quiet setting of the college was quite different from the hustle and bustle of Boston. He mentioned in one of his articles that although the team was nick-

named the Tigers, the players prefer to be known as the Country Gentlemen. When Neely returned from Atlanta, he spoke to Hern in his office.

"Well, I'd rather Boston knew our offense so we could try a lot of trick stuff," Neely told him. "The boys love fancy plays. In fact, every now and then they make one up on the field; and if I don't recognize a play, I'm sure Boston coach Frank Leahy won't.

"That McFadden put a lot of these gray hairs on my head. I don't discourage him any. He's a right smart tailback; and if he feels he has worked the team into a bad spot, I like to see him get reckless. We've scored a few touchdowns on plays I've never seen before. Here's how our huddle works. When the boys come back into it to get the play from Banks, some of the boys may say, 'That halfback on my side was out of position on that play. Let's give him old 93.' Banks says, 'No, but let me know what he does on this next one.'

"If that defensive back makes the same mistake twice, Banks calls for a play through him. He doesn't need to be told what plays to call, generally speaking. Once in a while I see a chance and send in a tailback to take Banks' place but not very often."

There was no question that "Bonnie Banks" McFadden was the local hero. Since he was Clemson's first All-American, he was idolized by all the youngsters in town. They called him "Banksie." The previous year he was also named an All-American in basketball and quite possibly was the first college athlete to achieve such status in two sports. He was thin and willowy, standing about 6'3" and weighing 174 pounds, and he had an engaging personality to accompany his good looks. He claimed he could catch rabbits by hypnotizing them, simply by wiggling his ears.

James McFadden grew up in a small town in South Carolina called Great Falls.

"Why, there's no such place," said McFadden one day to Hern on the steps outside of the barracks. "It's kind of a crossing. Everybody is kind of a colonel there. Every time an auto goes through Great Falls, the colonels line up on the sidewalk and shake their heads, muttering, 'Heavens to Betsy, what'll they think of next?' I don't know how many people are there, but I'm sure that every one of them is living."

A friendly type with a fine sense of humor, McFadden would stop between classes to talk to anyone who called to him. One day one of the yard men stopped him. He didn't even talk football. Instead, they discussed whether or not a local widower with seven sons should marry a widow with 13 sons and daughters, which was the big social topic around town. Until it was settled, the widower would do his courting on Sunday evening. McFadden couldn't help solve the problem.

"It was like this one old guy around here who was married five times and shot two of his wives," McFadden told Hern. "He admitted shooting them in the legs with a little bird shot. He said, 'It probably didn't do so much harm, and it certainly did them good. But, gosh, that was back when I was a middle-aged man.'"

Not only was McFadden a local hero, but he had earned a reputation around the state as well. Once, when he was a sophomore in high school, he got off a punt that traveled so far that the officials stopped the game to measure it. A short time after he was named an All-American, Governor Burnet R. Maybank gave a speech in Clemson to honor McFadden.

"Banks," said the governor, "your making the All-America team is worth $10,000 to the state of South Carolina."

"Gov," shouted McFadden, "you just put that in writing—on a check."

McFadden had solid support in the backfield from Shad Bryant and Charlie Timmons. And the three of them operated behind a big, bruising line led by Joe Blalock, George Fritts, Bob Sharpe, Tom Moorer, and Walter Cox. Actually, Cox filled in for Howard Payne, a fine guard who was switched to the backfield, and developed into the squad's finest blocker. But their hidden strength was their defense, which had allowed only 42 points in the nine games they played that season. Before the Cotton Bowl the only loss Clemson suffered occurred in the second game of the season when they were nipped by Tulane, 7-6.

A crowd of 20,000 may seem small today,

but that many people came to the Cotton Bowl on a cold afternoon in Dallas to see little Clemson go against the big eastern power, Boston College. It was the largest crowd that Clemson had ever played before.

After a scoreless first period, the Eagles scored in the opening minutes of the second quarter. Alex Lubachik kicked a 26-yard field goal to push Boston College in front, 3-0. After McFadden put the Eagles in the hole with a quick kick, the Eagles didn't hesitate to punt the ball back to Clemson. Starting on their own 43-yard line, the Tigers mounted a drive. McFadden led the way with a 12-yard run and a 16-yard pass. Timmons crowned the drive by plunging for a touchdown from the one-yard line. Bryant missed the extra point, but Clemson led, 6-3. Nobody expected that the halftime score would be the final score as well. McFadden played brilliantly on defense, knocking away Boston quarterback Charlie O'Rourke's passes time and again while averaging 43 yards on his punts.

"Clemson is every bit as good as they were cracked up to be," praised Leahy. "We lost to a great team, one of the best I have ever seen. I have the satisfaction of knowing that while we were beaten, the game wasn't lost on a fluke."

Yet, Clemson didn't get to fully savor its victory. There were reports after the game that Neely had been offered a five-year contract to coach Rice. Neely wouldn't comment. Several weeks later, he did indeed leave Clemson to take the Rice job.

1940 COTTON BOWL
January 1, 1940
Dallas, TX

CLEMSON	0	6	0	0	– 6
BOSTON	0	3	0	0	– 3

BC—Lukachik 34 FG
CU—Timmons 2 run (Kick failed)
Attendance: 20,000

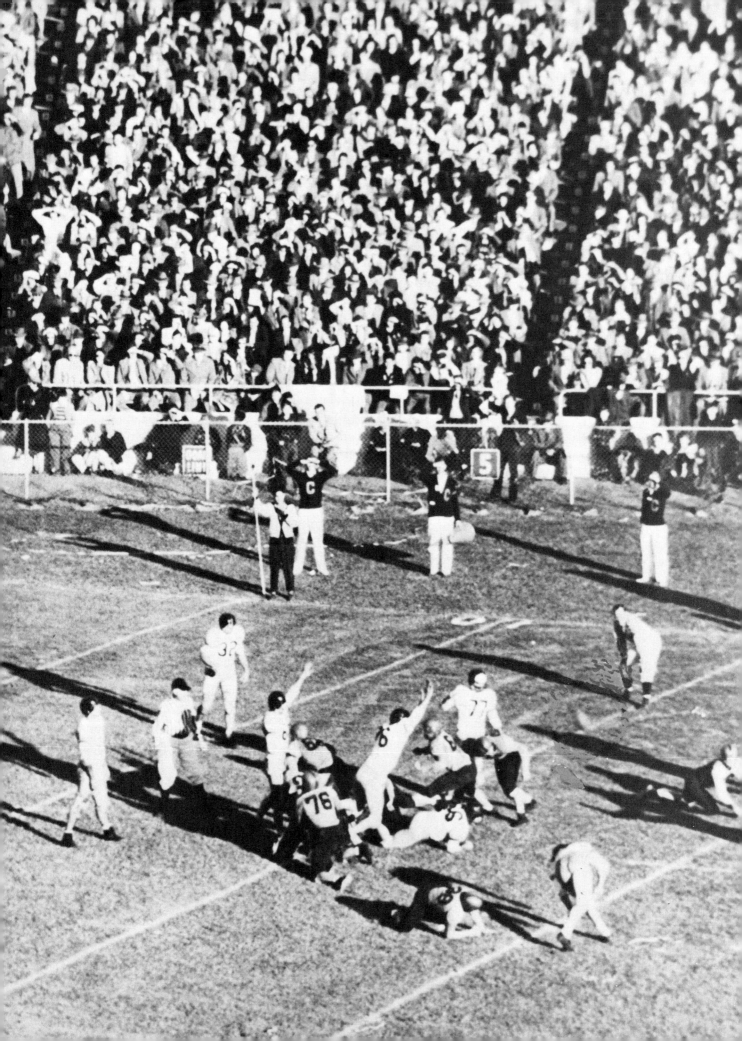

7

1949
GATOR BOWL

"This Is The Best Team I Have Ever Coached"

Although Clemson finished with identical 4-5 records in 1946 and 1947, coach Frank Howard must have suspected the future would be brighter. He scheduled ten games for Clemson in 1948 and the Tigers went out and won all of them. No college team in the state of South Carolina had produced an unbeaten season in 48 years, and it was such a momentous accomplishment that the Tigers were toasted at a gala banquet in Eppes Restaurant in Greenville that was attended by 300 guests and chaired by the governor of South Carolina, J. Strom Thurmond. Since the governor was himself a Clemson alumnus, the occasion was that much more meaningful to him.

"I am proud of Frank Howard," Thurmond began in his after-dinner speech. "I'm glad that he was named coach of the year, an honor he deserved. I appreciate the fine work he has done. I am proud of the team because it is a South Carolina team and because it is my team. The team has brought fame to South Carolina and to Clemson. Dr. Poole could advertise in every paper and periodical in the United States and couldn't get the publicity that you, the Clemson team, have brought to Clemson. The prestige this fine championship football squad has given to the institution, the state, and the nation has increased the value of every diploma Clemson has issued or will issue. This fame will last for years."

But coach Howard was only hoping it would last long enough to beat Missouri in the Gator Bowl. The experts around the country didn't think it was likely. Despite the fact that Clemson, Michigan and California were the only undefeated teams in the nation, the forecasters established Missouri as a one-touchdown favorite. The analysts were convinced that Missouri had played a much tougher schedule. In addition they felt Missouri's coach, Don Faurot, was more of a household name than was Howard and his squad of Tigers, who had more often been called "Country Gentlemen." The experts were not impressed with the knowledge that Clemson had scored 250 points while yielding only 53 to their opponents.

Maybe because his team had managed to go unbeaten, or perhaps it was because this was his first bowl game as head coach that Howard became more superstitious. When he arrived in Jacksonville for the game, Howard brought along two suitcases. One contained his clothes, and the

Jack Miller booted a 32-yard field goal in the fourth period
which enabled Clemson to edge Missouri, 24-23.

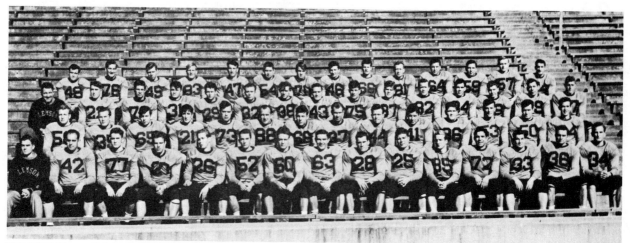

The 1948 Tigers finished the season unbeaten with an 11-0 record.

other was packed with an assortment of charms. If the charms meant anything, then Missouri was in for a long afternoon. Howard's good luck trinkets included a horseshoe a friend had given him before Clemson had beaten South Carolina in the traditional state fair game, the tooth of an Indian tiger, which was reputed to have brought luck to many wartime fliers, and a hat that he took with him on every road game, that had been given him by a Clemson haberdasher. It didn't end there. Each member of the football team carried a good luck buckeye nut. They were given to the players by the Pickens, South Carolina, weekly newspaper editor, Gary Hiott. It was a reminder that the Ohio State Buckeyes were one of the two teams that had defeated Missouri.

Howard had put together a fine backfield. As usual, the defense was powerful, but it was the offensive punch of the Tigers that was the team's strongest point. Tailback Bobby Gage had gained over 1,000 yards during the season, most of it with his passing. Fred Cone was a young, hard-running fullback, and Bob Martin, the team's captain, was a veteran quarterback. The star of the backfield was wingback Ray Mathews. He had led the Southern Conference in scoring with 78 points and had beaten out North Carolina's highly heralded "Choo Choo" Justice, who had 66. Only a sophomore, Mathews had gained 573 yards rushing and had caught 13 passes for 363 more yards. He capped the regular season by scoring all three touchdowns in a 20-0 victory over The Citadel.

"He's my old faithful," Howard said. "We couldn't operate without him."

In truth, Missouri represented a stern test for the Tigers. They had easily won eight of ten games. Faurot, who had invented the Missouri Split-T, had produced an explosive offense. More impressive, Missouri had averaged a little better than 36 points a game and their line outweighed Clemson's by five pounds per man. Other than the Buckeye game, Missouri's only loss was to Oklahoma, the Big Seven champion, and Missouri had finished in the runner-up spot behind the Sooners.

"As soon as I knew we'd be playing Missouri, I went over to Duke to visit my ole buddy Wallace Wade," Howard said. "We didn't know much about that Split-T, and Duke had played Missouri the year before and got beat 34-7. I spent the whole day learning about the formation from coach Wade. When I was ready to leave, he asked me if I was going to use his defense. When I told him I wasn't, he wanted to know why I had wasted his time and mine. I told him that it hadn't been a waste at all, that I had learned plenty, especially what defense not to use.

"Honestly, before the season began I thought maybe we might win six; and again I thought maybe we might lose six. I probably chewed more tobacco that year than ever before. If I had to guess why we had such a good season, I'd say it was because we all pitched in with the material we had, worked hard and played hard."

Howard, indeed, worked his team hard before the Gator Bowl. He really hadn't been pleased with the way his team played in the final two games of the season against Auburn and The Citadel, although they won both. He had only two weeks to get the Tigers ready for their biggest game of the year, and he didn't spare any time. He put the Tigers through rigorous practices before they left for Jacksonville; and once there, he drilled them in secret workouts.

"We've been slipping, going backward," Howard told reporters. "Those last two games didn't look very good from where I was sitting. I'm afraid they slacked up in general when they read how those last few games were sure-fire bets....No, we aren't trying to work out any special defenses for Missouri. We're just trying to play football. Missouri's Split-T is, as far as I'm concerned, another T. If you're smart and fast, you can break it up without a lot of tricky defense...I don't give a damn which is the best team. We want to win."

Almost all the seats, except the ones in the end zone, were filled by game time. A crowd of 35,273 was in the stands, which was the largest crowd ever to see a football game in Jacksonville. Clemson went to work quickly by recovering a Missouri fumble on the 19-yard line and scoring five plays later on a one-yard plunge by Cone. Later in the period, Cone scored again from a yard out to give Clemson a 14-0 lead.

In the second quarter, Missouri struck back. They scored early in the period; and then with five minutes remaining in the half, they tied the game at 14-14. Nothing appeared to be going right for Clemson at this point. The halftime ceremonies ran too long, and the Clemson drill platoon had to shorten its presentation.

However, Clemson took the second half kickoff and marched straight down field. The touchdown that put them back on top again, 21-14, came on a tricky pass play from Gage to Johnny Pulos that fooled Missouri completely. Near the end of the quarter, Missouri added a safety when Gage misplayed a punt. The two points trimmed the Tigers' lead to 21-16 when the third quarter ended and the stands were in pandemonium.

Midway through the final period, Clemson added to its lead. Jack Miller booted a 32-yard field goal that stretched the Tigers' edge to 24-16. They needed it, too, because Missouri moved quickly after taking the kickoff and scored on a 20-yard pass play. In the closing minutes of the game, however, Clemson hung on to its 24-23 lead and ran the clock out with three first downs.

"This is the best team I have ever coached," said Howard. "Missouri scored last and chiseled our lead to 24-23. They kicked off to us, and we moved into their territory but had a fourth and three situation at the Missouri 41. A decision had to be made, whether to run and try to keep possession or kick and give Missouri another chance to score.

"Bobby Gage decided to go for it. I turned to Pop Cohen, our backfield coach at that time, and said, 'Old man, if they make it, I'll be a great coach. If they don't, they might ride me out of Clemson.' Gage gave the ball to Fred Cone, our fullback. He met a stone wall and I thought we'd had it, but he slid off and found a hole a little more to the outside and made six yards and a first down at the Missouri 35. That one six-yard play stands out in my mind the most, and this boy Cone is the best player I ever coached."

1949 GATOR BOWL
January 1, 1949
Jacksonville, FL

CLEMSON	14	0	7	3	–	24
MISSOURI	0	14	2	7	–	23

CU—Cone 1 run (Miller kick)
CU—Cone 1 run (Miller kick)
UM—Entsminger 2 run (Dawson kick)
UM—Entsminger 1 run (Dawson kick)
CU—Poulos 9 pass from Gage (Miller kick)
UM—Safety, Gage pass grounded in end zone
CU—Miller 32 FG
UM—Bounds 20 pass from Braznell (Dawson kick)
Attendance: 35,273

8

1951 ORANGE BOWL

"Read The AP Poll If You Want To Know About Clemson"

In 1950, the Tigers were undefeated once again. There weren't many other teams in the country that could match Clemson's 8-0-1 record, the tie having occurred in a 14-14 game against South Carolina that had been played on a rain-swept, muddy field at Columbia. In fact, some experts believed that Clemson had the best single wing attack in the country. The Tigers were ranked tenth in the final college poll, the highest position they had ever achieved. It should have brought them recognition and respect. Strangely, it didn't produce either.

Coach Frank Howard, who was usually jovial and never one to worry about things, seemed a bit concerned after a celebratory banquet, one of the many he attended following Clemson's excellent season. He had just finished a dinner of ham, red eye gravy, and hominy grits; yet, the unflappable Howard was concerned. Only several days earlier, Clemson had been invited to play in the 1951 Orange Bowl game against the University of Miami. That alone should have pleased him. But once again, the grapevine had it that the Miami populace was disappointed about playing little-known Clemson.

"Shucks, we've won the only two bowl games we've been in, which don't seem to mean much to some folks," Howard said. "They ought to read the AP poll if they want to know about Clemson."

The anti-Clemson sentiment that had erupted in Miami moved a former Tiger alumnus, Gene Plowden, to act. He was in a good position to do something, too, since he was a sportswriter for the Associated Press in Miami, and he was tired of the derogatory stories he had seen about the school. He wrote a cleverly worded letter to Howard that was carried on the national wires. Plowden wrote:

"Personal note to Frank Howard, head football coach at Clemson College:

"Dear Frank:
"You and your players can do a great job of 'educating' South Florida football followers when the Tigers meet the University of Miami Hurricanes in the Orange Bowl here New Year's Day. The storm that broke

Wingback Ray Mathews drives for yardage against Miami.

when the selection was announced almost a week ago hasn't subsided yet.

"'Who is Clemson?' was a familiar cry. 'Who have they played? What town is it in? I never heard of it. Is it a new wonder drug or something?'

"Many seem to have taken the choice as a personal affront. Some said even Miami's beloved Hurricanes were insulted. One writer commented that he thought Clemson was some sort of animal being added to the Ringling Brothers and Barnum and Bailey Circus.

"'The choice of Clemson to meet the Hurricanes was a surprise,' said one of the more charitable writers. 'Some will applaud. Others will object. Some of the fans are yelping over the choice of Clemson. I concur from a publicity standpoint we did not come up with a scoop, but I do think that Clemson has a good football team and that our chances for an exciting contest are very good. If you are disappointed, accept it in good spirits. After all, it's not the first time the Orange Bowl committee has disappointed you.'

"Another writer wrote: 'There's no use having apoplexy over Clemson's selection. We're stuck with it, so let the disappointment go at that.'

"We know Clemson ranked 10th in the Associated Press football poll, while Miami was 15th; and you had a good point when you said, 'Tell them to read the AP poll if they want to know about Clemson.' You saw Miami whip Missouri, 27-0, on the Hurricanes' home grounds, the same team Clemson walloped, 34-0, early in the season in Missouri.

"I thought you summed it up nicely the other day when you said: 'They don't have to worry about us. The people will see a good football game. There are a lot of schools with older traditions than Clemson, but there aren't many with a better team. You can't play tradition.'

"You are right, Frank, and the records show Clemson fared pretty well against Boston College in the Cotton Bowl in 1940 and against Missouri in the Gator Bowl two

years ago. As a Clemson alumnus, I may be a bit biased; but I do believe this Orange Bowl will rank with the best, and I've seen some thrillers. So, bring your boys down and show these Miamians a thing or two, Frank. They can stand a little enlightening.

"Sincerely,
"GENE PLOWDEN
"(Clemson '24)

"P.S. By the way, you don't happen to have a couple of Orange Bowl tickets lying around, do you, Frank? There isn't a one left in town."

The Orange Bowl was the only bowl to present two unbeaten teams. Miami, like Clemson, had a 8-0-1 record. (The Miami tie was in a game against the University of Louisville, 14-14.) While the selection committee for the Orange Bowl was unanimous in its selection of Miami, they were openly split regarding Clemson's appearance. Several of the members had voiced support for twice-beaten Alabama. Yet, Howard was gracious in accepting the invitation to participate, knowing, of course, that the Gator Bowl officials also wanted Clemson if the Orange Bowl had collapsed.

"I'm very happy that Clemson is to play in the Orange Bowl with such a worthy opponent as Miami," Howard said when the Orange Bowl committee finally made up its mind. "Our boys deserve all the credit. They have played for the team's success as a whole and not for individual glory. I believe we have more outstanding players than other teams, and in the interest of all of them, the school, the alumni, and the state, I'm thrilled to death. We hope to play a good game. I am sure we will."

One of the outstanding players Howard was referring to was fullback Fred Cone, who was playing his final year for Clemson. Cone not only enjoyed his best season, but was also the team captain. He had led the Tigers in rushing, with 845 yards, and in scoring, with 92 points, and was selected on the All-Southern Conference team. Howard believed that the 180-pound Cone was the best fullback in the country. And there was wingback Ray

Mathews, who had topped the Tigers in rushing the previous two years, who was also ending his career. Howard also had a good-looking prospect in newcomer Billy Hair at tailback. He had passed for three touchdowns against Duquesne and ran for two more, and he also tossed two touchdown passes against Furman. The remaining members of Clemson's strong backfield were blocking backs Windy Wyndham and Dick Hendley and wingback Jackie Calvert. They had scored a total of 329 points, while the usually strong defense had limited the opposition to just 63 points during the season.

The biggest pre-game rumor to circulate was that Howard had received several offers from other colleges. Howard could be close-mouthed when he wanted to and merely brushed off any comment.

"Aw, hush," he would say. "I got a little New Year's date with Miami to worry about right now."

Despite all the pre-game furor about Clemson, a crowd of 65,181 attended the contest. Once again, it was the largest crowd that any Clemson team had played before, and they were determined to perform well. They got as far as the Miami 37-yard line after the opening kickoff, but they stalled. After Miami was stopped, Clemson got the ball again but couldn't get a first down. After an exchange of punts, the first quarter ended scoreless.

Early in the second period, Hair was sent into the game. He immediately ran for seven yards and then threw a 45-yard pass to Bob Hudson on the Miami four-yard line. On third down, Cone took it from the one. Charlie Radcliff added the conversion to give underdog Clemson a 7-0 lead. Although the Tigers were in Miami's territory most of the second period, they couldn't score again by the end of the first half.

Hair ignited the Clemson offense once again in the third quarter. He completed three passes in a 75-yard drive, the last one for 21 yards to Glenn Smith for a touchdown. Radcliff missed the extra point, but Clemson led, 13-0. Miami struck back quickly for two touchdowns; and when the period ended, they had grabbed a 14-13 lead. Clemson's big play came midway during the final period, when Miami was backed up on its goal line. The Hurricanes' star runner, Frank Smith, tried to get some running room by taking a pitchout in the end zone. However, Sterling Smith, an unheralded non-scholarship guard, broke through and nailed the Miami runner for a safety that gave Clemson a 15-14 lead. The game ended some seven minutes later with the happy Tigers carrying Smith and Howard on their shoulders around the Orange Bowl.

Howard said years later that he would never forget the crowd noise or what Sterling Smith had done that day.

"I thought the stadium was caving in from the noise," Howard said. "When Sterling ran off the field after getting that safety, his daddy came down out of the stands and started hugging and kissing him like crazy. That night he took his son's game jersey and wore it all over town. I never saw such a proud parent in my life."

1951 ORANGE BOWL
January 1, 1951
Miami, FL

CLEMSON	0 7 6 2	–	15
MIAMI (FL)	0 0 14 0	–	14

CU—Cone 1 run (Radcliff kick)
CU—G. Smith 21 pass from Hair
   (Kick blocked)
UM—Mallios 5 run (Watson kick)
UM—F. Smith 17 pass from Hackett
   (Watson kick)
CU—Safety, F. Smith tackled in end zone
   by S. Smith
Attendance: 65,181

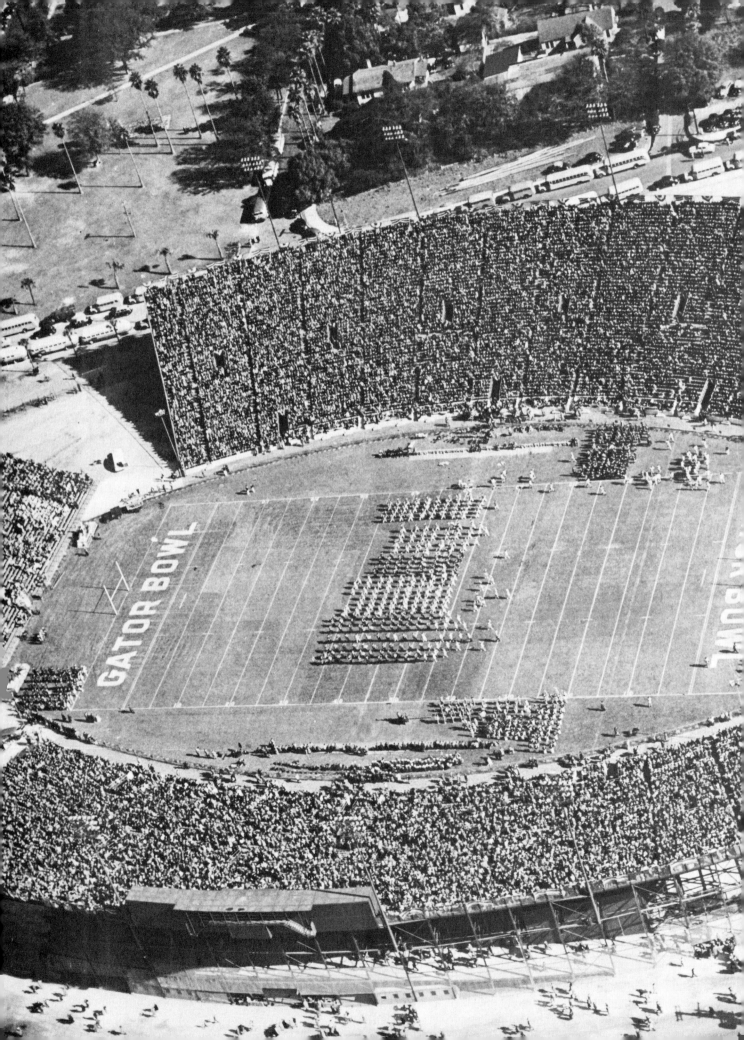

9

1952
GATOR BOWL

"We Knew We Were In The Wrong"

In 1951, the presidents of the 17-member Southern Conference schools decided that it was time to deemphasize football. A week after the season began, they had recommended that the conference ban bowl competition by member schools effective that year. The presidents' actions only served to underscore the discontent of some schools, Clemson and Maryland among them, who were intent on building their football program. No one realized it at the time, but the eventual outcome of the presidents' meeting resulted in the formation of the Atlantic Coast Conference in May of 1953.

By December, an ominous cloud hung over the Clemson campus. It placed a shadow on another winning season, one which the Tigers completed with a 7-3 record. Their success had earned them another bowl bid, this time to the Gator Bowl, in which Clemson would face Miami in a rematch of their thrilling Orange Bowl meeting in 1951. In late November, Clemson had polled conference members for permission to play in the Gator Bowl and received a negative answer. Nevertheless, they decided to accept the Gator Bowl offer, which was a direct violation of the conference's rule. Since Maryland had accepted a bid to play Tennessee in the Sugar Bowl, the Southern Conference found itself embroiled in a volatile situation.

Rumors began to circulate that Duke and North Carolina might withdraw from the conference if Clemson and Maryland were not expelled. Other stories were heard that Clemson and Maryland would bolt the conference on their own if they received such a harsh penalty. Both schools learned their fate at a December 15 meeting in Richmond. By a vote of 12-5, the conference placed Clemson and Maryland on one year's probation, which forbade any of the other members to play the two schools in 1952. The ruling took six games away from Maryland's schedule and five from the schedule Clemson had arranged. Coach Frank Howard, who was in Richmond when the probation was announced, voiced his complaint.

"I'll tell you, I don't think it's right," exclaimed Howard right after the meeting. "And I just want everybody to know that I don't think it's right."

Later that night in Richmond, where the meetings were conducted,

Howard did not sleep well. He was still a bit stunned by the action taken at the meetings.

"It was like I woke up this morning and found myself in Russia—if I had slept any to wake up," he said. "It used to be that in America a fellow could work hard and get along all right. I'm not so sure now. Down at Clemson we've been minding our business for a long time—and trying to win a few football games. We figured that a Gator Bowl bid came as the result of hard work.

"We knew the Southern Conference presidents were against the bowl games; and when they turned down our request for the right to go, we knew we were in the wrong. We came up here to Richmond to take our punishment like a man. I don't know what kind of punishment they call it, but tearing up our schedule is a little bit harsher than what we expected. Shucks, I don't mind it as much as some of the teams we are playing. It's going to hurt them more than us."

Meanwhile, Howard had to concentrate on getting his squad ready to meet the University of Miami for the second straight time. There was no love lost between the two schools, either. Howard gave his squad four days off for the Christmas holidays and told them to come back lean and mean. He warned them that Miami would be ready for them since they were still smarting from the previous year's defeat. He showed them a quote in the newspaper that Miami coach Andy Gustafson had made just before he dismissed his squad for the holidays.

"This is our chance to get even with a team that was awfully lucky to beat us in the Orange Bowl last year," said Gustafson.

That was enough to add fuel to the fire that had been simmering in Miami for a year. Howard realized it, too.

"We're cooking up a few new plays. But in the main, we'll stick to old-fashioned single wing, country style," Howard said. "We're beginning to look better with a little more shine on our offensive plays. Yeah, I think we improved some in our last four games of the season, but we're still not clicking consistently. I think our boys in the fourth period against Auburn looked better than even our Orange Bowl team looked at any time during the 1950

Billy Hair returned the opening kickoff 72 yards to Miami's 26 yard line but the Tigers failed to score.

campaign."

The Tigers really came alive the final four games of the season. Up until that juncture, they appeared mediocre with a 3-2 record. Then they roared past Wake Forest, 21-6; Boston College, 21-2; Furman, 34-14; and Auburn, 34-0. It was this strong finish that attracted the Gator Bowl officials to Clemson. Howard accomplished wonders after graduation removed the four mainstays of his 1950 backfield—Ray Mathews, Fred Cone, Jackie Calvert, and Dick Hendley.

In the four ending victories, Clemson had scored 110 points while surrendering only 22. Most of the offense was supplied by tailback Billy Hair and end Glenn Smith, both of whom were named to the All-Southern team. Hair's passing produced 1,004 yards, and his running accounted for 698 more. Smith caught seven touchdown passes and led the Tigers in scoring with 42 points.

Howard was still rankled when he arrived in Jacksonville five days before the game. He

Quarterback Steve Fuller (1975-78) holds a number of records.

Tiger cheerleader Mary Barnes.

The Tiger mascot does his number
on the slide trombone.

The first time the Tigers wore orange pants
was against South Carolina in the final game
of the 1980 season.

Clemson fans clearly demonstrate who is No. 1.

...e isn't room for another sticker.

What's more appropriate than orange soda
in toasting Clemson as the No. 1 team of 1981?

...ie Bauman (1977–80) was a cause célèbre
...e 1979 Gator Bowl game against Ohio State.

g can "hold that Tiger" once the band strikes up.

There is nothing prettier than a Tiger paw.

The Tiger cheerleaders and mascot get ready to entertain the hometown fans.

rterback Homer Jordan led the Tigers to an unbeaten season
the national championship in 1981.

The Clemson defense moves in on Herschel Walker of Georgia
in 1981 game in Death Valley. Clemson defeated the Dawgs, 13-3.

A quiet moment before a game.

Mr. Knickerbocker sells more Tiger souvenirs
than any store in South Carolina.

Running back Cliff Austin set a new single game
rushing mark by gaining 260 yards against Duke in 1982.

Tigermania starts at a young age.

Painting the Tiger paw on a main road.

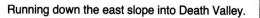

Running down the east slope into Death Valley.

Defensive tackle Ray Brown leads the Tigers off the field after the 1982 Orange Bowl win.

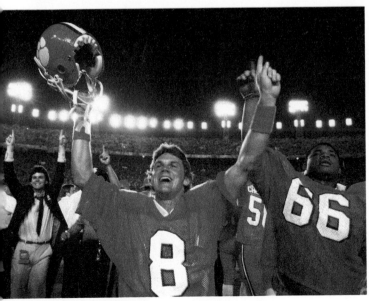
of Tiger players is apparent
e 22-15 Orange Bowl victory over Nebraska
er taking the No. 1 national ranking.

uttle looks for yardage
Nebraska in 1982 Orange Bowl game.

Coach Danny Ford expresses his view to an official.

The 1982 Orange Bowl Champions are rated the No. 1 college team of the 1981 season.

Even a Tiger has to relax sometime.

The Orange Bowl trophy.

poked sarcasm at the censure that had been inflicted on Clemson by the conference.

"They say we are bad," snapped Howard. "Well, if going to bowls makes you bad, I'd like to rot a little bit. Other conference teams can't play us because we're going to a bowl, but they can play Tennessee and Georgia Tech and Miami. They're going to bowls, too.

"But, I'm more concerned with the game we're getting ready to play. I think we're going to have a fine game. Miami has a pretty good team, better than last year's; and I don't know whether we can beat them or not. I don't know whether they can beat us. It's a toss-up.

"I must say the boys came back from the Christmas holidays in good shape. There wasn't too much evidence of overstuffing at the Christmas tree, but we're still working hard. We have to do our best to get ready to win if we can."

Clemson was appearing in its third bowl game in four years. They were a successful bowl participant, too, having won all three games. While the crowd wasn't anywhere as large as the one that turned out for the previous year's Orange Bowl, it was, nevertheless, a record Gator Bowl throng of 37,208 that was made comfortable by a sunny afternoon.

It didn't take long for the fans to become excited. Hair brought the crowd to its feet on the kickoff by racing 72 yards to Miami's 26 before he was pulled down. The Tigers were in excellent position to drive for a touchdown, but they only gained six yards on four plays and had to give up the ball.

With three minutes left in the first period, Miami drove 82 yards for a touchdown. Harry Mallios took a pitchout on the 11-yard line and raced to the corner of the end zone. Elmer Tremont accounted for the extra point, and Miami led 7-0.

In the second period, the Hurricanes scored again. They got the opportunity when they blocked Hair's punt on the Clemson 33-yard line. This time Mallios cracked over the two-yard line, and Tremont converted again to send Miami into a 14-0 halftime lead.

While the opening half was fairly evenly contested, the Tigers appeared fired up in the third period. Yet, they couldn't score. They held the edge in the final period and again came up empty. Despite holding Miami without a first down the entire second half, Clemson still lost the first bowl game in its history, 14-0. They simply made too many mistakes offensively.

1952 GATOR BOWL
January 1, 1952
Jacksonville, FL

CLEMSON	0	0	0	–	0	
MIAMI (FL)	7	7	0	–	14	

UM—Mallios 11 run (Tremont kick)
UM—Mallios 2 run (Tremont kick)
Attendance: 37,208

10

1957 ORANGE BOWL

"I Told Them I Was Going To Resign"

Clemson won its first ACC title in 1956 by winning all four of its conference games and was asked to play in the Orange Bowl. Overall, the Tigers finished the season with a 7-1-2 record. The only loss they had suffered turned out to be a very embarrassing one, 21-0 to the University of Miami which went on to close its season with an 8-1-1 record. However, Miami was ineligible to participate in a bowl game that year, and since Clemson's loss occurred near the end of the season, it left a bad impression on football fans in Miami. They weren't too excited about the coming Orange Bowl attraction.

The Tigers' opponent, Colorado University, wasn't a household name either when it came to post-season bowl games. They had appeared only once before, against Rice, in the 1938 Cotton Bowl, and their 1956 record wasn't very impressive. They finished with a 7-2-1 mark, underscored by the fact that they weren't even the champions of the Big Seven Conference. Oklahoma had won the crown, but they were ineligible to return for a second straight time by the conference rules. Oklahoma had dealt Colorado one of its losses, 27-19, while Oregon inflicted the other, a 35-0 rout. So, it was only natural that the Clemson-Colorado pairing created yawns in Miami.

Unfortunately for Clemson, on the day they left for Miami, a normal three-hour trip turned out to be a seven-hour nightmare. The plane they had chartered for the trip never arrived at the Greenville airport. It wasn't until hours later that Pan American resolved the quandary by dispatching one of its clippers to rescue the stranded Clemson players, who had been waiting for four hours.

It didn't take long to remind coach Frank Howard that he was back in Miami. No sooner had he arrived in the terminal than a local reporter asked him if his team was anxious to play a good game because of the 21-0 beating they had taken on November 16. It rankled the mild-mannered Howard a bit.

"Ain't they ever going to forget that?" he snapped. "We lost only one game, but we made the mistake of losing it here. Remember, Texas Christian took a good licking from Miami, too; but they ain't snakebit. They went right to the Cotton Bowl. I believe my boys will be high for this one.

Halfback Joel Wells scored two touchdowns against Colorado, one on a 58-yard run.

Colorado fullback John Bayuk scores one of his two touchdowns in the second period to open scoring.

They'd better be."

Howard then hustled his players towards a fleet of cars that had been waiting for hours. He couldn't wait to get to the University of Miami practice field, although it was late in the afternoon. He looked back at the reporter.

"They're in pretty good shape," Howard remarked, "but I gave them four days off for Christmas; and they may have put on a little fat that we'll want to whittle off of them."

Both Clemson and Colorado relied almost totally on their running game. Passing was practically non-existent in the thinking of both Howard and his adversary coach, Dallas Ward of Colorado. However, there were extenuating circumstances. In the last five games of the season, Clemson hadn't thrown a single pass. However, it wasn't until Howard arrived in Miami that he revealed that his quarterback, Charlie Bussey, had injured his hand and couldn't throw. It made tackle Bill Hudson wonder.

"I like to say we used the running game to set up our punting game," laughed Hudson. "I used to play end, and coach Howard wanted

to move me from end to tackle. This was when our quarterback wasn't that good, but I still wanted to catch passes. So when I said something to him, coach Howard replied, 'Son, with our quarterbacks the way they are, you've got as good a chance catching passes at tackle as you do at end.'"

Joel Wells was the main reason Howard preferred to run. The senior was the key in Clemson's Split-T offense and set an ACC rushing record with 803 yards. The reason Colorado relied on its running game was John "Beast" Bayuk, the spinning fullback out of its single wing attack. Bayuk was a powerful, 220-pound piano-legged runner, and complete opposite of the speedy Wells.

As usual, Howard tried to stir interest in the game. Five days before the game he spoke before an audience of some 3,500 people at a Chamber of Commerce sponsored luncheon in the Bayfront Park Auditorium. The guests got a sample of Howard's wit.

"We overwhelmed and humiliated Missouri in the Gator Bowl," said Howard. "The score was 24-23. We humiliated Miami in the

Orange Bowl. The score was 15-14. Now, I've been coaching here for 26 years because the Clemson alumni are fine folks. Not too many are soreheads. We used to have the single wing, and folks stopped wanting to play us. Oklahoma is the only team which used the true Split-T. The rest of us have a lot of versions. I do know we can be deceptive. Our quarterback will fake handing the ball to a halfback and give it to the fullback. I've even seen him give it to the opposing tackle.

"But folks in South Carolina ought to all be backing us. After all, ain't we bringing them more national publicity than anybody else? None of the other teams have been going to bowl games like we have in recent years."

It wasn't Howard's fault that the Orange Bowl wasn't sold out for the first time in 15 years. There were 72,552 fans who turned out on a hot, 75 degree afternoon, leaving 3,000 seats empty. The first quarter action turned out to be the way Hudson described it earlier. Neither team mounted an offense, and each had to punt the ball away all three times they had it.

However, Colorado fans began to cheer in the second period. Early in the quarter, Bayuk scored from two yards out to culminate a 75-yard drive and give the Buffaloes a 6-0 lead. A short while later, Bob Strabsky intercepted Bussey's pass on the Clemson 47-yard line and returned it to the 10. Three plays later, Boyd Dowler followed a block by Bayuk around end to score from the six-yard line and send Colorado into a 14-0 lead.

They weren't finished. A partially blocked punt gave the Buffaloes possession of the ball on the Clemson 26. In just one play, Howard Cook raced into the end zone for Colorado's third touchdown. The conversion attempt was no good; and Colorado, seemingly on the way to a rout, led at halftime, 20-0.

It was a different looking Clemson team that came out for the third quarter. The Tigers took the second half kickoff and drove 69 yards with Wells scoring from the three-yard line. The next time Clemson got the ball, Wells brought the crowd to its feet. He broke through a hole over right tackle and scampered 58 yards for a touchdown. The game had a new look.

The Tigers still had the momentum when the fourth period began. They recovered a Colorado fumble on the 11-yard line. Three plays later, Spooner went over from the one-yard line to tie the game. Bussey kicked his third extra point to give Clemson its first lead of the game, 21-20. It was an exciting comeback.

But then a strange thing happened. Bussey tried an onside kick, and guard John Wooten recovered for the Buffaloes on the Colorado 47. It took Colorado only eight plays to regain the lead when Bayuk scored from the one-yard line. The extra point gave Colorado a 27-21 edge. Clemson's final hopes for a victory ended when Bussey's pass was intercepted on the Colorado 17 late in the game.

Howard's impassioned halftime plea had almost turned the game around.

"I told them I was going to resign," revealed Howard. "That was it. I told them I was going to hand in my resignation if they didn't play better in the second half."

Bussey took the blame for the loss. He had called the onside kick without consulting with the coaches. He felt he could catch the Colorado team by surprise. At the time, eleven minutes still remained in the game and he was convinced Clemson would need another touchdown to win.

"I cost us this game," he said with tears in his eyes. "I made a couple of bad mistakes. I shouldn't have called that onside kick."

1957 ORANGE BOWL
January 1, 1957
Miami, FL

CLEMSON	0	0	14	7	– 21
COLORADO	0	20	0	7	– 27

UC—Bayuk 2 run (Indorf kick)
UC—Dowler 6 run (Cook kick)
UC—Cook 26 run (Kick failed)
CU—Wells 3 run (Bussey kick)
CU—Wells 58 run (Bussey kick)
CU—Spooner 1 run (Bussey kick)
UC—Bayuk 1 run (Indorf kick)
Attendance: 72,552

11

1959 SUGAR BOWL

"Clemson Is The Best Football Team We Met"

By 1958 the ACC was becoming established as a strong football conference, and Clemson was emerging as one of its stronger teams. That season, the Tigers won the title with an 8-2 record. It was the fourth straight year in which Clemson won at least seven games. During that period, the Tigers produced a 29-9-2 record. Although they were recognized as a powerful force within the conference, they still hadn't quite earned the national recognition which goes with the success they had achieved the past four years. Still, Sugar Bowl officials were impressed enough with Clemson to give them a bid to the 1959 Sugar Bowl.

Now it was the New Orleans press that was not pleased with the committee's selection. No sooner had Clemson accepted the invitation than the critics roared their disapproval. Although the game had been a sellout as far back as November 5, anti-Clemson sentiment was high. The self-proclaimed experts had good reasons to be pleased with the selection of local favorite LSU. The Bayou Tigers were rated the nation's number one team. In addition, they were also a colorful team. Led by All-American running back Billy Cannon, they were favorites of the press because of their lightning-crack defensive unit named the "Chinese Bandits." The practice of coach Paul Dietzel of maintaining three full teams (besides the "Chinese Bandits" there was the "Go Team" and the "White Team") also brought them attention.

Coach Frank Howard felt it could be 1957 all over again for Clemson, only worse. Even before he took his Tigers to Biloxi, Mississippi, for the final days of preparation, critical newsmen had been making derogatory remarks about his team. The game was a complete mismatch they said and made reference to the fact that the nation's oddsmakers established LSU as 16-point favorites. In a prestigious bowl game having the magnitude of the Sugar Bowl, with its 82,000 seats, that was quite a lot.

What troubled the critics was Clemson's record. Certainly, judging LSU's record wasn't difficult; the team won all ten games which it played that season. After analyzing Clemson's record, the experts had established a sound case for themselves. The Tigers had to rally four times during the final minutes of each game to beat Virginia, 20-15; North Carolina, 26-12; Vanderbilt, 12-7; and Wake Forest, 14-12. They also cited a

The white-shirted Chinese Bandits of LSU caged the Tigers in a tense struggle, 7-0.

26-6 loss to South Carolina and a 13-0 defeat to Georgia Tech before Clemson closed out its season with three straight victories.

Although Clemson didn't have the range of talent that LSU had from employing 33 players for each game, the Tigers were loaded with strong runners. Howard made use of eight players and they each gained 130 yards or more. Doug Cline led the rushers with 438 yards and was supported by Rudy Hayes, Mike Dukes, Bill Mathis, Harold Olson, George Usry, Charlie Horne, and Bobby Morgan. Howard also had two good quarterbacks, Harvey White and Lowndes Shingler, both of whom had missed several games during the season due to injuries. Clemson was strong up front as well, being led by All-American candidate tackle Lou Cordileone.

Of course it bothered Howard any time Clemson was placed in the position of underdogs, but he was used to it, as well. In Clemson's other bowl appearances, they had had the same role. Before leaving Clemson for the Sugar Bowl, he joked about the situation over his morning coffee.

"Shucks," said Howard, "anybody knows a skinny mountain tiger can whup a fat swamp tiger any time."

But, when Howard arrived with his team in Biloxi, he was even better prepared to fire back at the critics. Sportswriter Pete Baird of the New Orleans Times-Picayune wrote in one of his columns:

"Oh, Frank Howard, we beg of you to warn that team of yours that LSU now reigns supreme; and when it reigns, it pours."

Not to be outdone, Howard wrote back in his best verse:

"Mistuh Baird, we got yo' note,
But we ain't got no feahs;
Cause when the final sco' is wrote,
We'll float home on yo' teahs."

Then, in a speech to the Biloxi Chamber of Commerce, Howard rolled out his homespun psychological attack. Not only did he loosen up the guests with laughter; more importantly, he loosened up some of his players who were in the audience.

"Look here," began Howard waving some clippings from the local papers. "This is what they think of us down here. You know, we hear so much about Cannon and those Chinese Bandits and White Team and Go Team that we thank our stars we have some boys who don't scare easily. They know, too, that if they watch Cannon too closely, they'll find that fellow Johnny Robinson running them ragged around ends; and if they watch Robinson and Cannon, that big guy, J. W. Brodnax, will smash right down through the middle. So, I don't know exactly what we're going to do, 'cept show up.

"This coaching business will get you if you let it. More letters come in from alumni and even small boys and girls telling me what I have to do about Cannon and the Chinese Bandits. If I didn't have a coaching job, I'd be between the shafts of a plow. But with all its trials, coaching beats plowing. I've always found you meet a lot of dumb guys in the newspaper and radio business, and tonight's no exception."

As was always the case, Howard's humor delighted those around him, even the press. Yet, Howard's psychological ploy didn't go unnoticed by LSU coach Paul Dietzel. In fact, he became unhappy with what he described as a psychological edge being enjoyed by Clemson.

"If Frank Howard had planned it, he couldn't have had it any better," said Dietzel. "He is saving every one of those news stories to show to his players. By game time he'll have that Clemson team on fire with the desire to win. They have, in effect, a tremendous psychological advantage. We approach the game knowing this, and it's our job to convince our boys what they are up against."

The morale on the LSU team was high. They had 33 regulars, which made for 33 happy players. Their extensive use in each game captured the imagination of the press. The "White Team" or first team was used both offensively and defensively. The "Go Team" was strictly an offensive unit, and the celebrated "Chinese Bandits" operated only on defense.

It was a cool 44 degrees when LSU kicked off. Despite all the pre-game banter of a mismatch, a crowd of 82,000 turned out, with the majority of the fans rooting for LSU. Clemson couldn't do anything after receiving the kickoff, and neither could LSU in their first offensive series. Near the end of the period, the Bayou Tigers had reached the Clemson 25-yard line when time ran out.

On the first play of the second quarter, Tiger end Ray Masneri pounced on a LSU fumble on the 23-yard line to end the threat. Yet, during the remainder of the period, Clemson couldn't get its offense untracked. The furthest they ever advanced was to their own 44.

LSU had two good opportunities to score and failed both times. Midway through the period, LSU had reached the Clemson 20-yard line. On fourth down, they had lined up for a fake field goal attempt. However, quarterback Warren Rabb's pass intended for Cannon in the end zone was too long. In the closing minutes LSU almost scored. Brodnax tried to leap over from the one-yard line but fumbled as he reached the goal line. Cline recovered to save a touchdown. LSU had dominated the first half action, gaining 137 yards to Clemson's 69 and producing seven first downs to Clemson's two. Still, the game was scoreless.

The first time Clemson had the ball in the second half it appeared as if the Tigers would score. However, Usray fumbled on second down; and LSU recovered on its own 28-yard line. As the third-quarter clock was winding down, LSU got a break. Mathis was standing back to punt on Clemson's 10-yard line. Center Paul Snyder got off a bad snap that hit Cline, who was in the backfield to block, on the leg. The ball rolled to the 11-yard line where LSU recovered. After Cannon got only two yards on two carries, he was set to run again. Instead, he threw a halfback option pass to end Mickey Mangham for a nine-yard touchdown. Cannon proceeded to kick the extra point that gave LSU a 7-0 lead. Nobody realized at the time that it would be the only touchdown in the hard-fought contest.

Clemson came close to scoring the last time they had the ball during the game. They had begun a drive at the end of the third period from their own 17 that had reached the LSU 24-yard line. About five minutes remained when the Tigers attempted a screen pass that failed. The play was well designed, but Usry dropped the pass and Clemson's hopes with it.

"Clemson is the best football team we met this year," Cannon said after the game. "They really hit. I don't know his name, but number 74 (Lou Cordileone) gave us fits. Anytime I looked up, he was on my back."

The sad part was that Clemson outplayed LSU in the second half. They ended up with 12 first downs to LSU's 9 and out-rushed LSU, 168 yards to 114. If Usry had held on to White's short pass on the LSU 24-yard line, the outcome might have been different. Usry had blockers in front of him to produce a big gain.

"Hell, I think we'd have beat them if they held onto that little screen pass," said Howard. "I was going for that two point conversion to beat them."

1959 SUGAR BOWL
January 1, 1959
New Orleans, LA

CLEMSON	0	0	0	0	– 0
LSU	0	0	7	0	– 7

LSU—Mangham 9 pass from Cannon (Cannon kick)
Attendance: 82,000

12

1959 BLUEBONNET BOWL

"The Most Points Scored Against TCU In 56 Games"

Clemson closed its 1959 season with an 8-2 record, disposing of Furman in Greenville, 56-3, to win its second consecutive ACC title. But nervousness filled the air on the Clemson campus due to the fact that the Tigers had not received a bid to a major bowl. It was something they had been accustomed to in recent years. They were hopeful, because appearing in a post-season bowl game would make this the third time in four years, and their record indicated they deserved an invitation. Not only were they the ACC champions, but they had finished 11th in the final national poll.

While the football team returned to Clemson, coach Frank Howard remained in Greenville, hoping to celebrate a bowl bid with members of his staff, the press, the Clemson officials and guests in the banquet room of a local hotel. Although there had been other celebrations during the season after big wins over North Carolina, 20-18 on opening day, South Carolina, 27-0 in the final Big Thursday game, and Wake Forest, a 33-31 victory that clinched the second consecutive ACC crown, this one was special. For one thing, Howard considered this year's team possibly the best one he coached. Then, too, Clemson was anxious to snap a streak of three straight bowl losses.

The bowl picture was still unsettled. Clemson's participation in one depended on the results of other games involving Georgia-Georgia Tech, Alabama-Auburn, and Miami-Florida, all traditional rivalries. As the nervous Clemson family waited, the fuzzy picture began to clear as each of the games ended. Georgia defeated Tech and accepted an invitation to play Missouri in the Orange Bowl. However, when Tech was given a bid to meet Arkansas in the Gator Bowl, Clemson trainer Fred Hoover moaned.

"How can they pick Tech?" he asked. "They lost four games and got beat by a team that lost 50-0. How can Gator do that? They just can't pass us up. Why, with a little luck we could have gone undefeated. We're still being ribbed about the flu epidemic that hit the team the week before the Tech game, but the truth is we had a lot of sick boys. I'm sure we could have beaten Tech if we would have been at full strength."

Clemson had lost to Georgia Tech, 16-6, in the third game of the sea-

Ron Scrudato, on bottom, scored Clemson's final touchdown of the game.

son., After winning four games in succession, they stumbled against Maryland, 28-25. They were a veteran team with many of the players having played in two bowl games, the Orange in 1957 and the Sugar in 1959. Analyzing the bowl situation, Clemson officials determined that the only two bowls that remained unfilled were the Liberty Bowl in Philadelphia and the Bluebonnet Bowl, launching its first year, in Houston.

In the midst of all the speculation that was going on, Howard was called to the telephone. He got up from his chair and went into another room. The minutes seemed like hours. Then Howard sent word that he wanted his assistant coaches to meet him in his room. The suspense continued. Later, when Bob Bradley, Clemson's sports publicist, entered the banquet room, he was immediately asked whom Howard was talking to.

"Don't know," answered Bradley. "The head man's still in the room on the phone. We should know any time now."

Howard returned with his coaches. He had a twinkle in his eyes as he approached the head table and banged on a glass with a spoon for quiet.

"Ladies and gentlemen," he began. "I just finished talking to some people on the telephone about a bowl game and have accepted an invitation to play TCU in the Bluebonnet Bowl in Houston, Texas, December 19th. We didn't get no guarantee. That guarantee stuff is all paper talk. Ain't none of them bowl games going to give you a guarantee, but we'll do all right. We're going to be given about 10,000 tickets to sell at $5.50 apiece. They have probably as fine a football stadium out there at Rice as there is in the country. It holds about 72,000, so let's try and fill it.

"I've played in the Rose Bowl and ole Clemson's been to the other big bowls, so this will be something new for us. A little variety is good for you. Maybe some of the boys will go out there and meet a millionaire's daughter, and that wouldn't be so bad. I'm looking forward to playing ole TCU, and I know we will represent the ACC in the same manner we have in past bowl games. Now let's eat."

Although Clemson's bowl record was 3-3, they nevertheless had played exciting football with but one exception: when they had been beaten 14-0 by Miami in the 1952 Gator Bowl. Other than that, all their games had been decided by seven points or less. Once again, just as it had been in all their bowl dates, the Tigers were established as underdogs. This time the oddsmakers made TCU, who also was 8-2 and ranked eighth nationally, an eight point pick.

TCU was big and rugged. They had a pair of solid performers in all-American tackles Don Floyd and Bob Lilly (who went on to star with the Dallas Cowboys), guard Roy Lee Rambo, and running back Jack Spikes, and were the top defensive team in the Southwest Conference. Clemson had a pair of standout tackles in Lou Cordileone and Harold Olson and had offensive punch in quarterback Harvey White; fullback Doug Cline, who topped the Tigers in rushing for the second straight time with 449 yards; and halfback Billy Mathis, who led the ACC in scoring with 70 points.

"I believe we're ready to play," Howard said. "Usually, it's pretty easy to get a team up for a bowl game. This year there are no special gimmicks. The New Orleans newspapers had been pretty critical of us last year before the Sugar Bowl, but you know something? We might show some of those other bowls. It looks like we'll have a great crowd. Boy, I love them big payoffs."

The crowd was not that big. Only 53,000 turned out on a damp, humid day with the temperature at 57 degrees at game time. Clemson moved after the opening kickoff. They reached the TCU 41-yard line before Cline fumbled the ball away. However, when the period came to a close, the Tigers had reached the TCU nine-yard line.

They got as far as the four, where they had to settle for a 22-yard field goal by Lon Armstrong and a 3-0 lead early in the second quarter. Midway through the period, TCU scored when speedy halfback Harry Moreland slipped out of the backfield and caught a 19-yard touchdown pass. The half ended with TCU in front, 7-3.

There wasn't any excitement the entire third quarter. Neither team threatened; both were determined to keep the ball on the ground. The period went by quickly with Clemson and TCU only having the ball twice.

In the final period, however, Clemson exploded. White brought the crowd to its feet with a 68-yard touchdown pass to Gary Barnes. Armstrong converted and Clemson went in front, 10-7.

The next time Clemson got the ball, they scored again. This time Lowndes Shingler hit Tommy King down the middle with a 23-yard touchdown pass. Shingler missed the extra point; and Clemson led, 16-7. When they gained possession again, the Tigers scored for the third straight time. They drove 63 yards in seven plays, with Shingler accounting for 46 of them on a 35-yard run and an 11-yard pass. Ron Scrudato went the final yard for the touchdown, and Armstrong added the conversion to push Clemson into a 23-7 lead. The Tigers had scored 20 points in seven minutes to seal the victory. Their final total of 23 points was the most scored against TCU in 56 games.

Clemson's first touchdown, the 68-yard pass to Barnes, turned out to be a prudent second-guess by Howard. The veteran coach admitted that he had called another pass play but yielded to his younger assistant coach Charlie Waller's call instead. Howard refused to describe the pattern that got Barnes open.

"Shucks," he said, "I want to use that pass again next year. Just say he goes down and cuts out."

Co-captain Paul Snyder, who played an outstanding game at center, tightly clutched the game ball. The senior center wasn't about to give it up to anybody. He had reason not to.

"I didn't get one during the season, and I told them I was going to keep this one," said Snyder.

1959 BLUEBONNET BOWL
December 19, 1959
Houston, TX

CLEMSON	0	3	0	20	– 23
TCU	0	7	0	0	– 7

CU—Armstrong 22 FG
TCU—Moreland 19 pass from Reding (Dodson kick)
CU—Barnes 68 pass from White (Armstrong kick)
CU—King 23 pass from Shingler (Kick failed)
CU—Scrudato 1 run (Armstrong kick)
Attendance: 55,000

The 1959 Clemson team closed out its regular season with an 8-2 record.

13

1977
GATOR BOWL

"The First Bowl Appearance In 17 Years"

The invitation to play Pittsburgh in the 1977 Gator Bowl marked a milestone in Clemson's football history. It marked the first appearance of the Tigers in a bowl game in 17 years, and it also signaled the restoration of Clemson's football prowess on the national level. During the transitional period after the 1959 Bluebonnet Bowl, the legendary Frank Howard had retired in 1970 and two of his successors, Hootie Ingram and Red Parker, were forced to resign after failing to rebuild a winning football program.

Yet, in his first season as Clemson's new coach, Charley Pell did just that. The Tigers completed an 8-2-1 campaign and a second place finish in the ACC. Pell, who had been an assistant on Parker's staff the year before, brought in a new coaching staff that dramatically improved the Tigers. Nobody had figured the Tigers would roar back so loudly after wining only five games during the consecutive losing seasons.

"I felt that we'd be good sometime during the year because of all the hard work that our players and coaches had put in," said Pell. "But, at the start of the season, I didn't know when we'd be good or how good we would be. Somewhere during our first three games, our players realized that they could be a good team. I think we found out just how good we could be the next weekend when we went on the road for the third straight week and beat Virginia Tech. We played well when we could've been flat. Our team showed a lot of poise and character at that point, and that's when I began to feel that we could be really good."

Clemson opened its regular season with a tough 21-14 loss to Maryland. After that they won seven games in a row, beating Georgia, 7-6; Georgia Tech, 31-14; Virginia Tech, 31-13; Virginia, 31-0; Duke 17-11; North Carolina State, 7-3; and Wake Forest, 26-0. In the final three weeks, they tied North Carolina, 13-13; lost again in a tough game against Notre Dame, 21-17; and beat South Carolina, 31-27.

The star of the revved up Clemson offense was quarterback Steve Fuller, a junior who blossomed under Pell's coaching. Named ACC Player of the Year, Fuller completed 106 of 205 passes for 1,655 yards and eight touchdowns. The passes he threw were the most by a Clemson quarterback since Tommy Kendrick attempted 267 in 1970, which remains the

Quarterback Steve Fuller looks to make things happen against Pittsburgh.

111

school's record. Still, the 1,655 yards that Fuller gained with his passes was a new Clemson mark of achievement. Fuller looked forward to the excitement of playing as he anticipated what was the first bowl game of his career.

"We've got to play crazy," said Fuller. "We can't afford to get out there and feel them out. We'll be wild out there. It'll be a crazy football game. With our fans, a road game doesn't seem so much like a road game. We know we'll have 20,000 people there no matter where we go. Our people are different from anybody in the world. They're wild and even obnoxious to some people, but I think they're the greatest."

The game was being looked upon as a duel between two fine quarterbacks, Fuller and a senior at Pittsburgh, Matt Cavanaugh. Cavanaugh received some mention as an All-American. He had more bowl experience, too, having played in the 1977 Sugar Bowl when Pittsburgh was voted the nation's number one team after trouncing Georgia, 27-3. Fuller, though, tried to play down the anticipated quarterback battle.

"It's not going to be two people out there shooting for the spotlight," remarked Fuller.

Yet, there was no discounting the presence of Cavanaugh. Like Fuller, he was the key to his team's offense. Among other things, his being a drop back passer caused Clemson to change its defensive strategy. Clemson's star linebacker Randy Scott appeared ready for the challenge.

"He doesn't drop back as deep as a lot of quarterbacks, and that means we won't be able to pressure him as much from the corners," pointed out Scott; "but we've got a few wrinkles set up for him that I'm pleased with. We're going to have to try and send some people in through the line to put some pressure on him. We run basically a college defense, and a lot of things they do are similar to the way the pros play."

Cornerback Rex Varn was aware that the Tiger defensive backfield was facing, in Cavanaugh, the best quarterback they had seen all year.

"They have got by far the best passing game we will face," said Varn. "Their receivers run pro routes, and they all go to the ball well. The secondary is going to have to remember to stick with the receivers because even if Cavanaugh gets trapped, he can fire a pass to anybody downfield. We're going to have to disguise our covers real well. I'm not sure just what we'll have to go to most, but we won't be able to let Cavanaugh know what cover we're in. If we do, he'll pick us apart. What makes it even worse for us is they don't just pass on normal passing downs like the other teams we have played all year. They pass whenever Cavanaugh wants to, and we haven't faced anybody who equals his caliber all year. I feel the passing game will be the key. That's something we'll definitely have to contain."

On paper, the teams appeared evenly matched. The Panthers gave up 11.7 points a game, and the Tigers 11.9. Both had 8-2-1 records, and each lost to Notre Dame. Pittsburgh was ranked 10th in the writers' poll, and Clemson 11th. Another oddity was that Pell and Pittsburgh's coach Jackie Sherrill both played football at Alabama under coach Bear Bryant, and both were in their first seasons as head coaches. Sherrill felt that possibly his team this year might be better than last season's, even though All-American running back Tony Dorsett had graduated.

"We do more things with the football," explained Sherrill. "Last year what we did most of the time was hand the ball to Dorsett. Defensively, we are more aggressive than last year. The difference in the game this week will be one or two plays. Depending on how some of the other games come out, the winner could end up being ranked between fifth and eighth; and don't forget, Clemson played Notre Dame better than we did. Clemson hides linebacker Randy Scott as much as they can. He's come up with some very big plays, and the secondary supports very well. On film, I think they are as good as anybody we played."

A new attendance record was established as 72,289 fans, 41 more than the crowd at the 1969 game, paid their way despite the threat of showers. They didn't have to wait long to see the first touchdown. The first time Pittsburgh got the ball after a Clemson punt, Cavanaugh hooked up with Elliot Walker for a 39-yard touchdown pass. With 1:07 left, Pittsburgh scored again on a 24-yard field goal by Mark Schubert. Fuller tried to bring Clemson back, but his pass was intercepted on the Pittsburgh 18-yard line just as the period was coming to an end.

The Panthers used the interception as a springboard for another touchdown in the opening minutes of the second quarter. This time Cavanaugh hit Walker with a 10-yard touchdown pass to complete an 82-yard drive. Clemson finally got some points on the scoreboard following the kickoff. Obed Ariri booted a 49-yard field goal to bring the Tigers to within two touchdowns, 17-3. The half ended 10 minutes later without any further scoring and with Pittsburgh clearly in charge.

Cavanaugh continued to find success with his passes in the third quarter. He threw his third touchdown pass of the game, this time hitting Gordon Jones for 10 yards. Pittsburgh's lead increased to 24-3 and held until the end of the period.

Clemson needed to score big in the fourth period to pull out of impending defeat. They couldn't do it. Instead, Cavanaugh combined with Walker for a 25-yard touchdown pass, and Schubert kicked a 21-yard field goal to overwhelm Clemson 34-3.

"From this point on we're going to be an experienced bowl team," said Pell. "I'm smarter today than I was yesterday. I learned a whole lot from losing, like pass defense for one thing. We played too cautious, and that's my fault. I need to apologize to the team. I didn't prepare them for this game. We have the opportunity to be a fine football team next year. We came a million miles from last January. This has been a Cinderella ballclub. It's done what no one said it could do."

1977 GATOR BOWL
December 30, 1977
Jacksonville, FL

CLEMSON	0	3	0	0	— 3
PITT	10	7	7	10	— 34

UP—E. Walker 39 pass from Cavanaugh (Schubert kick)
UP—Schubert 24 FG
UP—E. Walker 10 pass from Cavanaugh (Schubert kick)
CU—Ariri 49 FG
UP—Jones 10 pass from Cavanaugh (Schubert kick)
UP—Schubert 21 FG
UP—E. Walker 25 pass from Cavanaugh (Trout kick)
Attendance: 72,289

14

1978 GATOR BOWL

"I Know More About Woody Hayes Than He Does About Me"

It appeared that happiness had returned to the Clemson campus. The students were elated with the success that Charley Pell achieved his very first season in 1977. The affable Pell was also well liked by the alumni; however, it didn't last. A month before the 1978 Gator Bowl against Ohio State, turmoil invaded the locker room. Pell, who had served a brief two years as head coach, unexpectedly resigned. In 1977, he produced an 8-3-1 record and a trip to the Gator Bowl. In 1978, he did even better. The Tigers finished the season with a 10-1 record and their first ACC championship in eleven years.

Now, just prior to the Gator Bowl, Pell was announcing that he would be leaving Clemson to take the head coaching job at Florida. He then said that he would coach the Tigers in the Gator Bowl, even though young Danny Ford had already been named as his replacement for the 1979 season. Ford would take over the recruiting and the football program immediately, but Pell would still be the head coach for the Gator Bowl game. It was a clumsy situation and the alumni weren't happy. The players felt that Pell had deserted them. The entire squad of 73 Clemson players signed a petition supporting Ford as head coach for the Gator Bowl game. The petition also said they intended to make the game against Ohio State one of their better ones. It was obvious it would be best for everyone if Pell would resign.

When he accepted the Florida job, Pell asked Ford to accompany him as his assistant coach. The two men had both played for coach Bear Bryant at Alabama and had coached together at Virginia Tech. When Pell got the Clemson job in 1977, he brought in Ford to assist him. Ford was happy at Clemson, and it hadn't taken long for school officials to ask him to stay on as Pell's replacement. He was popular with the players, and Pell himself had recommended him for the football program. Ford was so anxious to redeem Clemson's football prestige that he didn't even bother to ask for a contract and immediately went to work. He had no other alternative, of course, since Pell took two defensive assistants with him to Florida. Ford was short on help and had only three weeks to get the Tigers ready.

"There have been too many other things to do, like recruiting and

Just before he is brought down, quarterback Steve Fuller gets off pass against Ohio State.

115

Obed Ariri kicks a 47-yard field goal in second period that gave Clemson a 10-9 halftime lead.

practicing for the Gator Bowl to sit down and sign a contract," said Ford. "I decided we could do all that later. Clemson is a college that has good people working for it, and I will go by what they say. If I can't trust the people I work for, then I'm in the wrong business. Certainly, we are going to change some things, but not just for the sake of making changes. We've got a first-class operation started at Clemson, and it will continue that way. We'll still ask for what we think is right to expect from players, things like getting their education, attending class, and working hard on the football field."

Ford was determined to have his squad work harder in preparation for this year's Gator Bowl against Ohio State than they had last year when they were walloped by Pittsburgh. Not only did he work his team hard on the practice fields at Clemson, but he ordered his squad to report to Jacksonville about a week earlier than the last year. This time the Tigers were in nearby Daytona for Christmas; and Ford, who even worked his team on Christmas Day, had closed practice sessions.

"You never know what to expect," said Ford, who wasn't taking any chances of being spied upon. "I will be very surprised if we don't play

well this time. That is the job of the coaching staff, to make sure we play well. If we get them ready, we have the people who can stand up against anybody in the country. I've learned one thing, and that is you better have danged good people helping you. If you do, you've got a chance; if not, you don't. Last year we didn't come here until after Christmas, and then we did a lot of sight-seeing. We just tried to do too much that didn't have anything to do with getting ready to play."

Ford was really in a tough position. His first game as a head coach was a big, pressure-packed bowl contest. Not only that, but in coach Woody Hayes of Ohio State, Ford was going up against a legendary figure much like Bear Bryant. In his 33 years as a head coach, the last 28 at State, Hayes had compiled a record of 238-71-11. But Ford had this to say:

"I know more about Woody Hayes than he does about me. He's probably done forgot more football than I'll ever know. I guess if I stopped to think about it, there could be a lot of pressure in this situation, but I haven't had time to think about it. I've been the head coach now just a few very long days. One thing I've learned since being head coach is that you

116

don't change as a person; you just don't get enough sleep.

"Really, I ain't playing Coach Hayes. And Coach Hayes ain't playing me. I'm looking forward to our kids playing in the Gator Bowl, but I don't know how much I look forward to it myself. I'll be so nervous I won't know where to look. I may not know if I'm in the right stadium. I guess it will be like the first time I ever put the uniform on, and the butterflies will leave after the first few plays. For sure, it won't take people long to make a judgment about me. Normally, a new coach takes over in spring drills, and all the public can do is read about him. My first game will find 70,000 in the stadium, and I don't know how many million looking on television." This was Ford's way of making light of the situation.

The endorsement he received from the players gave him a secure feeling. He felt certain they would be ready to play a good game. They had played outstandingly all season, losing only to Georgia in the second game of the campaign before going on to win nine consecutive games. They ranked seventh in the nation's ratings. The Tigers were also a veteran team, many of them had played in last year's Gator Bowl. Quarterback Steve Fuller, for the second straight time was voted the ACC's Player of the Year. Fuller had an All-American receiver in Jerry Butler, who caught more than half the passes Fuller threw.

Ohio State was ranked 20th in the polls. They finished the season with a 7-3-1 record. Hayes had an excellent freshman quarterback, Art Schlichter. Ron Springs was his best runner. However, the Buckeye strength was in All-American linebacker Tom Cousineau, who had 277 tackles during the season, an average of better than 20 a game. Hayes was a veteran of post-season games as Ohio State was making its 13th bowl appearance.

A crowd of 72,011 was there. Ohio State got the ball and drove 63 yards before being stopped on Clemson's one-yard line. It was the closest they came to scoring. At the end of the first period neither team had scored.

Early in the second period Bob Atha gave the Buckeyes a 3-0 lead when he kicked a 27-yard field goal. Clemson came back after the kickoff with a fine 80-yard drive. Fuller him-

self got the touchdown on a four-yard run. Obed Ariri added the extra point to give Clemson a 7-3 lead. Yet, Ohio State came back with a 78-yard march. Schlichter ran for the touchdown from the four-yard line. Steve Gibbs blocked the extra point try; and State led 9-7. However, with just five seconds left on the clock, Ariri booted a 47-yard field goal to give the Tigers a 10-9 halftime edge.

In the third period, Clemson added to its margin. Fuller directed the Tigers on an 84-yard drive with Cliff Austin scoring from the one-yard line. Ariri's conversion gave Clemson a 17-9 advantage when the period ended two minutes later. Midway in the fourth period the tension increased. Ohio was driving and Schlichter scored from a yard out. He then tried to run for the two-point conversion that would have tied the game, but was stopped by Jim Stuckey. But it was Charlie Bauman who secured Clemson's 17-15 victory. In the closing minutes he intercepted Schlichter's third-down pass on the Clemson 24-yard line. The play created a fracas on the sideline which resulted in Hayes being assessed two 15-yard penalties for unsportsmanlike conduct. He took several swings at Bauman and had to be restrained from any further outbursts.

After the game, Ford was reminded that he was the only unbeaten coach in the country.

"I think I'll resign tomorrow," smiled Ford. "I'll tell you, if all the games are like this one, I don't know if I'm going to enjoy this."

1978 GATOR BOWL
December 29, 1978
Jacksonville, FL

CLEMSON	0	10	7	0	— 17
OHIO ST.	0	9	0	6	— 15

OSU—Atha 27 FG
CU—Fuller 4 run (Ariri kick)
OSU—Schlichter 4 run (Kick blocked)
CU—Ariri 47 FG
CU—Austin 1 run (Ariri kick)
OSU—Schlichter 1 run (Run failed)
Attendance: 72,011

15

1979 PEACH BOWL

"These Seniors Have Won 27 Games In Three Years"

Before he began his first full season as head coach, Danny Ford faced a major rebuilding job. The ACC championship team that he had coached for only one game in the 1978 Gator Bowl had lost 15 starting offensive and defensive players, and everyone was expecting that Clemson would be going through a period of rebuilding under a new coach. However, Ford fooled everyone by producing a team that went 8-3 and finished second in the ACC.

The Tigers opened the season by blanking Furman, 21-0. After losing to Maryland the following week, Clemson won four successive games, including a 12-7 victory over Georgia. Following a close three-point loss to North Carolina State, 16-13, Clemson beat Wake Forest, 31-0, in its final home game before taking to the road. They beat Gator Bowl-bound North Carolina, 19-10; came from behind with a dramatic 16-10 win over Notre Dame; but stumbled against South Carolina, 13-9. The victories over two national powers, Georgia and Notre Dame, made officials of several bowls take notice.

The Peach Bowl engagement in Atlanta against Baylor was Clemson's third consecutive bowl appearance, something that had never happened in the school's history. It marked a decisive resurgence in Clemson's goal to establish itself as a big-time power. Before the Gator Bowl in 1977, Clemson had had only one winning season in nine years. Although the Bears were 7-4, they finished 19th in the national polls, just one notch below Clemson. Baylor was the first Southwest Conference opponent Clemson had played in 14 years. The last time occurred in 1965 when the Tigers beat TCU, 3-0; and Clemson was meeting Baylor for the very first time. Ford realized the importance of playing a great game against Baylor. It was essential to the future success of his recruiting program and would help establish a winning atmosphere.

"Our team has been to bowl games for the past two years," said Ford. "I think they kind of like the taste of honey they've gotten with the bowls, and they want some more, but we've got to get past Baylor first."

Ford had given his squad three weeks off following the loss to South Carolina at the end of the season. What he had planned for them when they returned was a series of two-a-day practices in Charleston using the

Lester Brown hurdles over from a yard out
to give Clemson an early 7-0 lead against Baylor.

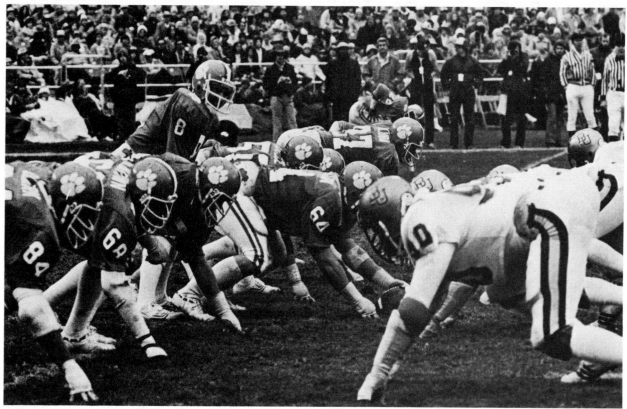

Quarterback Bill Lott looks over the Baylor defense.

facilities of The Citadel. He outlined four days of workouts there before taking the team to Atlanta for the final five days of preparations. While his players were enjoying the long layoff, Ford was busy putting in long hours on the road recruiting. He was anxious to get back on the field.

"I realize the team has been away from organized drills for about four weeks, and there are bound to be some sore muscles," said Ford. "But we have just a little over a week to get ready for Baylor, and the youngsters are going to have to look past the pain. We're just going to try and get our timing back between now and game time. We won't change much from what we did all season long. What we did the last nine games was good to us, and there's no use in trying to put a mess of new stuff in. It would confuse us more than it would Baylor."

By the time the Tigers arrived in Atlanta, the players had worked out all the kinks. Ford cut the workouts to once daily and didn't get any argument from the players. At the end of the week Ford expressed his satisfaction.

"We've improved a lot since we've been in

Atlanta," said Ford. "We've got our stuff down pretty well. It's just a question now of repetition and making sure the players know all their assignments. We ought to be pretty good considering the amount of work we've put in. The players worked real hard."

Linebacker Bubba Brown agreed. The sentiments he expressed represented those of the other players as well.

"While we were in Charleston, we were working on our conditioning. We were out of shape for a while. Since we came up here to Atlanta, the two-a-day practices we had in Charleston paid off. Now we're more relaxed and back into the rhythm of our normal defensive and offensive strategies and also getting back into the game itself."

Jim Stuckey, Clemson's All-American defensive tackle, had to concentrate on the team's strategy, more, perhaps, than any other member of the defense. He had been one of Clemson's stars all season long. As a senior, he was playing his final game.

"I've been double and triple teamed most of the season, especially in the last four or five games," Stuckey pointed out. "It's been frustrating. A lot of our fans haven't been able to understand why I'm not in on a lot of tackles, but I know I'm doing my job; and the coaches and my teammates know I'm doing my job. They're going to be gunning for me, to see how good I am."

Clemson's middle guard Charlie Bauman remarked about another kind of pressure. Once he got to Atlanta, he was the center of controversy by the press. Invariably, everyone who interviewed him wanted to know about the Woody Hayes incident the year before in the Gator Bowl. The references bothered Bauman, who, like Stuckey, was playing his last game.

"I don't like to talk about it," Bauman said. "Why? Because right now I'm known as the guy Woody Hayes hit. I'm a football player; and I'd like to be known as a football player, an All-Atlantic Coast Conference middle guard or an All-America or something. I'd hate to see something like that distract from the win over a Big 10 team because it was a big win for us as well as the ACC. I got a phone call from him about the third week after it happened. I was fascinated. He didn't apologize because that's not his way. He asked how I was doing and congratulated me on the victory, stuff like that."

The Peach Bowl appeared to have two teams that would concentrate on defense. During the season, Clemson's opponents averaged only 8.4 points a game. The Tigers ranked seventh in total defense and 10th against the rush. On the other hand, Baylor gave up 15 points an outing.

Of the crowd of 57,371, those who knew football were expecting a low-scoring game. Yet, the second time they got the ball, the Tigers scored. Lester Brown went in from a yard out, and Obed Ariri added the conversion to give Clemson a 7-0 lead which held up when the first period came to an end. However, Baylor bounced back in the second quarter to score twice and take a 14-7 halftime lead.

Ariri got the Tigers closer to catching Baylor on the opening series of the second half. He booted a 40-yard field goal to trim Baylor's margin to 14-10, but Baylor answered back. First, Robert Bledsoe kicked a 29-yard field

goal; and then the Bears scored another touchdown with just over three minutes remaining to take a 24-10 lead. In the final period, Baylor's defense kept the Tigers in check until 20 seconds were left to play. Chuck McSwain scored from the one-yard line, and Bill Lott completed a two-point conversion on a pass to Jeff McCall to trim Baylor's edge to 24-18. Clemson's hopes were raised when the Tigers recovered an onside kick with 19 seconds left. After Lott completed a pass to Perry Tuttle for 30 yards, he tried another that was intercepted on the Baylor 30-yard line. It was all over.

"This is the first time in a long time that Clemson has lost two games in a row," Ford said, "but nobody ever gave up. We fought until the end. We can't let this wipe out the accomplishments we made to get this far. We couldn't protect the punter. When you have two punts blocked, you don't deserve to win. We lost it on the kicking game, as far as I'm concerned.

"I was proud of the way our youngsters hung in there right to the very end. We can be proud just for bringing Clemson to a post-season bowl. Those seniors have won 27 games in three years, and there are a lot of seniors who would have liked to have won that many."

1979 PEACH BOWL
December 31, 1979
Atlanta, GA

CLEMSON	7 0 3 8	– 18
BAYLOR	0 14 10 0	– 24

CU—L. Brown 1 run (Ariri kick)
BU—Taylor 3 pass from Brannon (Bledsoe kick)
BU—Holt 24 pass from Brannon (Bledsoe kick)
CU—Ariri 40 FG
BU—Bledsoe 39 FG
BU—Cockrell 7 pass from Elam (Bledsoe kick)
CU—McSwain 1 run (McCall pass from Lott)
Attendance: 57,731

121

16

DANNY FORD

"I Told Them I Don't Fear Anybody"

Ｔhe orange baseball cap sat back on Danny Ford's head as the youth-
ful-looking Clemson coach put his squad through a light workout in
Memorial Stadium. Ford was satisfied with the drill and after a half
hour had gone by, he blew his whistle. The players circled the coach who
spoke for about two minutes. At the end, they let out a big cheer that
reverberated throughout the empty stadium and then they jogged off the
field to the locker room at the west end of the stands. It is a routine that
Ford puts his players through every Friday afternoon before a home
game. By early evening, the team and coaches would be at a hotel in Anderson where they would spend the night.

Ford, the 21st coach in Clemson history, was ushered in under a cloud.
Just after Clemson completed a 10-1 season and was preparing to meet
Ohio State in the 1978 Gator Bowl, Charley Pell, who had restored Clemson's football fortunes in the two years he was head coach, announced he
had accepted the head coaching position at the University of Florida. The
abruptness of Pell's move caught Clemson officials by surprise, created in-
dignation among the school's followers and sent shock waves across the
tranquil Clemson campus. The popular support that Pell had received
during his two winning seasons evaporated as quickly as the dew under
the South Carolina sun. His son, Carrick, who was eight years old at the
time, was harassed by other students. Clemson fans became more vocal
when Pell remarked, "I'm splitting, and I may never come back." One
banner that hung from a building in downtown Clemson read, "Pell is a
traitor." And, almost overnight caustic bumper stickers that read, "To hell
with Pell," began to appear.

"One thing Pell said was that one reason he was leaving and going to
Florida was that he didn't think Clemson would ever have a chance to win
a national championship," recalled Brian Clark, who was a senior offensive guard back then. "He thought the school was too unknown."

In the two years that Pell coached the Tigers, he compiled an 18-4-1
record, second only to the 19-3-2 mark produced by John Heisman in his
four years as coach at the turn of the century. In addition, Clemson had
not appeared in a bowl game for 17 years prior to Pell's taking them to
one his first year in 1977. Pell still wanted to coach the team in the Gator

Ford holds daughter Ashleigh Lynn on knee. Oldest daughter Jennifer Renee holds onto dog as Ford's wife Deborah smiles at it all.

tee, at age 30, Danny Ford became the youngest Division I coach in the nation.

"When the comittee was interviewing me, the biggest item was my age," said Ford. "They talked about fear and awe. I told them, I don't fear anybody. The only thing I'm afraid of is snakes. If I see a snake, I take off running. Pell probably recommended me because I had the title of assistant head coach, but there were others on the staff just as qualified. There was no sense fighting each other if someone else wanted the job in the worst kind of way. But we had a good group of assistants, and there was no jealousy. The best thing Clemson did was to act very, very swiftly. They didn't drag it out. They could have gotten a lot of coaches to come to Clemson."

Ford's appointment was a popular one with the players. After Pell's hasty departure, they regrouped quickly under Ford. Meanwhile, Ford received an unexpected gift from fervent Clemson alumni. A week before the Gator Bowl, they presented him with a sleek powder-white Jaguar. Ford knew that the car had been intended for Pell and that after he left, the alumni had said, "What the hell. Let's give the car to Ford, baseball cap and all." Ford's secretary, June Roach, jokingly admitted that he would have preferred a pick-up truck.

Ford was stepping into a pressurized situation. He had less than three weeks to prepare for the Gator Bowl. Nevertheless, the players responded and went out and defeated Ohio State, 17-15. Because of the Woody Hayes' incident, more publicity was given to the Ohio State coach than the fact that Ford in his first game as head coach had won a bowl game.

"It was a thrilling win for Clemson," said Ford. "Some things happened that took away from the game itself. The easiest part was talking to the players during the game. I had already done that all year as the offensive line coach. The hard part was that there were so many things I didn't understand about what a head coach should be doing. I was nervous. I didn't want Clemson to be embarrassed like it had been the previous year when we lost to Pitt, 34-3. You're trained to do everything. But until you coach your first game, you don't know what you can do."

Ford had never been a head coach before,

Bowl. But athletic director Bill McLellan, under pressure from Clemson's powerful alumni, got him to resign. Exercising dipomacy, McLellan didn't publicly display any resentment.

"I was real disappointed when he left," said McLellan. "Emotions got into it with a lot of people, but it was a business decision. Charley was an awfully good organizer, a very intense person. He was a demanding taskmaster, and he started to achieve excellence here."

Before he left, Pell recommended to the athletic board that Ford replace him. After only 23 games at Clemson as an assistant coach, Ford was to be the new head coach. It took the athletic board just 48 hours to appoint Ford. On December 5, after just two extraordinary meetings with the athletic commit-

124

A tense moment during a game occupies Ford's attenti

Ford's popularity is evidenced as he signs autographs for group of youngsters.

not even in a Pop Warner League. He began as a graduate assistant at Alabama in 1970 and 1971. The next two years he was a full time assistant. Ford then became an assistant coach at Virginia Tech for three years before Pell brought him to Clemson as his assistant in 1977. Yet, Ford knew what winning was all about. At Alabama, he played on three bowl teams. Later, as a graduate assistant and as an assistant coach, he participated in four more bowl games.

Bob Bradley remembers an incident from the first year Ford came to Clemson as an assistant in 1977. The Atlanta Constitution had a story about the young assistant coach and intended to describe him as the "highly regarded Danny Ford." However, because of a typographical error, the phrase came out "highly retarded Danny Ford." After reading the story, Ford showed the article to Bradley.

"Can I sue 'em for that?" asked Ford.

Bradley pondered the question, leaned forward on his desk and dispatched a stream of tobacco juice into a paper cup. Then he looked seriously right at Ford.

"Danny, you're gonna have to prove 'em wrong first," Bradley drawled.

There is a refreshing candor about Ford, a lot of country in him. He is most happy wearing a baseball cap, chewing a wad of tobacco and driving a pick-up truck with his fishing gear in the back. He often talks about fishing with his father in Gadsden, Alabama, just like he used to do as a kid. When he can't find the time to fish, he prefers to remain at home with his family, a pretty dark-haired wife named Deborah and three young daughters.

"Being a head coach was something I always knew I'd do," said Ford. "I didn't know whether it would be in high school or a small college or what, but I knew I wanted to do it."

In his first full season as a head coach in 1979, Ford produced an 8-4 record despite having lost 15 starters from the 1978 team. The fourth loss occurred in the 1979 Peach Bowl against Baylor, 24-18. Two of the three regular season losses were by only three and four points. It was quite a rewarding season for Ford. One of the biggest wins occurred against Notre Dame. Although a heavy underdog, which most teams are when they play at Notre Dame, Clemson overcame a 10-0 halftime deficit to defeat the Irish, 16-10. It marked only the third time in Notre Dame's colorful football history that the Irish lost their season's home finale.

The youthful Ford has driven the Tigers to a 36-10-1 record his first five years as coach.

Wearing a quizzical look, Ford wonders where the bear came from.

Ford was somewhat surprised by his team's success that year. Before the 1979 season began, Ford knew the Tigers' strength was their defense. Later he admitted the defense turned out better than he expected. They allowed only an average of eight points a game. He discovered that the offense was weak but was quick to point out that "they came a country mile" by working hard week after week. He also was of the opinion that the season's success would help considerably in recruiting for the 1980 campaign.

"We have to get the right kids," said Ford. "As a result of our winning program the last couple of years, we are able to recruit up and down the east coast now. If we recruit well, we can be anything we want to be."

Clemson football appeared to be on the way back after three consecutive winning seasons. The Tigers' reputation grew because of their appearance in three nationally televised bowl games. However, in 1980, the program suffered a temporary setback when Clemson finished with a mediocre 6-5 record. Once again Ford's integrity prompted him to shoulder most of the blame for the team's lackluster performance after winning four of its first five games. Ugly whispers were heard about his being too young to be a head coach and that perhaps he wasn't really qualified for the job. Ford admitted that he was still learning by his mistakes, but he refused to be discouraged. His goal was to be successful.

"I can look back and see I made some kind of mistake just about every day," said Ford. "Not big things necessarily, but things like not stressing a point or not talking enough to a particular player. There were times during the 1980 season when I overreacted. I would worry about every rumor that I heard. I probably worried more about those rumors than I did coaching. The toughest thing to say is, 'I failed,' and we failed five times in 1980. When you lose, you doubt yourself, your plans, whether the players are playing as best they can. Losing creates doubts like winning creates momentum and confidence.

"Looking back, I see that I overreacted to losing. I didn't give the players enough credit for what they overcame. Every time you walk on the football field, you don't expect them to be perfect, but I was impatient. We failed to realize how many youngsters hadn't been around Clemson's program. It was the biggest rebuilding job we've had since I've been here."

Bowl-conscious Clemson fans were looking for bigger things in 1981. If there was any pressure on Ford, he didn't show it, although he realized his critics would be quick and vocal. After just two full seasons of coaching, Ford had reached a crossroad early in his career. He was aware he had to win and win big, and he did a lot of soul searching in the lonely months before fall. The only sweet memory he had remaining from the 1980 season was a 27-6 triumph over nationally ranked South Carolina in the final game of the year.

The biggest decision Ford made during those months was an internal one. He decided to delegate more responsibility to his assistant coaches. In that way, each coach would be responsible for his particular area. He reasoned that it would provide more cohesiveness within that unit and contribute to the single purposeness of the entire team, which was to provide leadership all around in winning together. He demanded more organization in planning and its ultimate execu-

Ford and friend Samar

tion. Although he just turned 33 years old, it appeared that Ford matured overnight in the months following the 1980 season.

"In 1979 we had a pretty good team, 8-4," said Ford. "Coaching was fun. Coaching was easy, but all of a sudden we were 6-5 in 1980. And I wasn't ready for that. I don't care if I was 33 or 53. In no way had I prepared myself to be an average coach with an average team. You're supposed to prepare. But I wasn't prepared for being sorry, and I was doing a sorry job. All of a sudden coaching was hard. We changed our plans in midstream in 1980, and that was the worst thing we could have done. It was a young team, and they really needed guidance. A 6-5 record wasn't the end of the world; but we took it, golly, like Clemson collapsed.

"We were young offensively in 1980, and they weren't ready to play. We played too many young people, and experience means everything in this game. There are some things about the season I won't ever forget. I know a little more about people now, and there are some people, people I call zeroes, that I don't want anything to do with."

A determined Ford faced the 1981 season with a sprinkling of optimism. The organizational changes he made along with his approach to the campaign itself gave him more inner confidence. For one thing, he decided to take Mondays off, not only to utilize it for recruiting high school prospects but primarily to provide his coaches with the opportunity of working together without any interference from him. Then, too, he delegated the responsibility of formulating the game plan to his assistants. Ford also realized that it was important to retain the personal touch he had with his players as an assistant and determined to remain close with his seniors. The squad was a bit more experienced than the year before, and there was guarded talk that perhaps the Tigers were good enough to make a strong push for the ACC championship.

"In planning for the 1981 season, it was the first year that we could say we had enough people to be a pretty good football team before the freshmen came in," said Ford. "We didn't have to turn to the new players for help. It wasn't like the previous year, going into the

In taking over from Charley Pell before the 1979 Gator Bowl, Ford, at the age of 30, became the youngest Division I head coach on record.

season wondering how a guy will react to playing in certain situations. All our guys didn't have tremendous experience, but they did have experience. Our coaches felt good about who we had on the field. We all felt a little more confident about things.

"I think our reputation of being a tough, intimidating team suffered in 1980. We lost some of the edge. We turned into too much of a finesse team. We lost a lot of respect from some of our opponents. I don't think people dreaded to play Clemson. We will need to be a more physical team. We need to take control of the line of scrimmage. I want us to be a team that our opponents are not looking forward to playing."

Ford himself appeared prepared. Yet, neither Ford nor anyone on his coaching staff anticipated just how successful Clemson would become in 1981. They swept through the ACC and finished the season unbeaten with an 11-0 record, the first time that had happened since 1948. By season's end, the Tigers were voted the number one team in the nation, an honor they had never received before. They secured

rd directed Clemson to the greatest season in the school's history in 1981. Duke was one of twelve teams that fell fore the unbeaten Tigers who finished the season ranked as the number one team in the country.

131

their ranking when they defeated Nebraska in the Orange Bowl, 22-15. Even Ford couldn't believe it.

"I wouldn't have bet on all this happening," said Ford. "No one could have imagined it either way. Not too many folks could have imagined we would have the type of year we had, being number one. Then it's very unusual for somebody who's been in coaching the short time I have to get that award. I just hope our staff and administration took a lot of pride in the honor because it's theirs more than mine.

"I was closer to the seniors in 1981 more than any group I've ever had. I spent more time with that group than any other. What you want from your seniors is to keep you in touch with the whole squad. They're always in touch with everybody's feelings on the team. Their job was to keep the squad in touch with me through them. They did a great job. They were like coaches."

Ford also enjoyed another personally rewarding moment in 1982. A week after Clemson ended its regular season, Ford went to Birmingham, Alabama, to see the Auburn-Alabama game. Being there was very meaningful to Ford. He wanted to watch his college coach, Bear Bryant, record his 315th victory, one which would establish a new record among coaches. The trip also helped bring back Ford's memories of Alabama and Bryant.

"I had a good time," recalled Ford. "That was the first game I enjoyed in a long time. There's so much emphasis put on winning. Winning gives you something to be happy about, but this was the first time in I don't know how long that I just sat back and enjoyed a football game. As an assistant coach, I had to worry about how the line was doing. As head coach, I have to worry about the team.

"Where I grew up, you hope to go to Alabama or Auburn, whichever is winning at the time. The recruiters don't say anything negative to you. Everybody talks to you like you're the best player in the world. They make you feel like you're wanted. That's the toughest thing for recruits, when you get to like a recruiter. The toughest thing you ever have to do is say no to somebody you like. I was playing football, and all of a sudden no more foot-

Ford and his staff sweat out a tense moment.

In his first game as head coach, Ford directed Clemson to a 17-15 victory over Ohio State in the 1979 Gator Bowl.

ball. I'm supposed to be a grown man and supposed to go out and make a living, but I was a football player. That's what I wanted to do. Doggone, I didn't want to go out and work."

Instead, Ford remained in college. He graduated in 1970 with a bachelor's degree in industrial arts. However, he decided to become a high school coach and studied for a master's degree in special education. His reasoning was simple. He felt he could earn more money with a master's. Bryant helped him along by adding him to his coaching staff as a graduate assistant in 1970 and 1971. It was during those early coaching years that Bryant developed the foundation of his coaching philosophy.

"The best thing about Bryant was that he was not afraid of change," said Ford. "He's not stubborn. If you've got long hair, that doesn't mean you can't start for him. If you've got a mustache, that doesn't mean you can't block. If you can't play in this offense, that doesn't mean you can't play in that one. He was coming off a 6-5 season my senior year, running the 'I' and the multiple offense. He came into

a coaches' meeting in August and said, 'We got to make a change. We're going to use the wishbone. If you want to learn about the wishbone, I'll teach you; if you don't, I'll help you get a job somewhere else.' That was that. If he stuck with the 'I,' I don't think he could have broken the record."

Ford has already thought about how many more years he intends to compete as a coach. Down deep, he's a laid-back type of person, honest-to-goodness country. Even after the most successful season in Clemson's long history when they reached the pinnacle in 1981 and the euphoric feeling that remained in every nook of the school was enough to make a coach think of coaching forever, Ford's thoughts were of the other side of life. His baseball cap rested high on his head, and a small wad of chewing tobacco came to a halt on one side of his mouth as he spoke just one week after defeating South Carolina.

"I'm gonna go home for a week; and I ain't gonna do nothing but maybe buy me some hay, feed the cows, and go fishing some with my daddy," said Ford. "My daddy and me have a little land we rent from my uncle. That's where I'll be most of the time.

"Twenty years of doing this kind of stuff—I don't know. I don't know. How do people do it for 20, 25 years? I want to get where I can retire. First of all, there's so many things I want to do. This was one of them, and it came early for me. You always dream of being a head coach and always work to be undefeated. Then, when you do it, when you have the opportunity or are forced to do it, whichever comes first, you ask yourself is that all there is to it? I think most of all, what you try to do as a coach is the best you can and get on to winning, winning, winning. It's always winning.

"You should feel like you're on top of the world, but I don't feel any different than I did in 1980 when we were 6-5. You feel like once it's done, it should be all over, but everything just keeps on coming at you. It should be the greatest feeling in the world, but there is always something else for you to do. I would love to be out in the woods today, fishing or hunting. I could just sit out there and watch them cows graze or just chew on a weed."

Mark Twain would love him...

134

17

1981 SEASON

"A New Beginning For Clemson Football"

The 1980 campaign, when Clemson stumbled into mediocrity with a 6-5 record, haunted Ford all winter. He had believed his squad was capable of being in a bowl game that year, but three close losses to Georgia, North Carolina State, and North Carolina by a combined total of only 13 points had made it only an average season. The team began its bid for a successful 1981 record, and another bowl trip, months before spring practice. Beginning the first week in January, the players began working out regularly on their own in the weight room or jogging around the practice field.

"I didn't think wide receivers had to lift weights like everybody else, but I was wrong," disclosed star flanker Perry Tuttle, one of the squad's seniors. "It wasn't that bad, either. I just worked to keep my muscles toned up. The important thing to do was keep my speed, and I actually increased my speed. In 1980 I ran a 4.42 in the 40-yard dash, and now I got it down to 4.40."

Ford was pleased with what he saw when it came time for spring practice, and the players' attitude of renewed dedication pleased the coaching staff. The athletes' bodies were trim and hard from their off-season workouts. The team looked snappy in the Orange and White scrimmage which officially brought an end to the three-week practice.

"This spring we've tried to open up and look at all our possibilities," observed Ford. "I think that last year we were too limited by what we wanted the team to be. This year we're going to try to do what our team can do best.

"We have several areas of concern, namely defensive end, linebacker, and the kicking game. The main worry is our kicking game. We have to find a replacement for Obed Ariri. I'm hoping that we won't have to depend on our field goal kicker as much this year, but we need to find one. We've got a guy off the soccer team, but I can't even say his name."

Ford was referring to Donald Igwebuike, an untried freshman. Igwebuike and Ariri were both from Nigeria. While at Clemson, both men played two major sports at the same time: soccer and football. Igwebuike had a tough act to follow. Ariri was the first and only one to kick field goals on Saturday and soccer goals on Sunday, setting Clemson field goal

Clemson players run down the hill on the east end of Death Valley.

records in the four years he performed, among them most career points, 288; most field goals in one game, four; most field goals season, 23; most field goals career, 63; and the longest field goal made, 57 yards.

Yet, that August, Ford had a good feeling about the approaching season. He counted 53 lettermen, which was abundant, indeed. If he wasn't concerned about his offense, it was because of the fact that he had all eleven starters back at their positions. And, he had a way to open his offense more. The key was junior quarterback Homer Jordan. While only a sophomore in 1980, he broke Steve Fuller's total offense record for a season by passing and running for 1,683 yards.

"The fans around here didn't know much about Homer," said Ford. "We knew he was a football player. We didn't know he was a quarterback. Early on he was very, very quiet—very, very shy. Didn't talk much at all. There was never a question of his having ability. See my fist? He was always like this, tight, nervous; and in the beginning he deserved the criticism because he was coming out there like he was playing basketball, dribbling the ball."

In his quiet way, Jordan was determined to play at quarterback. He was under great pressure. He was the first black quarterback ever to play for Clemson and would be subjected to sharp criticism should he fail to fulfill Ford's expectations. As a freshman in 1979, Jordan was nothing more than a back-up to quarterback Billy Lott and played very little. Before the 1980 campaign, he was listed primarily as a defensive back. It was obvious then that the coaching staff didn't have much confidence in him as a quarterback. Although he had led Cedar Shoals High School in Athens, Georgia, to an 11-1 record his senior year, coaches at the University of Georgia didn't think much of Jordan's ability either and passed him by. "Clemson told me I'd have a shot at quarterback, so I took it at that," said Jordan.

When he discovered that he was being switched to the defensive backfield after spring practice in 1980, Jordan pleaded with the coaches to give him a shot at quarterback. They agreed. When he reported to practice that fall, Jordan was rated no better than a third-string quarterback on the depth chart.

Hardly encouraging. Yet, Jordan worked hard, and his confidence grew every day. Three days before the Tigers opened their season against Rice, Ford named Jordan as his starting quarterback.

"The thing I did that probably hurt him last year was to start him against Georgia in Athens in the second game," said Ford. "He didn't play very well, and we got beat, 20-16. He was back home, playing in front of all those people and was nervous. If I was smart, I should have figured all of that out. But he hung in there after that and finished the season strong. The rest of the squad now has confidence in him."

Much of the inner strength to succeed that Jordan possesses comes from his mother, Alice. After her husband died, she worked at two jobs for 13 years to support Homer and his three sisters. She worked as a cashier at an insurance company from 8 a.m. until 4 p.m. and later, at night, from 11 p.m. to 7 a.m. as a hospital nurse.

"My time for sleep was after dinner was through and the dishes were done," said Alice, "but on football nights that was impossible. Little Homer would come to me and say, 'Momma, you're coming to the game, aren't you?' And I'd say, 'Yes, Little Homer, I'll be there.' But here's something I never told him: A lot of times I'd just watch the first few minutes of the game, long enough for him to look up and see me in the stands. Then I'd go back in the car and rest until the fourth quarter.

"He was determined to go to college and play football, as little as he was. One night some of his friends carried Homer into the house like he was on a stretcher. Later that week I said, 'Little Homer, you're not going to try and play, are you, when you're so hurt and all?' And he said, 'Yes, Momma, I am.' And that was that."

By his junior year in 1981, Jordan was ready to take command. Tuttle noticed it.

"Homer's grown up so much," said Tuttle. "It really started with the last four games of 1980. Before that, he was never really sure of himself. When it was time to check off a called play at the line, Homer didn't know what to do. I would put my arm around him and say, 'Homer, don't worry. The coaches have confi-

inding a replacement for kicker Obed Ariri
as one of Ford's concerns before the 1981 season.

139

The 1981 Clemson cheerleaders had plenty to cheer about during the season. From left, Mary McNeil; Rick Conte; Pat Hook; David Pinion; Kathy Anderson; Scott Gallaway; Karen Lawing; George Helmrich; Jennifer Hemphill; Bill Grainger; Sheri Nix; Russel Ragen; Danny Pechthalt and Ricky Capps.

dence in you. Go with your instincts.'"

If he had done that, perhaps Clemson would have won more games that season. But he was simply nervous. It showed in one game near the end of the season against North Carolina in which Clemson lost, 24-19. The Tigers had a chance to win but suffered a frustrating defeat.

"We had a first-and-goal on their one-yard line with a minute and a half to play," recalled Jordan. "The coach called the same play—fullback up the middle—three times. I saw their end crashing, and I knew that it wouldn't work, but I wouldn't check off the play."

In 1980 the offensive unit moved the ball well between the 20-yard lines but consistently failed to get the ball into the end zone. An assertive Jordan, with a full season's experience tucked under his belt, was the answer for 1981. Jordan knew what was expected of him. During the summer, he had worked on improving his passing and timing with receivers. He had accepted the previous season's frustrations as being a learning process.

"The talk around here this year has been about which bowl we want to go to," said Jordan. "So many players are returning, including the entire starting offense. We worked together all last year and know each other really well. Now we can't wait to get started. Everyone feels this is going to be our year."

Nobody wanted to have a winning season more than Tuttle. The fleet wide receiver, whom pro scouts ranked as one of the best in the country, wasn't named to the 1981 preseason all-ACC squad in a poll of the ACC coaches.

"I went home one weekend this summer, and the first thing I do when I get to the house is pick up the paper," said Tuttle. "I looked at the headlines that said, 'Tuttle Left Out.' It made me kind of mad; and the first thing I thought was, you know, they still don't respect me."

It didn't matter to Ford what the other coaches around the conference thought about Tuttle.

"I know how good he is," said Ford. "Pro scouts tell me there aren't that many great receivers around this year and that teams who are going to be looking for wide receivers will give Perry a look very, very early in the draft.

Perry runs excellent routes, and right now he's running his routes two-to-one better than he was last year; but what makes him as good a wide receiver as there is anywhere in the country is that he has three years of experience."

The knowledge that Ford was going to open up the offense more pleased Tuttle as he prepared for his fourth and final season. In the last two years, he had caught every touchdown pass that was thrown. He needed only 572 more yards to surpass Butler as Clemson's all-time leading receiver. The Jordan-to-Tuttle combination was being compared by some as being even better than the Steve Fuller-Jerry Butler union several years earlier. It was no wonder that Tuttle was anxious for the season to begin.

"We're going to pass more," said Tuttle. "We're going to take more chances on first and second down. We're going to open up a whole lot more things. That's going to help me and our weak side receiver, Jerry Gaillard, too. When we start going to the back side of the offense, it will eliminate a lot of double coverage, a lot of three-on-two coverage that we saw so much last year. I think more people are going to realize how good a receiver Jerry is. Hey, the main thing is that we've got a number one quarterback; and Homer is a good one. Last year we went into the season not knowing who was going to be the number one quarterback. We kept shuffling quarterbacks in and out the first two or three games. Now we know who's number one. It's no longer a guessing game."

With his passing game apparently sound, Ford had to sort out his running game. He had a long list of backs but none in the game-breaker category. The best of the bunch was Chuck McSwain, a junior tailback who was the team's leading rusher in 1980 with 544 yards. However, McSwain was hampered in the daily workouts by a pulled leg muscle.

"We don't have a great running back yet," said Ford. "We just don't know what the situation is. McSwain has a muscle pull, so he's got to be behind right now. He is a big, strong back who really hasn't showed the kind of speed that he has. At times he's made everybody here excited about what he can do. Jeff McCall has improved a lot at fullback, and Cliff Austin has gotten a lot tougher. Both have good speed. But we haven't had one back stand out consistently. Different ones have looked good on different days."

The four practice fields off to the right of the Jervey Athletic Center were a beehive of sweaty bodies toiling under a hot August sun. The regular season opener against Wofford College was less than two weeks away. The players labored in the burning heat of two-a-day workouts. After one morning workout, some of the players openly showed signs of fatigue. Yet, offensive line coach Larry Van Der Heyden wanted more effort. He called his group together and then sent them back on the field. They ran a play which didn't measure up to the standards that Van Der Heyden required. He clearly made it known.

"You either give us an hour and twenty minutes of what we want, or we'll stay out here three hours until you get it right," shouted Van Der Heyden.

Wide receiver Perry Tuttle had a good feeling about the 1981 campaign.

The players responded. They finished their workout on an upbeat, hustling, and with lively chatter.

The shriek of the air horn sounded like a sonata to the players as the morning drills concluded. They would run from all four fields to listen to Ford. He reminded them not to get started on any bad habits and stressed teamwork. He also told them they were looking tired from so much practice and that if their legs felt heavy with fatigue to take it a bit easy in the afternoon session.

Ford himself put in long hours. He spent most of them on defense in long meetings with his staff. A solid defense was vital to any success the team would have in the approaching season. The past success of Clemson teams has always been accented by a strong defense. The Tiger defense often ranked among the best in the nation. In 1980 it had been weak. They yielded an average of 304 yards a game. On three occasions their opponents scored more than 30 points on Clemson. Four others scored over 20 points. Overall, they gave up an average of better than 20 points a game, more than double the previous year's efforts. While most of the blame was pointed at the defensive backfield, a good deal of it should have been directed at a weak pass rush.

"If you give somebody all day to throw, anybody can complete a pass," remarked Ford. "We lost a lot of respectability on defense and have to work very hard to restore that respectability. We weren't a very good defensive football team. Our defensive end play was terrible. We just couldn't contain people. The defense is going to have to gain respect. We want them to play tough and ornery like they have in the past."

The standout on the defense was linebacker Jeff Davis, who was returning for his final season. He had been credited with 160 tackles in 1980, the most in the ACC. Among the total were 108 first hits, a new Clemson record. Davis was easily a first team All-ACC selection.

"Davis is the best I've ever had," said Ford. "No linebacker I've played with or coached hits as hard as him. I didn't see anyone last year who came close to Jeff's ability, and I am sure there aren't too many in the country that

can compare with him."

It was high praise, indeed. While he was an assistant at Alabama, Ford worked with Woody Lowe and Barry Krause, both of whom earned All-American honors. It was obvious that Ford expected Davis to be his defensive leader.

"When I hear him say things like that, it makes me feel good and makes me want to play that much harder," says Davis. "I don't want to prove him wrong. I usually let my actions speak for themselves; but I'm going to be more vocal this year, trying to pick everyone up. I'll talk to people; and if I can make a big hit, it can be contagious.

"Last year the defense didn't play in the Clemson tradition. A lot of people did things against us they hadn't been able to do before. Instead of coming together to stop it, everyone began worrying about what everyone else was doing. People were saying this guy isn't doing his job or that guy isn't. We weren't working with each other. We've got to get back to where we're supposed to be. The guys know what needs to be done. We've got to have a team effort. The line helps the linebackers and defensive backs do their job and vice versa. We had too many individuals on defense and we weren't enough of a team. The Clemson defense is supposed to be swarming like bees, helping each other out. We got away from that last year.

"We can see a different attitude this year. Things are different. Everybody has matured more. We know we have to have a good season and go to a bowl game to get back the respect we deserve. Some people may be overlooking Clemson this year, but that's good. That's the way we like it."

Still, two weeks before the opener, Ford didn't like what was happening during one afternoon workout. After about an hour, he dismissed the entire squad. The players trudged back to the locker room.

"We were playing today like we did in a lot of games last year," Ford explained to those who questioned him about stopping the practice. "We were making too many mistakes. If we played Wofford today, they'd have beaten us, 50-0. I could say it was a hot day or that we had injuries or that classes had started, but

Clemson was scheduled to open the season against Villanova, but when the Philadelphia school dropped football, Wofford accommodated the Tigers for the first time since 1940.

that would be passing the buck. We were just making too many errors. I felt we needed to call it off and let the guys get things out of their system that are apparently preoccupying their minds. In general, we did not deserve to be playing in the Valley if we were going to fumble, throw interceptions, and have penalties; but there will be another day to regroup. We will get it right."

The regrouping came even faster than Ford expected. The next day the senior members of the squad met with their coach. They wanted to know why they couldn't talk about the problems they were having on the field right then and there and start over. Clearly, a new attitude had permeated throughout the squad. It was a new beginning for Clemson football.

GAME 1: WOFFORD

The season-opening game against Wofford was truly an accommodation by the small South Carolina school. Villanova was originally scheduled to play Clemson; but when the Philadelphia school abruptly dropped its football program, it left Clemson with an opening-day void. Quickly, Clemson athletic director Bill McLellan reached for the phone and called Wofford's athletic Director Tom Sasser, who also happened to be the Terriers' football coach, and agreed on the game.

Surprisingly, there was a tinge of nostalgia attached to the meeting. Wofford was one of three schools that helped launch Clemson's

143

football history back in 1896. In beating Wofford, 16-0, Clemson was able to make its very first season in intercollegiate football a winning one. Yet, over the years, the rivalry never fully matured. The last time Clemson and Wofford played was in 1940 when the Tigers roared to a 26-0 victory. In all, the schools had faced each other eleven times with Clemson winning eight of the occasions.

The September 5 opener was the earliest in Clemson history. Nevertheless, the Tigers have been quite successful in opening day games. Their record of 62-14-9 translates into a winning percentage of .788. It is quite high, indeed, when considering that the Tigers' overall winning percentage in the 85 years they have been playing football is .557.

The last time Wofford beat Clemson was in 1933, 14-13. Nobody figured it could happen again. The two institutions went their separate ways since the last time they had met 41 years ago, Clemson ambitiously competing in big time college football while Wofford remained in small college circles. It was not lost on Sasser, who made no pretensions about playing Clemson. Not since 1957, when the Terriers lost to South Carolina, 26-0, had Wofford faced a Major Division I school.

"I think you know when you're playing one of the better teams in the ACC and you read somewhere they're picked in the Top 20, it seems like the reality of their team gets more real the closer you get to the game," said Sasser. "But still, we scheduled this game knowing what it could mean to us. I still think all the pluses are there, and the players are looking forward to it. I didn't go into this thinking we would be able to play Clemson and be on a par with them, but I felt we have a pretty good team; and if the chemistry goes right, who knows?"

Actually, the game itself figured to be a breather for Clemson. It was the easiest one of the eleven-game schedule and at the same time the toughest one of Wofford's list of opponents, albeit it was the easiest trip since the Terriers were only a short distance away on Interstate 80. They were quite familiar with Death Valley even though they had never played before a crowd of over 60,000 people before.

"We are not looking at Wofford any differently than we did Rice or Furman," said Ford in reference to Clemson's last two season-openers. "I have great respect for their staff and team. They concern us in a lot of ways. They were 7-2-2 last year and ranked nationally. Their wing-bone offense may be the hardest we'll have to prepare for all year, and you know their people will be playing ten feet taller.

"I'm just anxious to see if our guys are ready to be the football team they say they want to be. Our kids are confident about the season, but they're not cocky. I feel like our people are a pretty mature group. They're thinking they're going to be good. I'm thinking with them. I believe they can accomplish whatever they want to. I just want to see how high they set their goals."

Earlier in the week it was feared that Mc-Swain's troublesome muscle pull would sideline him for the opener. Although he wasn't quite fully recovered by game day, he was ready to play. He needed only 13 yards to reach the 1,000 mark in his career. Also ready was Tuttle, who had suffered a slight ankle injury at one of the mid-week practices. Tuttle needed only two receptions to become only the third player in Clemson history to catch 100 passes in a career.

Under a hot sun, Wofford received the opening kickoff of the 1981 season. Igwebuike buried the kick in the end zone, and the Terriers put the ball in play on the 20-yard line. They surprised the sold-out crowd by keeping the ball for over eight minutes and reaching the Clemson seven-yard line before finally being stopped. Don Hairston gave the Terriers a 3-0 lead with a 24-yard field goal.

Tuttle immediately made his presence felt. He returned Hairston's kickoff 38 yards to position a Clemson field goal. Igwebuike displayed a powerful leg when he tied the game with a 52-yard field goal.

It wasn't until six minutes had gone by in the second period that Clemson got the lead. It came suddenly and dramatically. Jordan and Tuttle combined on a picture book 80-yard touchdown pass that had Tiger fans roaring. Bob Paulling's conversion gave Clemson a 10-3 edge. The next time they got the ball the

Tigers scored again. Jordan completed an eight-play, 76-yard drive by running the last 14 yards around left end on a keeper. Paulling's kick made it 17-3, minutes before the first half ended.

Clemson received the second half kickoff and marched 73 yards for a touchdown. Jordan recorded his second touchdown pass of the game when he hit wide receiver Frank Magwood with an 11-yard throw. Paulling's kick stretched Clemson's lead to 24-3. Just before the third quarter ended, Clemson scored again. Jordan scored his second touchdown by going over from three yards out. Paulling added the extra point to give the Tigers a 31-3 bulge.

On their first series in the final period, Clemson scored its fifth touchdown. McSwain sped around left end for five yards to complete a 56-yard drive. Igwebuike converted; and the Tigers led 38-3. Wofford finally scored again when they recovered a fumble on the Clemson 39-yard line. Ten plays later, Barry Thompson hit tight end Dirk Derrick with a 15-yard scoring pass. Hairston's conversion made it 38-10. Clemson closed out the scoring a minute from the end when Jeff McCall broke over right tackle for ten yards for a touchdown. Paulling booted the extra point that made the final score 45-10.

Tuttle collected his two receptions, finishing up with four. McSwain got his 13 yards, piling up 51; and Clemson had its first victory of the season as expected. Ford was relieved to get the first game out of the way because he found out some things about his team.

"I saw a lot of good things out there, especially on offense," said Ford. "Of the things we saw wrong, there's nothing we can't correct. They had an excellent game plan in the first half and ran us ragged with their misdirection plays. We just had a whole lot more depth than they did. If we hadn't thrown the big bomb, it could have been 3-3 at halftime."

WOFFORD AT CLEMSON
September 5
Weather: Partly Cloudy, 83°
Attendance: 59,313

CLEMSON	3 14 14 14	— 45
WOFFORD	3 0 0 7	— 10

WC—Hairston 24 FG
CU—Igwebuike 52 FG
CU—Tuttle 80 pass from Jordan (Paulling kick)
CU—Jordan 14 run (Paulling kick)
CU—Magwood 11 pass from Jordan (Paulling kick)
CU—C. McSwain 5 run (Igwebuike kick)
WC—Derrick 15 pass from Thompson (Hairston kick)
CU—McCall 10 run (Paulling kick)

GAME 2: TULANE

There were two areas of concern that confronted Ford as he began his preparations for Tulane. One, of course, was the game itself, which is a way of coaching life every week. The other, although not directly involved with the actual playing of the game, could most decidedly affect it. It was the off-field influences of playing in the Superdome in frivolous New Orleans that occupied Ford's mind most of the week.

For one thing, Clemson had never played a game indoors before. That wasn't all. They were playing their first night game in five years, which didn't seem too important except for the fact that it allowed the players a lot of free time before the game with the city's famed French Quarter a nearby distraction. Since the New Orleans Saints play in the Superdome, the artificial surface with its pro layout of extra hash marks evident, a giant instant replay television screen high above the field, and the enormity of the Superdome itself, all created a worry for Ford. Yet, he approached the challenges clinically.

"Playing in the Superdome, the Astroturf, a night game, that's all new to us," said Ford. "We're concerned about the fact that the playing field designed for NFL standards has four hash marks instead of two. We're going to add two hash marks to our practice field to get accustomed to that.

"I also hope none of our players will be concerned about the instant replay system used in the Superdome. I don't want our defensive backs to be distracted. I don't know how we're going to prepare for the atmosphere of New

William Devane stops a Tulane runner as Johnny Rembert comes up to make sure.

Orleans because we don't have anything like that around here. Also, I don't have many experiences playing at night. I don't want the players sitting around the hotel all day, nor do I want them out sightseeing all day. I'm leaving it up to the players. Our seniors have made a lot of decisions for the squad this year, and I think they've made some good ones so far. We're going to prepare in every way we can. Our guys are old enough to know why we're going down there, and I know they're looking forward to playing in the Superdome."

It was obvious that Ford was depending on his seniors for leadership. That was clearly missing a year earlier; yet, it appeared to have returned. It was evident during the practices when the seniors expressed themselves by helping out others. Jeff Bryant, the team's senior All-ACC defensive tackle, was one of the leaders that Ford spoke about.

"When you have senior leadership, it makes

a lot of difference," said Bryant. "When it's a long practice, when it gets hard and it's hot, you've got to have someone step forward and lead the team and make people want to do the things we have to do. It's not so much verbally but physically you have to show them. It's something I've always believed in. I've always been a hard worker. I believe that you play like you practice. That's why I get on people when they get out of line. This is my football team. I've been here. I know the system. I feel like the underclassmen should help me to have a good season because it's my last, and I want to go out in style."

Clemson had not played Tulane since 1975. The Green Wave surprised the Tigers back then by beating them in Death Valley, 17-13. They first met in 1937; and Tulane won for the first time, 7-0. In the subsequent nine times that the teams have played each other, Tulane emerged victorious on six occasions.

Ford had a high regard for Tulane, who had lost a heart-breaking 19-18 decision in their opening game.

"They concern me quite a bit," said Ford. "We haven't seen a team with a pro style offense like this since the Wake Forest teams of 1978 and '79. Tulane is a better team than I would like to play this early in the season. I'm not sure we would have wanted to play them without having a game under our belts."

Clemson received the opening kickoff but couldn't do much. They managed to reach Tulane's 37-yard line from which point Igwebuike's 55-yard field goal attempt was short. Tulane took over at that point and drove to Clemson's 28-yard line before stalling. However, Vince Manalla booted a 46-yard field goal that provided Tulane with a 3-0 lead.

Misfortune struck Clemson following the kickoff. After failing to produce a first down, Dale Hatcher was sent in to punt from the 26-yard line. However, the ball was snapped over his head and rolled into the end zone. Hatcher managed to cover the ball for a safety that gave Tulane a 5-0 lead.

It wasn't until midway through the second period that Clemson finally scored. Defensive end Joe Glenn made it possible. He recovered a Tulane fumble on the 25-yard line to set up tailback Cliff Austin's four-yard touchdown run. Paulling converted to give the Tigers a 7-5 edge, which they kept when the half ended.

Clemson had an opportunity to score first in the third period but lost it. They recovered a Tulane fumble on the 33-yard line following the kickoff. Clemson got to the Tulane 16 which was close enough for Paulling to attempt a 33-yard field goal. Unfortunately, the snap was bad; and Paulling never did get the kick off. When the quarter ended, the score remained 7-5 as neither team could produce a serious scoring threat, although Clemson was driving at the end.

On the very first play of the fourth quarter, Paulling was on the field again. This time his 31-yard field goal attempt was good; and Clemson led, 10-5. It was apparent at this point that the tenacious Tiger defense would have to control the game. They met the challenge by intercepting a Tulane pass two plays after the kickoff. Minutes later, Paulling re-turned to the lineup. He looked at a 37-yard field goal try and came through to give the Tigers a 13-5 lead with just over twelve minutes remaining in the game. Nobody realized at the time that the game would end that way. Clemson's defense was the deciding factor, limiting Tulane to just five first downs and 177 total yardage. Ford was relieved when it was over with."

"I feel lucky to get out of here alive," said Ford. "There were a lot of mistakes in the game. I don't know how many, but they came from both sides. Offensively, we made a lot of mistakes; and we didn't score many points. I thought Tulane was a lot better team than they showed in the game films."

Although it wasn't pretty, it was a victory nevertheless. The players accepted it.

"It was a rough game," said Tuttle. "They were a real physical team, and I'm glad that we got out of this one the way we did."

CLEMSON AT TULANE
September 12
Weather: Indoors (Louisiana Superdome), 78°
Attendance: 45,736

CLEMSON	0 7 0 6	– 13
TULANE	5 0 0 0	– 5

TU—Manalla 46 FG
TU—Safety, Hatcher falls on bad snap in the end zone
CU—Austin 4 run (Paulling kick)
CU—Paulling 31 FG
CU—Paulling 37 FG

GAME 3: GEORGIA

It may have appeared insignificant at the time, but by winning its first two games Clemson achieved something they hadn't been able to do since 1970. More significant was the fact that the Tigers had to face Georgia in Death Valley. The Bulldogs were the number one college team in 1980 and owned the nation's longest winning streak, which consisted of 15 games.

The rivalry with Georgia was growing in in-

Quarterback Homer Jordan looks for running room against Georgia.

tensity. Some Clemson partisans felt it was almost as big as the rivalry with South Carolina. Actually, the series began in 1897. Over the years Georgia had dominated the rivalry, 33-13-3. Yet, more emphasis has been placed on the games played in recent seasons. Only 22 points have separated the two teams the last four times they faced one another with each team winning two games. It was in Death Valley in 1979 that Clemson last beat Georgia, 12-7.

The Clemson players realized how important that game against the nationally ranked Bulldogs was to them. By winning its first two games, Georgia was rated number four in the national polls. Although they had won their first two games, the Tigers were not ranked and were hungry for recognition. They were convinced a win over Georgia would make the pollsters take notice.

So intent were the players about the game that the senior members of the squad met with Ford in the middle of the week. They wanted Ford to allow the team to wear their orange pants against Georgia. Ford refused their request. He wanted to save them for the season-ending game against South Carolina. They had worn them the previous year against the Gamecocks when Clemson just barely managed to produce a winning season with a rela-

tively easy 27-6 triumph. Ever since then, Ford has held the orange pants in reverence, only to be worn against South Carolina. However, the Clemson seniors convinced Ford that the Georgia game was every bit as big and got the young coach to relent.

"I didn't want them to wear them, still don't want them to wear them but once a year against South Carolina; but I got overruled," admitted Ford. "I knew it was coming. I knew they were going to ask; and I said, 'No, I don't want to embarrass the orange pants. I don't want to take the glow off them. I don't want to take the chance. I want to wear them again when I know we can win.' They said, 'Well, we can wear them this week.'"

It was understandable why Ford was apprehensive at the prospect of playing Georgia. The defending national champions easily won their first two games against California and Tennessee. In junior running back Herschel Walker, the Bulldogs had the game's most publicized and dominating player. He had already established a bushel of Georgia records and had already accounted for 328 yards in the two games he played. Yet, Ford didn't want to place too much emphasis on Walker to prevent his players from being awestruck by him and not being able to concentrate on the game itself.

148

"The key to this game is not stopping Herschel Walker," emphasized Ford. "Quarterback Buck Belue and flanker Lindsay Scott are fine players who can kill you if you concentrate too much on Walker. We will be ready for Georgia, of course. We won't need to do much motivating as coaches for this game. We are playing the defending champions."

Quarterback Homer Jordan and defensive tackle Jeff Bryant, both of whom are from Georgia, had more incentive than others.

"It's getting bigger than the South Carolina game," remarked Jordan.

"For me, it's bigger," added Bryant. "I've been looking forward to this all year. We're playing the defending national champions with a 15-game winning streak and Mr. All-World."

The game was expected to be close. It began that way with a scoreless first quarter. Georgia did manage to threaten towards the end of the period. They had a first down on the Clemson 17-yard line; but after gaining four yards, Walker fumbled and safety Jeff Suttle recovered.

Even when the second period began, Jordan had trouble moving the offense. However, with about nine minutes left, he was given a great opportunity when safety Tim Childer intercepted Belue's pass on the Georgia 18. After moving to a first down on the eight, Jordan threw a touchdown pass to Tuttle that got the crowd of better than 62,000 to its feet. Paulling converted to give Clemson a 7-0 lead.

Near the end of the half, Clemson struck again. Walker again fumbled and middle guard William Perry recovered on the Georgia 34-yard line. Three plays later, with only eleven seconds showing on the clock, Igwebuike booted a 39-yard field goal to provide Clemson with a 10-0 halftime advantage which made Tiger followers happy.

However, Georgia managed to come back with the second half kickoff. They marched 56 yards, basically on two plays, a 21-yard run by Walker and a 14-yard pass completion from Belue to Scott, before being stopped. A 40-yard field goal by Kevin Butler managed to trim Clemson's lead to 10-3.

Early in the final period, Igwebuike gave Tiger fans more to cheer about. With 14:01 left in the game, he was accurate with a 29-yard field goal that extended Clemson's margin to 13-3. From then on, it was up to the defense; and they responded with swarming intensity to intercept Belue five times before the game ended while keeping Walker out of the end zone. Tiger fans celebrated well into the night.

"It was the biggest win I've ever had in football," beamed a happy Jordan. "It's going to be a lot easier going back to Athens. I can go home and talk a little bit."

Most of the other players felt the same way, still excited by the victory.

"This was probably the biggest game we were going to play all year," said linebacker Jeff Davis. "When we lost to Georgia last year, we kind of lost our morale; and it hurt us for the rest of the season. We know the rest of the games are important, but we had to win this one."

"This is the best I've ever felt after a football game," added defensive tackle Dan Benish.

GEORGIA AT CLEMSON
September 19
Weather: Clear, 69°
Attendance: 62,446

CLEMSON	0	10	0	3	–	13
GEORGIA	0	0	3	0	–	3

CU—Tuttle 8 pass from Jordan
    (Paulling kick)
CU—Igwebuike 39 FG
UGA—Butler 40 FG
CU—Igwebuike 29 FG

GAME 4: KENTUCKY

The convincing victory over Georgia awakened the nation's pollsters. After the third week of the young season, Clemson cracked the top 20 and was ranked 18th by United Press. The Clemson triumph was so impressive to United Press that Ford was also voted the Coach of the Week by their panel of experts.

"Danny, you dug yourself a hole Saturday,

didn't you?" quipped Frank Howard, whom Ford acknowledged as contributing some strategy to the offense. "Now ya got to win 'em all."

Ford looked up at Howard and quickly replied: "If I knew that staying in coaching would make me look like you, I'd get out right now."

The low-keyed Ford appeared to take the honors he and his team received in stride without any outward show of exuberance. While the United Press poll, the one voted upon by a panel of coaches, picked the Tigers 18th, the Associated Press in its poll of writers ranked Clemson a notch below, as 19th. Whatever, Clemson was beginning to generate some national recognition.

"Being Coach of the Week is an honor, but I wish our whole team had been named instead of me," said Ford. "They did the work. We didn't have one hero against Georgia; we had about 25. Since we don't play this Saturday, we're not making them practice the first couple days of the week; but after that they can't be heroes anymore. They have to get back to work. We try to work our way up all season, but we're really not concerned about the polls. It's good recognition for our outstanding university and our outstanding team. They certainly deserve it."

While the players earned their brief respite, Ford and his staff immediately began to get ready to face the University of Kentucky in Lexington. The Wildcats were another team that held a series edge over the Tigers, winning six of the seven games they played. The last time they played, in 1971, Kentucky won, 13-10, in Death Valley. The lone Clemson victory occurred in 1938 when the Tigers blanked the Wildcats, 14-0, in Lexington.

Although Kentucky had lost two of its first three starts, they nevertheless were a dangerous opponent and couldn't be taken lightly. After opening with a 28-6 victory over North Texas State, the Wildcats lost two tough games. One was to Alabama, 19-10, and the other was to Kansas, 21-16. Not only did Ford display a worried look about Kentucky, but he also felt the game was a pivotal one for Clemson.

"Before the season I felt the Tulane game would be a very, very important game in our season," said Ford. "We won that, and I didn't have enough foresight to look ahead on the schedule to see Kentucky sitting there. Now Kentucky is a lot bigger game than we thought it would be at the time. That'll be the turning point for us, I think. How we handle that game on the road will tell whether we're a really good team or a pretty good team. It'll be a tough one because we don't play them every year.

"Honestly, I worry about this game more than any we've had or will have on our schedule. Kentucky is so close; they're so close to winning. They are a team that's hungry to win. They ought to be 3-0. They had those two games against Alabama and Kansas won. If they'd made two tackles, just two tackles, they'd be unbeaten. They're just snakebit. We've seen the Alabama film; and they just whipped Alabama up front, on both sides of the football. It's just that they don't look like they've decided if they're going to be a throwing team, a running team, or a finesse team. They are the only team we've seen that doesn't have an option play. They're also trying to decide who their quarterback is going to be."

Ford had his own problems. It revolved around his running game. He wasn't getting maximum mileage out of his tailback position. Although he had used a number of runners there, none seemed to establish themselves as a take-charge guy. Tailback Cliff Austin led the running attack with 171 yards. Right behind was Jordan with 160. Jeff McCall, the fullback, had 139 yards, while Chuck McSwain, the Tigers' leading rusher in 1980, had been bothered by a leg injury and had contributed only 78 yards from the tailback spot. Ford had room for concern.

"Right now Homer Jordan is touching the ball about 40 percent of the time for us," said Ford. "That's too much. We've got to come up with a play or something that will get our tailbacks some yards. We've still got plenty of things to work on to become a good football team."

Unbeaten Clemson lured a sellout crowd of 57,453 fans to Commonwealth Stadium. Neither team could get a first down the first time they had the ball. On its second series, the

Kentucky defense converges to stop tailback Brendon Crite.

Wildcats drove 47 yards in eleven plays, at which point Tom Griggs booted a 40-yard field goal that sent Kentucky into a 3-0 lead. When the quarter ended, the troubled Clemson offense did not produce a first down.

Clemson's offensive woes continued in the second quarter. Yet, the Tigers appeared ready to score when Jeff Bryant recovered a fumble on the Kentucky 16-yard line. They moved for a first down on the six where they failed on four successive runs by Austin. They never seriously threatened the rest of the period except for a 49-yard field goal attempt by Igwebuike that fell short six seconds from the conclusion of the first half.

Clemson looked like a different team when they took the second half kickoff and drove 83 yards in 13 plays with Kevin Mack slipping off tackle for a six-yard touchdown run. Paulling added the extra point that gave the Tigers a 7-3 lead.

Some two minutes later, defensive end Andy Headen positioned Clemson's second touch-down by recovering a fumble on Kentucky's 21-yard line. After only six plays, Jordan raced into the end zone from three yards out. Paulling's kick gave Clemson a 14-3 edge when the third period ended.

Midway through the final period, the Tigers secured their victory. They put together an 87-yard drive in 12 plays that consumed more than six precious minutes. McSwain carried for 41 of the yards, scoring a touchdown from two yards out. Paulling's kick provided Clemson with its final margin of victory, 21-3.

"The team came out and played like Clemson should play in the second half," said Ford, obviously relieved, "but they didn't play a lick in the first half, offensively or defensively. We couldn't establish anything in the first half; we were lucky to be down 3-0. We're very delighted to get out of here."

Still, Kentucky coach Fran Curci was impressed with the Tigers.

"Clemson is the better football team," said Curci. "They're the best team we've played to

151

date. Their defense is equally as good as Alabama's. Their front four is the best I've seen."

CLEMSON AT KENTUCKY
October 3
Weather: Sunny, 63°
Attendance: 57,453

| CLEMSON | 0 | 0 | 14 | 7 | – | 21 |
| KENTUCKY | 3 | 0 | 0 | 0 | – | 3 |

UK—Griggs 40 FG
CU—Mack 11 run (Paulling kick)
CU—Jordan 3 run (Paulling kick)
CU—McSwain 3 run (Paulling kick)

GAME 5: VIRGINIA

The heady air that permeated the environs of Clemson was quite understandable. Just 48 hours after their triumph over Kentucky for their fourth straight success, the unbeaten Tigers cracked the elite top ten in the national polls, not just one of them but both of them. Clemson was ranked ninth in the Associated Press vote and tenth in the United Press one. It meant a great deal to the school and its legion of followers. Only three other times were the Tigers ever considered good enough to be included in the Top 10. In 1950, they were tenth in the final regular season poll. In 1978, they were ninth and then climbed to sixth in the final balloting after defeating Ohio State, 17-15, in the Gator Bowl.

Clemson was now entering the second phase of its schedule. The Tigers' first four wins had been secured against non-conference opponents. Their trip to any bowl would begin in earnest the fifth week with the campaign against Virginia, the first of seven consecutive ACC games. The Tigers were ready to start their hunt for an ACC title in Death Valley.

By now, Ford was developing a reputation of being the most worried 33-year-old in the country. Even though Clemson was undefeated and Virginia hadn't won any of the four games it played, Ford had a frown on his face. He didn't even find any solace in learning that the Cavaliers had never beaten the Tigers in the 24 times they played each other down through the years.

"I'm very, very concerned about Virginia," said Ford early in the week, "more so than a lot of people would tend to think. I don't know how many of our players are yet, but it shouldn't take very long after they watch the film. The thing that worries me more than anything else about Virginia is that they know how to go out and beat people they're not supposed to beat. They beat Georgia at Athens a couple of years ago and beat Tennessee at Knoxville last year. They have realized that they can play with anybody and have come up with that one big, big upset every year.

"We should have gotten beaten last year. We won, but the only thing we did was let them know they could play with Clemson. They've scored a lot of points offensively with a lot of people injured this year, and we need to bear down as an offensive and a defensive team and a kicking team to become a football team at Clemson. Then we'll see if we deserve the recognition we're starting to get as a football team."

Deep down Ford wasn't really worried about Virginia despite what he was saying. Rather, he was worried that his own team would become complacent and not display the intensity they did both offensively and defensively in the second half of the Kentucky game. He was simply sounding a warning to anyone who would listen.

"I think our young people have got to do a lot to get themselves involved to win this week," said Ford. "Our seniors will have to do a better job of leadership this week. I'm anxious to see how the guys play this week. I think I'm just going to stand on the side and wash my hands of this one. If they want to be good, they can be good; but if they don't want to be mentally ready to play—I'm going to let them decide this week if they want to be a good football team or not.

"We should have a lot of reasons why we want to play well. We would like to stay where we're at in the national spotlight. It's our first conference game. We'd like to keep the defensive football team getting recognition and would like for the offensive team to continue

152

to give the performance it gave in the second half against Kentucky. So, we should have a lot of incentive to play well mentally and emotionally."

Physically, the Tigers were in excellent shape. The fact that wide receiver Jerry Gaillard, who missed the last two games, was ready to play again gave them an even healthier look. Even so, Ford decided on some offensive backfield changes. McSwain was named to start at tailback over Austin, and Mack was picked to open at fullback ahead of McCall. It was one way to stir the waters of complacency.

A threat of rain hovered over Death Valley on Homecoming Day. Maybe it was a good omen at that. In 1977 when Virginia appeared at Homecoming, it rained; and Clemson calmly went out and blanked the Cava-

liers, 31-0. This time it took the Tigers a while to get started. It wasn't until there were 22 seconds left in the first period that they got on the scoreboard. Igwebuike kicked a 22-yard field goal to give Clemson a 3-0 lead.

It wasn't until time was winding down in the second quarter that Clemson scored its first touchdown. They did so quickly. Jordan connected with Tuttle for a 20-yard completion. On the very next play, Tuttle got 22 more on an end around. Austin then brought the crowd to its feet when he broke loose around right end on an exciting 43-yard touchdown gallop. Paulling's kick sent the Tigers into their dressing room with a 10-0 halftime lead.

Taking the second half kickoff, Clemson kept right on going and scored its second touchdown. Except for one 16-yard pass, they

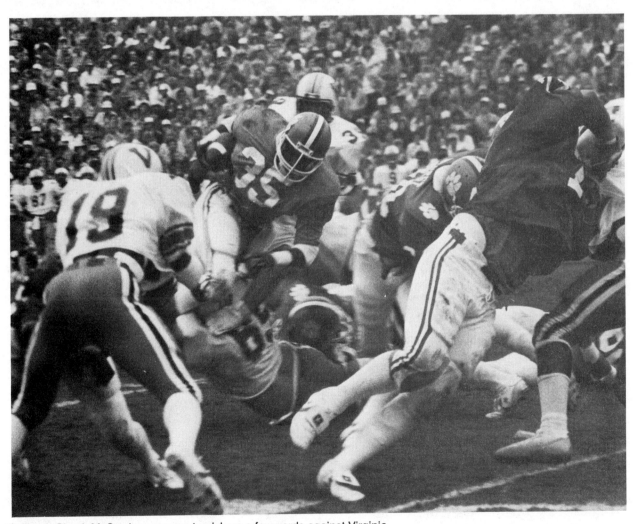

Tailback Chuck McSwain manages to pick up a few yards against Virginia.

153

Cliff Austin ran for two touchdowns in Clemson's 38-10 victory over Duke.

kept on the ground, driving 77 yards in 11 plays. McCall got the final five yards for the touchdown. Paulling's conversion attempt was good as Clemson stretched its lead to 17-0.

The next time the Tigers got the ball, they scored again. This time they traveled 67 yards in 13 plays. Jordan mixed his plays well, completing all three passes he threw. Austin slammed over left tackle from a yard out. When Paulling made good on his conversion, the Tigers extended their margin to 24-0.

They added to it early in the final period. The first time they got the ball, they scored once more. After they reached the Virginia 16-yard line, they were held in check. However, Igwebuike was accurate with a 32-yard field goal attempt that sent Clemson into an insurmountable 27-0 bulge with only ten minutes remaining in the game. Much to the delight of the Homecoming crowd, it ended that way. The defense basked in glory. It was the first time since 1979 that Clemson had shut out an opponent.

"Our goal was to keep them from scoring," said defensive end Bill Smith, "and anytime a defense can keep a team from scoring, it's got to help your offense. They ran to our weak side in the second half and did a good job un-

til we adjusted, but we really got serious when they got near the goal line. We had to stop them to preserve the shutout."

The defense was determined to achieve it.

"People have been getting three points on us, and we have been wanting that goose egg real bad," said linebacker Jeff Davis. "A lot of people thought we would take Virginia lightly, but we've got a lot on the line. We deserve our ranking. With a goose egg, there's no way you can lose. That was a big thing for us today. We wanted it, and we talked about getting it all week."

VIRGINIA AT CLEMSON
October 10
Weather: Rain, 59°
Attendance: 63,064

CLEMSON	3	7	14	3	– 27
VIRGINIA	0	0	0	0	– 0

CU—Igwebuike 22 FG
CU—Austin 42 run (Paulling kick)
CU—McCall 5 run (Paulling kick)
CU—Austin 1 run (Paulling kick)
CU—Igwebuike 32 FG

GAME 6: DUKE

By now, some of the post-season bowl game executives were taking an interest in Clemson. A representative of the Peach Bowl was in the press box viewing the game against Virginia. Then, after the Tigers vanquished the Cavaliers, Mickey Holmes, the executive director of the Sugar Bowl, warmed to the thought of the Tigers celebrating New Year's Eve in New Orleans, even though it was still too early in the season for any serious deliberating along those lines. Still, Clemson's fast 5-0 start and its sixth ranking in the Associated Press poll was creating interest, especially to Holmes who remembered the Tigers' visit to New Orleans to play Tulane the second week of the season.

"When they came down here for the Tulane game, the Clemson people brought a bunch of $2 bills with Tiger paws on them," said Holmes, "and for the next week after that, the Clemson fans were the talk of the town. I would have my car radio tuned to a talk show, and that was the No. 1 topic. The fans were well behaved. It was Labor Day weekend, and I'm not sure one of the hotels was quite ready for the invasion; but they geared up pretty soon. The townspeople would love it if Clemson happened to be one of the teams in the Sugar Bowl."

The fact that Clemson was traveling to Durham, North Carolina, to meet Duke pleased the Blue Devils' coach Red Wilson about the prospects of a big gate. Duke, a private institution, doesn't draw many big home crowds; and the appearance of the Tigers represented added revenue at the box office in the presence of Clemson fans.

"We'll probably have 10,000 people coming from Clemson," said Wilson. "The Clemson people are great supporters. They are loyal, and I admire them for their loyalty. When Maryland and Virginia come to Duke, they won't bring anybody. We cannot fill the stadium with our own people. We just don't have the people to do it. That's why Clemson means so much to us because they do bring us a lot of revenue, and I want the Clemson people to know it."

That was strictly on the business end. On the playing side, it was a different story, not all sweet and mellow. The Clemson players were seeking revenge from Duke, because of last year's game at Death Valley. Duke, which was 0-5 at the time, walloped Clemson, which was 4-1, 34-17. The Tigers were humiliated, and the loss led to their downfall in producing a 6-5 season. The players didn't forget it and neither did Ford. He remarked that Duke would rather beat Clemson than any other team, which says a lot when considering that the Blue Devils have such intense intrastate rivals such as North Carolina, North Carolina State, and Wake Forest.

"They don't like Clemson," said Ford. "They're not impressed with Clemson and don't have any reason to be impressed with Clemson. Duke was an 0-5 football team last year when they came down here to the Valley. They came in here and did everything they said they were going to do before the game. And when you can do it, it ain't bragging. I just don't think our people thought Duke could beat us. I looked at the film of last year's game. We started with a touchdown and a field goal, and then we started going nuts. We had clipping penalties. We jumped offsides. I didn't even watch the second half because I knew it was going to get worse."

This time the Tigers had one of the best defensive teams in the country in preparing to make Duke its sixth straight victim. They had allowed only one touchdown all season and had kept their opponents out of the end zone for 16 consecutive quarters. The Tigers had averaged giving up 4.2 points a game, which ranked first in the nation among major colleges.

The offense, too, had appeared better. They had displayed more consistency than the last time they faced Duke. They moved the ball well in every game and made only seven turnovers in five games. In its last two games, Clemson had not suffered a costly turnover. Jordan had been the leader and had either run the ball or thrown it in 40 percent of Clemson's plays.

Still, the Tigers had an added factor: emotion. They couldn't wait to play Duke.

"This game has been in the back of our minds," said offensive tackle Lee Nanney.

"We've been taking our games one at a time, but Duke brings back a lot of bad memories. They made some derogatory comments about us after last year's game."

Once the game began, the Tigers took charge. The first time they got their hands on the football, they scored. Jordan led them on a 64-yard drive in seven plays with seldom-used Brendon Crite going over from the four-yard line. Paulling's conversion gave the Tigers a quick 7-0 lead.

When the second period opened, Clemson was working on an 80-yard drive that had begun late in the first quarter. They got down to the Duke three-yard line before stalling. Paulling made an appearance again, only this time to boot a 20-yard field goal that sent the Tigers into a 10-0 lead. The very next time Clemson took over on offense, they scored again. This time they went 49 yards in eight plays with Cliff Austin breaking loose on a 15-yard touchdown run. Paulling's conversion made it 17-0.

Austin wasn't finished yet. On the next series, he brought the crowd to its feet by shaking free up the middle for 77 yards before he was tripped up on the Duke four-yard line. Three plays later Jordan put the finishing touches on the 98-yard drive by sneaking over from the one. Paulling converted, and the Tigers were on their way to a romp, 24-0. Seconds before the half ended, Duke managed a field goal which still left them far short, 24-3.

Clemson wasn't about to let up. They took the second half kickoff and went 59 yards for another touchdown. Austin punched it across from two yards; and when Paulling tacked on the extra point, Clemson's lead ballooned to 31-3.

Duke managed to score a touchdown, being the first team to do so in 18 quarters of play against Clemson's defense. Quarterback Ben Bennett accomplished it with a 21-yard touchdown pass to split end Cedric Jones. However, Clemson answered back. Completing a 65-yard drive, Jordan hit Tuttle with a 29-yard touchdown throw. Paulling's kick restored Clemson's bulge, 38-10. It was the last scoring of the day. Clemson had its revenge.

"This was my best game at Clemson," said Jordan, who completed 13 of 19 passes for 198 yards and a touchdown. "The receivers ran great routes, and I had a good day throwing the ball."

Austin, also, had his best day, rushing for a career-high 178 yards and two touchdowns.

"We weren't ready to play last year," said Austin, "but we were ready this year. I think it showed."

Duke coach Red Wilson had seen enough.

"They are no doubt one of the top collegiate football teams in America," said Wilson.

CLEMSON AT DUKE
October 17
Weather: Sunny, 63°
Attendance: 26,000

CLEMSON	7 17 14 0	– 38
DUKE	0 3 7 0	– 10

CU—Crite 4 run (Paulling kick)
CU—Paulling 20 FG
CU—Austin 15 run (Paulling kick)
CU—Jordan 1 run (Paulling kick)
DU—McKinney 29 FG
CU—Austin 2 run (Paulling kick)
DU—Jones 21 pass from Bennett (McKinney kick)
CU—Tuttle 29 pass from Jordan (Paulling kick)

GAME 7:
NORTH CAROLINA STATE

The one ingredient confronting Ford as his undefeated Tigers roared to their sixth straight triumph was finding a method to keep his squad from getting complacent the rest of the season. After soundly drubbing Duke, Clemson moved up in the national polls. They were ranked fourth in the Associated Press register and fifth in the one sponsored by the United Press. It was a tenuous position. Any team would dearly love to cage the Tigers, and with four successive ACC games ahead, Ford kept his worried look.

He turned the pages of his book on motivation to keep the fire lit under his squad. Ford

156

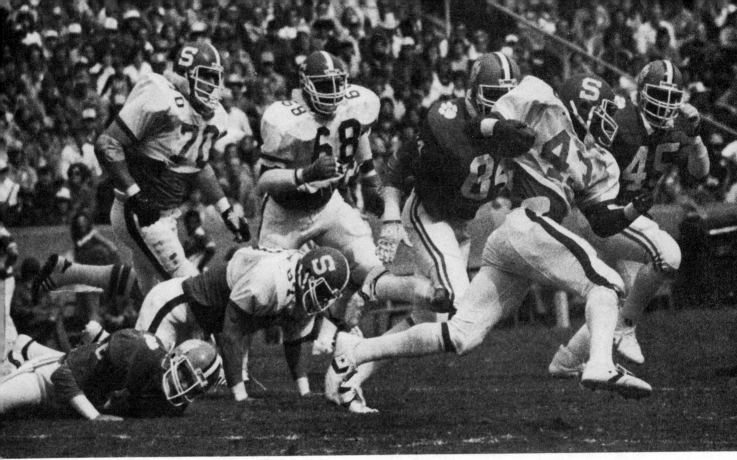
Defensive end Bill Smith (84) and linebacker Jeff Davis (45) chase State ballcarrier.

was determined to give his Tigers somewhat of a battle cry each week. The week before the Duke game he stressed how the Blue Devils had humiliated Clemson 34-17 the year before in Death Valley, of all places. Nothing like that is ever supposed to happen at Clemson.

Ford was looking for something he could use against North Carolina State, who were 4-2. He thought about reminding his players that the Wolfpack defeated them, 16-13, the last time they appeared in Death Valley in 1979 or the fact that State trimmed them 24-20 the past year at Raleigh; but that was much the same ploy he had employed the previous week with Duke. He needed something else. For a moment he thought he had found one. Ford was told that the Wolfpack had blocked at least one punt in every game they had played. Now, that was different. Ford gleaned the State statistics and shook his head when discovering that they had blocked only three punts. He tossed the sheet behind him with somewhat of a smile.

"That would have been a good one, but it just shows that you can't take somebody's word for it," said Ford. "Before the Kentucky game,

somebody told me that Kentucky had never won on television. I was all set to tell the kids that, but we got to researching it and found out they had won practically every game they had been in on television.

"Yet, for some reason Clemson hasn't had any success playing North Carolina State. We have had our problems against them. We've only won two out of the past 12 games. We turned the ball over three times to them last year, and they got 21 points. North Carolina State will do anything to win, from riding motorcycles on the field to wearing masks, but this is a key game for them. Any prayers they have about winning the conference will be gone if they don't win this one."

Still, Ford had to be heartened by the fact that Clemson was off to its best start in 33 years. His offense was beginning to jell, which was profoundly demonstrated in its performance against Duke. Led by the ever-improving Jordan, the Tigers uncovered a balanced attack that netted 563 yards, the third highest in Clemson history. Broken down, 323 came on the ground and 240 through the air. Although he was still looking for a take-charge running back, Ford nevertheless was getting

157

maximum production from his tailback spot. Austin, who came out of nowhere after an injury-plagued 1980 season in which he had only 78 yards, was Clemson's leading runner with 466 yards. McSwain, who started the last two games at tailback, had 303 yards. Combined, their totals came to 769 yards, which no one could fault.

Defensively, the Tigers remained the nation's top team in that department. They allowed only 5.2 points a game. They had been exceptionally tough on the ground, yielding only 94.7 yards a contest without surrendering a touchdown. Overall, Clemson had given up only two touchdowns in the six games it played.

"I'm glad to see the offensive team have a game like they did last week," said Ford. "Except for turning the ball over three times, we played just like it was diagrammed. Our offense is a little more diversified. We've got more threats. To beat Clemson early, if a team took Jordan away, they took 40 percent of our offense away. Half of the other 60 percent was Tuttle. With teams doubling him, it cut down that percentage even more. But all of a sudden the tight ends come around and then the tailbacks. That takes a lot off Jordan. Folks are now saying they can't just stop Jordan and beat Clemson. Last year he knew he was supposed to be the leader, but he was struggling like everybody else was. He's got confidence now, and the plus is that his athletic ability doesn't hurt him at all."

After his performance against Duke, the quiet-spoken Jordan moved to eighth place on the career passing list at Clemson with over 2,000 yards and ninth in career total offense with over 2,700 yards. He was looking at something else, however.

"There's nothing I'd like better than to bring a national championship home to Clemson," Jordan said.

It was a chilly 48 degrees when the teams

Safety Terry Kinard grabs State runner. Clemson was hard pressed to win, 17-7.

lined up for the opening kickoff. Austin picked up right where he left off the first time Clemson had the ball. He rushed for 15 yards in two carries but fumbled the ball away the third time he ran. State recovered on its own 41-yard line and moved for a touchdown from there. Larmount Lawson scored it with a 13-yard burst. Todd Auten converted to give the Wolfpack a 7-0 lead with half the period gone.

Clemson took the kickoff and got as far as the Wolfpack 23-yard line before being stopped. Igwebuike then booted a 39-yard field goal that narrowed State's margin to 7-3 when the first quarter ended.

Both team's defenses controlled the action the second quarter. It appeared as if the half would come to a conclusion without any more scoring. Yet, with just over three minutes remaining, Jordan quickly led the Tigers to a touchdown. He ran for 22 yards and passed for 22 more to account for 44 of the 65 yards the drive covered. Austin got the touchdown from a yard out, and Paulling added the conversion that gave the Tigers a 10-7 halftime lead.

However, the defense took over again, which resulted in a scoreless third quarter. It wasn't until midway through the final period that Clemson insured its seventh straight victory. The clinching touchdown came on a 52-yard drive. Jeff McCall produced it when he broke loose on a 15-yard run off tackle to score standing up in the end zone. Paulling again kicked the extra point to provide Clemson with a hard-fought 17-7 victory. What had made it a difficult victory was when the Tigers turned the ball over five times. It didn't go unnoticed by Ford.

"We always seem to turn the ball over against them," said Ford. "I don't think I had the team ready to play, but the longer we played the better we got. It's a shame I didn't have them ready. We weren't sharp today. We weren't clicking on 12 volts. Our defense did the job in the second half. At the same time, our offense took control of the line of scrimmage; and we were able to move the ball pretty good even though we didn't score the points we would have liked to. Right now I'm just glad we're still in the left-hand column. It's hard to fault a win.'

N.C. STATE AT CLEMSON
October 24
Weather: Partly Cloudy, 48°
Attendance: 62,727

CLEMSON	3	7	0	7	– 17
N.C. STATE	7	0	0	0	– 7

NCSU—Lawson 13 run (Auten kick)
CU—Igwebuike 39 FG
CU—Austin 1 run (Paulling kick)
CU—McCall 15 run (Paulling kick)

GAME 8: WAKE FOREST

There were some whispers around the Clemson campus. The Tigers had won their first seven games, and ever so quietly talk was heard about maybe Clemson would keep right on going in its last four games and finish the season undefeated. The Tigers were getting stronger in the polls, too. They climbed to the third spot in the Associated Press poll and the fourth position in the United Press poll. Never had a Clemson team been ranked so high. All they had to do was to keep on winning to maintain it, which is when the idea of an unbeaten season occurred to Tiger followers.

"That ranking could be good, and it could be bad," said Frank Howard. "They could lose anytime the way football is now. I don't think that will happen this week, but you always have a week when you don't play well. I really thought we'd be 8-3 this year, but I thought Georgia would beat us 'til I saw Georgia play. I'm glad to see us so high in the polls, but it kinda scares me, too.

"We could go a long way. Our defense is talented, and the offense don't fumble much; and we don't have many interceptions. We ain't beating ourselves this year. Most teams beat themselves on mistakes, and mistakes will beat your butt quick. Ford doesn't have a fancy offense, but it's adequate. The defense gives 'em the ball in good field position; and if it doesn't, the punter does. Them boys are coming along. They look good. All I do is sit back and think about what I would do from one play to the other, but the one thing I don't do is second-guess like a lot of people do."

Yet, he is close to Ford. He openly admires the job the young coach has done in turning the football team around after the 6-5 campaign of 1980. Ford realizes what Howard has meant to Clemson football all these years. It was Howard and his six bowl teams that first put Clemson on the football map. The two share many moments together.

"I talk with Ford and tell him what I think," said Howard. "I was close with Charley Pell, too. The only ones I wasn't close to were Red Parker and Hootie Ingram. They tried to do everything different from what I did just because it was different from the way I did things.

"Ford was young when he got the job, but he has done a helluva job. I tell people we got a lot in common. We're both from Alabama; we were both under 30 when we got to be head coaches, and we both won our first game. It so happens that my first one was Presbyterian, and his was Ohio State.

"But Ford is smart. He took some lumps last year, but he's getting a lot of help from Tom Harper. He was right in getting an old head to help him like I had me. A young coach needs an old head."

Harper had some personal recollections about Wake Forest, who were the Tigers' next opponent in Death Valley. Before he was an assistant coach at VPI for three years, Harper had been the head coach for one year at Wake Forest, in 1972. Although the Demon Deacons were 3-5 and were definitely the underdogs against Clemson, they played a wide-open brand of football with an offense that either lived or died by the pass.

"The thing that worries me about Wake Forest is that they can score from anywhere on the field," said Ford. "Every snap of the ball is like a two-minute offensive drill. They have a pass-controlled offense, and they are committed to throwing the ball. I'll bet right now that they'll throw the ball 60 times or more. They expect to come down here and beat Clemson with the passing game. They're too dangerous. We're going to have to work on rushing the passer because we're going to have to hurry them. We're going to have to take the football

and hold onto it for long periods of time. We want the people who can beat us to be sitting on the bench."

Ford had the Deacons figured right. They received the opening kickoff, and quarterback Gary Schofield began throwing the ball all over Death Valley. The first five times he touched the ball, he threw. When he tried for a sixth straight time, he fumbled and tackle Dan Benish recovered at midfield. With Cliff Austin leading the way, Clemson scored a touchdown in seven plays, all on the ground. Austin gained 43 of the yards, taking the ball over from the four-yard line. Paulling converted and Clemson jumped in front, 7-0.

The Tigers scored again the next time they got the ball. Again, they went 50 yards with Austin going in from the three-yard line. Paulling's kick made it 14-0. Near the end of the quarter, Wake Forest got on the scoreboard when Schofield hit Kenny Duckett with a 17-yard touchdown pass.

In the second quarter the Tigers erupted for five touchdowns. It was the biggest offensive display in Clemson history and sealed the Deacons' doom. First, McSwain scored on a one-yard run. Then Kevin Mack scored on a 10-yard run. Jordan got into the scoring act with a seven-yard keeper around left end. Jeff McCall made his presence felt by breaking away on a 24-yard touchdown gallop. McSwain got into the scoring column with a 16-yard run that mushroomed Clemson's lead to 49-7. Before the first half ended, Wake Forest managed to score a touchdown which seemed meaningless. Clemson had an insurmountable 49-14 lead.

It was now a question of how many points Clemson would score. On the first play of the second half, Jordan connected with Tuttle on a beautiful 75-yard touchdown pass to up Clemson's margin 55-14. After a Wake Forest field goal, Clemson scored once more when reserve quarterback Mike Gasque hit Tuttle with a 25-yard touchdown pass to give Clemson a 62-17. Moments later the Tigers scored again when McSwain swept around right end for a touchdown. When the quarter was over, Clemson led, 69-17.

There was no stopping the Tigers. They scored after five minutes of the fourth period

Clemson established a school and an ACC record in 82-24 drubbing of Wake Forest.

when Duke Holloman scored a touchdown from three yards away. Five minutes later, Craig Crawford broke loose on a 72-yard touchdown jaunt that further added to Clemson's lead, 82-17. The Deacons got one more touchdown before the carnage was over, which made the final score 82-24! Unbelievable.

Clemson established all sorts of records. The 82 points broke a 27-year-old ACC record; the total points eclipsed the school's record of 76

scored against Presbyterian. The 12 touchdowns was a new Clemson record, as was the 756 total yards they produced. The 161 yards Tuttle accumulated on pass receptions gave him 2,225 for his career, two more than Jerry Butler made.

"We've really been needing a game like that," said offensive tackle Lee Nanney. "Hopefully, it will silence the critics who said we didn't have an offense."

Tiger mascot Ricky Capps was glad it was

161

Fullback Jeff McCall scored Clemson's only touchdown in Tigers' tense 10-8 victory over North Carolina that brought ACC title.

over. He did progressive pushups to coincide with the score and had to quit after 382. That had to be a record, too.

WAKE FOREST AT CLEMSON
October 31
Weather: Cloudy, 58°
Attendance: 60,383

CLEMSON	14 35 20 13 – 82
WFU	7 7 3 7 – 24

CU—Austin 4 run (Paulling kick)
CU—Austin 3 run (Paulling kick)
WFU—Duckett 17 pass from Schofield (Denfield kick)
CU—C. McSwain 1 run (Paulling kick)
CU—Mack 10 run (Paulling kick)
CU—Jordan 7 run (Paulling kick)
CU—McCall 24 run (Paulling kick)
CU—McSwain 16 run (Paulling kick)
WFU—Cunningham 1 run (Denfield kick)
CU—Tuttle 75 pass from Jordan (Kick failed)
WFU—Denfield 22 FG
CU—Tuttle 25 pass from Gasque (Kick failed)
CU—C. McSwain 12 run (L. Brown kick)
CU—Holloman 3 run (L. Brown kick)
CU—Crawford 72 run (Kick failed)
WFU—Duckett 5 pass from Schofield (Denfield kick)

GAME 9: NORTH CAROLINA

Ford came up with a new ploy the week before the North Carolina battle at Chapel Hill, North Carolina. He had run out of adjectives, which he used to describe opponents at his weekly press conference, and turned to guard Brian Clark for help.

"How about stupendous, coach?" said Clark.

"I can't use it," replied Ford. "I don't know what it means."

Instead, Ford got the message across to his players by putting up a number of "Carolina On My Mind" posters on just about every available space in the Jervey Athletic Center, not that anyone at Clemson needed any reminding about how important the game against North Carolina was. It was without question the Tigers' biggest game of their unbeaten season, which had now reached eight games.

What was paramount in the Clemson-North Carolina meeting was the fact that the eventual winner would emerge as the ACC champion and automatically be awarded a major bowl bid. So attractive was the game that representatives of eight bowl events were attending with the hope of eventually landing the winner of the contest, which was looked upon as the biggest one in the state of North Carolina since anyone could remember.

Since the Tigers were the only undefeated team in the nation with eight victories,[1] they had inched their way to No. 2 in the Associated Press poll behind Pittsburgh and No. 3 in the United Press tabulation. Since North Carolina was ranked eighth in the AP and ninth in the UPI, it marked the first time ever that two schools from the same conference faced each other after being ranked nationally.

The game was so big that later in the week, on Thursday night, the school's Central Spirit Committee sponsored a Danny Ford Day pep rally at the Amphitheater in which a crowd of some 2,000 cheered late into the night. They even promoted a Danny Ford Look Alike Contest in which five youngsters dressed like the youthful coach, accented by a baseball cap on each head and a wad of chewing tobacco in each one's mouth. Deborah Ford, the coach's pretty brunette wife, was then asked if "any of them look like Danny?"

"I haven't seen him for so long I can't remember," smiled Deborah. Then she instructed the contestants to walk bow-legged and spit their chaw so she could decide for sure who most resembled her popular husband.

It was a big night, indeed—a marching band, a stage crowded with cheerleaders, Ford and his family, Ford's father, sister, uncle, several former teammates, his Sunday school teacher, high school teacher, and local sports editor, all of whom came from Gadsden, Alabama, to honor Ford. Clemson president Bill Atchley had issued a proclamation officially making it Danny Ford Day. The festivities relaxed Ford for one night, anyway.

"Coaching has become fun again," said Ford. "No big problems, yet. Everybody wants to play. At times last year when things weren't working, we had to say, 'Y'all stick around and play some.' Not any more.

"This team's surprised me. I just hope being No. 2 ain't a vacation. I hope we make a home there. We can have a program that's in the top 10. We've got the facilities, support, and program that a lot of youngsters want to be part of."

First Ford had to concern himself about North Carolina. If he was genuinely worried this week, he had reason to be. The Tar Heels, led by running back Kelvin Bryant and quarterback Rod Elkins, were 7-1, their only loss being inflicted by South Carolina two weeks earlier. Both Bryant and Elkins were troubled with injuries; yet, when considering the importance of the game, Ford expected both to play.

"We're preparing for Bryant; we're preparing for Elkins, and we're preparing for Lawrence Taylor in case he comes back from the pros," said Ford, emphasizing the seriousness of his game preparations. "It's their homecoming game, and it's a game that we've got to win to at least give us an opportunity to share the ACC championship. It should be a very, very close game and a very good matchup between two good football teams.

"I'm very concerned about how we can play physically with this team. We were out-muscled last year. With the exception of two games, we've always been pretty much in every game we play physically. The Peach Bowl game against Baylor in 1979 was one, and the North Carolina game last year was the other. Their game plan was to out-muscle Clemson, and I think they did it."

A standing-room-only record crowd of 53,611 overflowed Keenan Stadium on a sunny, cool day to witness the struggle for ACC supremacy. Clemson couldn't do anything after receiving the opening kickoff, and neither could North Carolina the first time they got the ball. The defenses of both teams were waging a fierce struggle in the trenches. The closest any team came to scoring was when Igwebuike was wide with a 50-yard field goal attempt, and the period ended scoreless.

In the early minutes of the second quarter, the Tar Heels broke through. Working on a 64-yard drive, Elkins, limping slightly from his sprained ankle, got North Carolina to the Clemson five before being stopped. Nevertheless, it allowed Brooks Barwick to kick a 22-yard field goal that gave the Tar Heels the lead, 3-0.

Clemson answered back. The Tigers took the ensuing kickoff and brought it down the field on a finely executed 81-yard drive in 14 plays. Jeff McCall got the touchdown on a nifty seven-yard burst off right tackle. Paulling converted to push the Tigers in front, 7-3.

It appeared as if the score would remain that way. However, with only 19 seconds left in the half, Dale Hatcher's punt was blocked from the 19-yard line, and the ball was recovered in the Clemson end zone that narrowed the halftime margin to 7-5.

Halfway through the third period, the Tigers got just a bit more breathing room. Igwebuike gave it to them when he booted a 39-yard field goal that sent Clemson into a 10-5 lead. However, just before the third quarter ended, Barwick kicked a 26-yard field goal that cut Clemson's edge to 10-8. The tenacious battle ended that way when both teams failed to come close to scoring in the final period. Clemson had its important win and a bowl bid in its pocket.

A large turnout of Clemson fans greeted the Tigers at the airport when they returned home. Ford still looked exhausted from the day-long pressure.

"We played too conservatively. We should have passed more," he said, "but we played some good defense when we had to."

CLEMSON AT NORTH CAROLINA
November 7
(Regional TV)
Weather: Sunny, 60°
Attendance: 53,611

CLEMSON	0	7	3	0	– 10
UNC	0	5	3	0	– 8

UNC—Barwick 22 FG
CU—McCall 7 run (Paulling kick)
UNC—Safety, punt blocked through end zone
CU—Igwebuike 39 FG
UNC—Barwick 26 FG

GAME 10: MARYLAND

Danny Ford claims he isn't superstitious. However, in the approaching days before the Maryland game, he certainly acted as if he was. He sat in his cluttered office sucking on a lemon, which he had done with regularity throughout his unbeaten season which had lasted nine weeks. Bob Bradley, the school's venerable sports information director, wanted to know if the lemon tasted good. Ford leaned back and smiled.

"Sweetest thing there is next to winning," said Ford. "When I played at Alabama, they gave us some red shorts with our initials on them. I wore them every game. They worked most of the time, but sometimes they didn't work. There are some things you don't change just because you want to change to show you're not superstitious. There are some things that you leave like they are because it doesn't hurt anything to leave 'em like that, but I don't believe you can call me superstitious. I just don't like to take chances. There are a couple of things I have done the same every week; but when you get right down to it, superstition doesn't get out there on the field and do any blocking and tackling. When it starts doing those things, I'll really start being superstitious, I guess."

More than superstition, Ford was puzzled by the lack of success Clemson had experienced against Maryland in recent years. In the last nine times they played each other, the Terrapins had won on eight occasions. What's more, Clemson was afflicted with its worst defeat since Ford became the head coach when Maryland walloped the Tigers, 34-7, last year at College Park, Maryland. It didn't seem to make any difference to Maryland, either, that this season's game was in Death Valley. The Terrapins had won the last four games played there in complete defiance of the Valley's tradition. It was no wonder that Clemson officials were expecting the largest crowd of the season at the Tigers' final home game.

Ford practically discounted the fact that Maryland's record was an unflattering 3-5-1. The Terrapins were 3-1 in the ACC where it counted most. If Maryland could continue its hex over Clemson, the Terrapins would have an opportunity to slice a share of the conference championship. That possibility did not escape Ford, who looked for every edge he could find, statistically or emotionally, to keep his Tigers roaring toward an unbeaten season.

"Maryland is one team in the conference our seniors have never beaten," noted Ford.

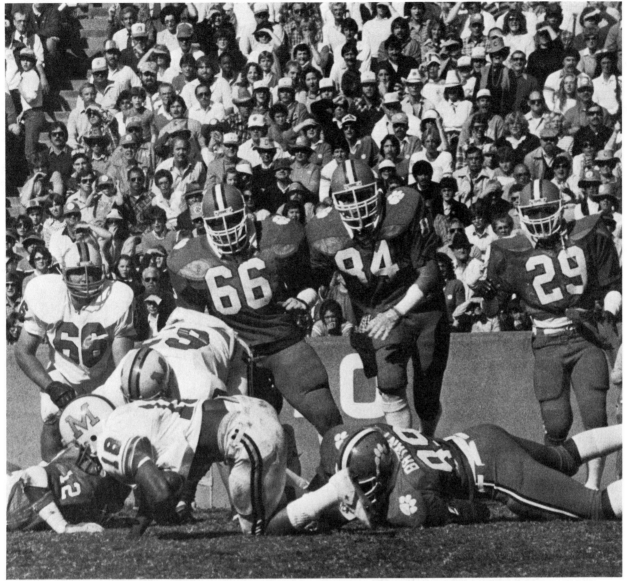

Defensive end Andy Headen, front, and defensive tackle Jeff Bryant, rear, bring down Maryland runner.

"Maryland lost some games in the conference that hurt them, but they can realize one goal—to take part of the championship. You've got to beat them to be a champion. I'm sure we will be favored; but if you look back at the record, Maryland's got Clemson's number and has had. It comes down to this being the most important game of the season. I said it before the season, and I'll say it again now for next year.

"If our guys can do what is expected of them, by whoever expects it, then I've got a story to tell. I can go to preaching. I can have a revival, anything I want, and tell what all they've overcome and what all they did; but until they do it, I ain't got a leg to stand on and talk about it. I keep telling them they are near being a great football team, but I can't say they are a great football team. They've got a chance to do something in football that nobody in Clemson has ever done, but they haven't done it yet."

The players were thinking about it, too. They had a snappy slogan from a James Bond movie to remind them, namely, "Diamonds Are Forever." It was a reference to the diamond rings the players would receive as champions of the ACC.

"We can't lose because we'd fall out of the ranking right quick," said Jordan. "People

165

would say we're just a Cinderella team, that we didn't deserve to be there. Southern Cal and Georgia can lose one or two and still be nationally ranked. Not us."

Jordan was clearly referring to Clemson's number two ranking in the Associated Press poll. The United Press still had the Tigers third. It was apparent, as Ford mentioned, that the game against Maryland was Clemson's biggest of the year. Jordan had received some unexpected incentive from outside the Tigers' lair for the game. After Maryland had lost to Tulane, 14-7, the previous week, Tulane coach Vince Gibson was quoted as saying, "Clemson won't defeat Maryland because of the lack of a consistent passing game."

"I didn't read it, but I heard about it," said Jordan without wanting to elaborate further. He had heard all he wanted to hear.

Jordan held the key against Maryland. He was expected to pass more often than in any other of the past nine games. The Terrapins' defense dictated it. They play a wide tackle six in which the linebackers position themselves right at the line of scrimmage. The strategy is utilized to stop the running attack, especially the wide sweeps that Jordan runs on the option.

The biggest crowd of the season, 63,199, sat in the orange seats in Death Valley on a cool, sunny day, expecting to see the Tigers win their first ACC championship since 1978 and only its second since 1967. After a series of misfortunes in which they lost the ball on an interception and a fumble, the Tigers finally scored just before the first period came to an end. Passing as expected, Jordan completed all four passes he threw in a six-play, 61-yard drive for a touchdown. The payoff was a 14-yard strike to Tuttle. Paulling converted and Clemson led, 7-0.

The Jordan-Tuttle combination struck again midway through the second quarter. This time Clemson went 88 yards for a touchdown. On second down, Jordan found Tuttle in the end zone from the five-yard line. Paulling added the conversion to send Clemson into a 14-0 lead. The next time the Tigers got the ball, Jordan again went to the air. It only took him three plays to get Clemson another touchdown. First, he hit with Tuttle for 30

yards, then Frank Magwood for 13, and finally, Jerry Gaillard for a 12-yard touchdown. Paulling kicked his third point to send Clemson into a 21-0 halftime bulge.

Clemson moved closer to the ACC title after a scoreless third period. There was only a brief moment of concern early in the fourth quarter when Jordan fumbled on the Tiger seven, and Maryland quickly scored on the next play. However, the tenacious Clemson defense preserved Clemson's 21-7 triumph. The fans knew what the victory meant by tossing oranges onto the field in anticipation of a trip to the Orange Bowl. Jordan had his biggest game of the year, completing 20 of 29 passes for 270 yards, while Tuttle caught ten passes to break Jerry Butler's career reception record and had one more game to add to his 140 total.

"Our primary goal before the season was to win the ACC championship," said a happy Ford. "Now we gotta get ready for another big one Saturday." He was already thinking about South Carolina.

MARYLAND AT CLEMSON
November 14
Weather: Sunny, 50°
Attendance: 63,199

CLEMSON	7	14	0	0	–	21
MARYLAND	0	0	0	7	–	7

CU—Tuttle 14 pass from Jordan (Paulling kick)
CU—Tuttle 5 pass from Jordan (Paulling kick)
CU—Gaillard 12 pass from Jordan (Paulling kick)
UM—Wysocki 7 run (Atkinson kick)

GAME 11: SOUTH CAROLINA

It was inconceivable to suspect that Ford would conjure any incentives for his players before the South Carolina game. The game itself said it all. Nobody in the state of South Carolina needed to be reminded of its importance. Their backyard rivalry had been nurtured with each passing year since they first began playing one another back in 1896. Yet, this time the contest took on a bit more meaning. The prospect of an undefeated season was a natural additive for Clemson, who was now ranked second in both of the weekly wire service polls. Pittsburgh, who was number one, and Clemson were the only two major unbeaten college teams in the country.

The Gamecocks would have loved nothing better than to upset the Tigers. They remembered last year's meeting in which Clemson salvaged a 6-5 season with a 27-6 victory. The loss caused further embarrassment to the Gamecocks, who were on their way to the Gator Bowl. Clemson also used the win as a springboard for its current success and, including that victory, had an unbeaten string of eleven games. The fact that Clemson was 10-0 and South Carolina 6-4 held relatively little meaning for the two rivals.

On paper, the Tigers appeared superior. They were averaging 28.7 points and 408 yards on offense. The focal point of the team's "I" offense was Jordan, who was averaging 183.1 yards a contest in total offense. He didn't make many mistakes, either. In 161 pass attempts, he had been intercepted only seven times. He peaked against Maryland by generating 312 yards, 270 passing and 40 rushing, surpassing the 300-yard plateau for the first time in his career. He was only 170 yards behind Bobby Gage, who was second on the career list in total offense. It was reasonable to assume that he would supplant Gage after the South Carolina game.

South Carolina's offense was pale in contrast to Clemson. Its drawback was inconsistency, largely based on the fact that coach Jim Carlen couldn't decide on who was his regular quarterback. He finally settled on junior Gordan Beckham after unsuccessfully attempting to make his offense more explosive by resorting to trickery. Although Beckham had passed for 1,121 yards, which was only 200 less than Jordan, he nevertheless was victimized by 14 interceptions, twice as many as his Clemson counterpart. The result was that South Carolina was averaging 266.6 yards on offense, well below Clemson's figure.

Yet, the strength of the Tigers' ten consecutive triumphs had been the defense. By allowing only 7.7 points a game, Clemson was rated second nationally. In seven of the games they played, they stubbornly held opponents to less than 100 yards rushing. In half of its games, the defense had not given up a single touchdown. Jeff Bryant up front and Jeff Davis from his linebacking spot led the Tigers' imposing defense. The pressure applied by the front line had allowed an opportunistic secondary, led by free safety Terry Kinard, to intercept 21 passes. By the same token, South Carolina's strength was also its defense, which had yielded 117 yards on the ground and 183 through the air.

Since South Carolina had a weekend off while Clemson was beating Maryland to clinch the ACC championship, Carlen had two weeks to prepare his team for the Tigers. The game was expected to attract the largest crowd of the season to Williams-Brice Stadium in Columbia for the 79th meeting of the series. The demand for tickets created a closed circuit television hook-up in the gymnasium of each school. Tiger fans had their slogan for this one in the form of bumper stickers that read, "11-0. A Chicken Kickin' Makes It Perfect!"

Both coaches knew the meaning of the game. Carlen expressed his sentiments on Monday.

"There's more hatred here than in other rivalries," said Carlen. "It's a stigma that has become hatred, and I'm not saying that's necessarily good for college athletics. I've been involved in rivalries before, but none of them compare to this one."

The following day Ford made his feelings known.

"I heard the word 'hatred' mentioned," began Ford, "but we don't hate. Hatred might not be the word that we would use because you're not supposed to hate people. We just dislike them this week. I think that's the way they feel about Clemson. It's a good rivalry, an enjoyable one and one I like to be associated with. I just hope it doesn't get ugly. There will be all kinds of talk and everything else this week, but it don't matter what is written or said. The team that's best prepared, the team that it means the most to, is the team that's

Chuck McSwain, who is stopped here, scored two touchdowns in Clemson's season-ending 29-13 triumph over arch rival South Carolina.

going to win."

The atmosphere was ready to burst at game time. Clemson took the opening kickoff but was stopped after three plays. Their opponents didn't wait long to score, which left the sold-out crowd of 56,971 stomping with excitement at the thought of an upset. The Gamecocks went 51 yards in eight plays with Johnnie Wright scoring a touchdown from a yard out. Mark Fleetwood's conversion gave South Carolina a quick 7-0 lead.

Again, Clemson's offense was ineffective. However, the defense came through. Attempting to punt, Chris Norman's kick was blocked by McSwain, and Johnny Rembert recovered the ball in the end zone for a Clemson touchdown. However, Paulling shocked Tiger fans by missing his first conversion attempt of the season after 31 straight to leave Clemson short, 7-6.

Yet, in the early minutes of the second period, Paulling atoned. He booted a 23-yard field goal to push Clemson in front, 9-7. After Jordan suffered an interception, Clemson scored again on its second series. Hollis Hall positioned it with an interception on the South Carolina 28-yard line. Six plays later, Jordan squirmed around left end for an 11-yard touchdown. Clemson then decided on a two-point conversion attempt which failed. Nevertheless, the Tigers led at halftime, 15-7.

South Carolina took the second half kickoff and drove 67 yards for a touchdown, with Beckham hitting Horace Smith in the end zone with a 10-yard pass. Beckham's two-point conversion try was foiled when he was sacked by Jeff Suttle, which preserved the Tigers' lead, 15-13. Clemson answered right back with the kickoff. Jordan led the Tigers on an 86-yard march, with McSwain getting the final yard and the touchdown. Paulling's conversion stretched Clemson's lead to 22-13 when the period ended four minutes later.

On their first series in the fourth quarter, Clemson sealed its victory. This time they went 80 yards for a touchdown with McSwain breaking loose up the middle on a 21-yard run. Paulling kicked the extra point, which gave the Tigers a 29-13 triumph and an unbeaten season. The Tiger Rag was heard all night—and all the way from Columbia to Clemson.

"I've told them all along they could be a great team if they continued to work and improve every week," exclaimed a happy but relieved Ford afterwards. "Now I'm ready to say it. This is a great football team."

The Orange Bowl committee thought so, too. They invited Clemson to be one of the participants on New Year's Day, and the bowl representative asked to talk with Ford. The phone went dead. An operator had mistakenly disconnected the call. "My God," grinned Ford. "He hung up on me!"

CLEMSON AT SOUTH CAROLINA
November 21
Weather: Partly Cloudy, 52°
Attendance: 56,971

CLEMSON	6	9	7	7	– 29
USC	7	0	6	0	– 13

USC—Wright 1 run (Fleetwood kick)
CU—Rembert, recovery of blocked punt in end zone (Kick failed)
CU—Paulling 24 FG
CU—Jordan 11 (Pass failed)
USC—Smith 10 pass from Beckham (Run failed)
CU—C. McSwain 1 run (Paulling kick)
CU—C. McSwain 23 run (Paulling kick)

18

1982
ORANGE BOWL

"We're Number One!"

An exhausted Ford decided to give his squad a week off following the South Carolina victory. The preparations for Nebraska, which Clemson would face in the Orange Bowl, could wait. He wanted the players to bask in the limelight of Clemson's first unbeaten season and highest ranking in 33 years, since the 1948 team won all eleven of its games. Ford also looked forward to the respite. It provided him with the opportunity to be in Birmingham, Alabama, for the Alabama-Auburn game, enabling him to share a milestone in coach Bear Bryant's long and successful career in which he was about to become the winningest coach in history. It was minutes after the game ended that Ford, himself, reached milestone. He was informed that Pittsburgh, which was ranked the nation's top team, was soundly upset by Penn State, 42-14, clearly opening the door for Clemson to be voted number one in both of the weekly polls conducted by AP and UPI. When he returned to Clemson on Monday, he learned about it officially from Bob Bradley.

"I think we feel just like everybody else who's been there," said Ford. "It doesn't mean anything until the bowl game is over, but it's a great honor for Clemson. We've done a good job every week, and we will be more proud if we can play well against Nebraska. The first goal was to win the conference title; the second, to go undefeated and get a major bowl bid; and the third goal, if we got that far, was to be the best team in the country. They have done an outstanding job all year, and I have to say this is a great football team. I want to emphasize the word great. They met the challenge every week and went 11-0 for the first time since 1948."

Clemson was the only unbeaten team in the country. They were overwhelmingly voted number one, being named on 63 of the 68 first-place ballots. They had become number one impressively, having beaten both Georgia and North Carolina when both were ranked in the top ten. Now, they could join Maryland as the only other Atlantic Coast Conference school to win the national championship, the Terrapins having accomplished it in 1953.

The Orange Bowl was the one the players wanted to play in. Clemson had appeared there twice before, in 1951 and again in 1957. Junior defensive tackle Dan Benish reflected the sentiments of the rest of his team-

Defensive end Bill Smith leads the Tigers out of the dressing room.

Quarterback Homer Jordan finds some running room around right end as tight end Bubba Diggs leads the way.

mates.

"The Orange Bowl seemed like the only place for us to go," said Benish. "We talked about a few other bowls, but the Orange is where we've wanted to go since the first of the season. We wanted to be number one, and the Orange Bowl can help us do it. It just seems like it was meant to be. Everything has been happening for us this season."

Yet, the season didn't surprise George Dostal. Not at all. Dostal is the team's strength-training director, who instituted a weight program for Clemson athletes six years ago. The training room had been a beehive of activity since last January, but it was quiet now. The players who were pumping iron from that time on a daily routine had all but left the campus to enjoy the time off that Ford had given them. The emptiness of the room only focused attention on a sign that Dostal had hung on a wall back in June. The message was clear.

"Believe: Clemson Tigers 11-0. In the Orange Bowl vs. Nebraska."

No one had talked about the sign back then. It was crudely made on the back of a workout card. Perhaps it was looked upon as a whim. Even Jeane Dixon in all her star gazing could not have been so accurate in forecasting the Clemson season exactly the way Dostal's sign had prophesied.

"I really believed it was possible," said Dostal. "There was a little bit of wishful thinking involved, but I believed in the kids' abilities. We had over 100 players working out this past summer. When I handed them over to coach Ford and his staff, I knew this was the strongest team we've had since I've been here. It's a dream come true. Call it an early Christmas present or New Year's present or whatever.

"We want to make our players as strong as possible from their toes to their heads. We think overall strength and stamina gives the players a mental as well as physical advantage. We go through three phases in our training— bulk strength, flexibility strength, and quickness. It's strictly strength work. We have nothing to do with steroids or excess water weight. We don't believe in it. Everyone does every type of training. It doesn't matter if it's Homer Jordan or Jeff Bryant. They do them all.

"Boyd Epley, Nebraska's strength coach, is a good friend of mine. He's had an outstanding program for a number or years, and I was hoping to play Nebraska so our programs could be compared. I'm delighted to be able to go against one of the top peers in the field. I'm just not making any prediction this time. I'm looking forward to going to Miami. If everybody plays up to their ability, I think we'll be happy when it's over."

The coaching staff wasn't taking any chances in preparing for Nebraska. Ford moved the entire football operation to Littlejohn Coliseum across the street from busy Jervey Athletic Center. Although it was somewhat of an inconvenience, it was a move the entire coaching staff approved. Ford wanted to make certain that his staff could labor with total concentration.

"When we got away from the football office, we got away from the telephones," said assistant head coach Tom Harper. "When you want to get something done, you've got to get away from the telephone calls, away from distractions. Danny Ford did a helluva job of organizing this season."

An appearance in a bowl game undoubtedly called more attention to Clemson's preparations. Yet, the coaching staff picked up right where they left off following their brief hiatus. Some of them couldn't wait to get back to work. The regimen was the same, with the exception being that they had more time to concentrate on Nebraska.

Normally, the work week begins at 7 o'clock every Sunday morning. It is a time that is utilized for each coach to grade the performances of his players from Saturday's game. Harper reviews the play of the defensive line; offensive coach Larry Van Der Heyden does the same for his unit, while the remaining coaches critique their players. At 11 o'clock, the staff meeting ends, allowing the coaches time for church and lunch before Ford's squad meeting with everyone at 3 o'clock.

The team is then split up into offensive and defensive units. One group watches film while the other lifts weights and jogs before switching schedules. At about 5 o'clock, the squad is dismissed for dinner, Later, the coaches return to their offices to break down film, which they do over and over. They work as late as midnight, looking for a fine edge.

"We'll look at the film on Nebraska in pairs," said Van Der Heyden. "We'll break down what their tendencies are. On offense, we want to know things like what they do on first down, second and long, second and short, third and long. We want to know what they do when the ball is on the left hash mark, what they do when the ball is on the right hash mark."

It doesn't end there. When the study is completed, the information is sent to the computer center at the other end of the campus. It is programmed scientifically, a computer printout is produced of Nebraska's tendencies in given situations. The next morning at 7 o'clock, Ford meets with his staff and leaves them to do more work on the game plan.

"We'll look at the film again," said Van Der Heyden. "Then we'll put Nebraska's defense on the blackboard. We break it down into fronts and coverages, and we'll go through each of our plays. We may find out at that time that some of our plays might be bad plays to run against a particular defense. You never try to run a bad play against a particular defense. We have an on-field scouting report. Then we'll run maybe two or three basic plays that we feel we have to be able to run against every defense."

Harper does just about the same thing, only his concern is defense. At 3 o'clock, he meets with the squad and goes over a scouting report. The session is short. The next day the coaching staff reviews the film again. That afternoon, Clemson's practice session is filmed with the offense and defense trying different plays and formations for Nebraska. That night, the coaching staff makes adjustments and begins honing the game plan.

"At that point, we'll plan what fronts and coverages we're going to use," said Harper. "We have to defend the field both horizontally and vertically, and we have to defend all kinds of situations on the field. We have to defend against short yardage, obvious passing downs, goal line situations, situations where you are defending the clock. We also have to defend against certain personnel, like a Herschel Walker type, when you have to get your stunt packages in order.

173

"Each member of the staff will look at our defense and say if he thinks we're going to be hurt by something we do. The defensive front is constantly trying to get a compromise with the secondary. We try to defend in something that is best for us and best for the secondary."

There was still more work to be done. On Wednesday, Ford goes over the game plan very closely. Later, he meets with his staff for more discussion. Following a heavy practice in the afternoon, the game plan is refined even further. Ford didn't want to leave any detail, no matter how small, unattended. The Nebraska game was the biggest one yet of the entire season. All that was left on Thursday was to review the week's work and finally complete the strategy. He just had more time to do it since the Orange Bowl engagement was still three weeks away.

After his weekly meeting with the senior members of his squad, it was decided that the Tigers would leave for Florida a week earlier than expected. Rather than spending the Christmas holidays at home, the players unanimously agreed to train at New Smyrna Beach before arriving in Miami the week of the game as scheduled by the Orange Bowl officials. Ford had listened to his seniors all season and depended on them for leadership. The next day, plans were formulated for Clemson to set up camp in the north Florida city just south of Daytona.

Before the squad left for Florida, they were toasted with orange soda. It was a novelty, indeed, the brainchild of Mark Avant, a vice president of the Pepsi-Cola Bottling Com-

Jordan rolls to his right looking to throw as tailback Chuck McSwain offers blocking support.

174

pany in Bennettsville. Avant designed an attractive can commemorating Clemson's outstanding season. It was orange in color; and besides the easily recognizable purple paws, the can contained the scores of all eleven Clemson games; the No. 1 AP and UPI poll rating; and the date, time, place, and opponent of the Orange Bowl. The Tiger Brew was an instant success. Originally, only 6,000 cases were planned; but because of the demand, it sharply rose to 30,000.

"We wanted it to be a collector's item," Avant said, "but if the demands keep up, we'll sell it to them."

The demand was there, all right. Mike Reese, the assistant manager of the Kroger store in Aiken, was selling Clemson Orange Soda for 55 cents a can. Jim Price, the manager of the Piggly-Wiggly in Kalmia Plaza, had them at 39 cents a can. He sold out and was waiting for more.

The weather in New Smyrna Beach was unseasonably cool when the Tigers arrived at The Islander Motel. Still, the players weren't thinking along the lines of any vacation. The seniors emphasized to Ford that they wanted the extra week in Florida to work. They wanted any edge they could gain on Nebraska, and to accomplish it, the players were willing to sacrifice their Christmas vacations while at the same time acclimating their bodies to the Florida temperature. The game meant too much to them. It not only represented an unbeaten season, but it also symbolized the national championship as well. Never in the history of Clemson football had such a possibility existed. It wouldn't be easy. The nation's oddsmakers didn't believe in Clemson. They made fourth-ranked Nebraska a six-point favorite.

"I think everybody on the team and everybody associated with Clemson University knows what is ahead—the national championship," said linebacker Jeff Davis, one of the team's senior leaders. "You can't make a better present for yourself than winning the national championship, and I'm trying to keep that in perspective. There's always time for fun after you've finished your hard work.

"I'm in pretty good shape. Once you get in shape, it's best to stay there. It takes every bit of two weeks to get back if you lose the edge,

Coach Danny Ford makes some halftime adjustments.

but I'd say that we're all in as good a shape as we were before the South Carolina game. One reason is even though we had a rest from 11 games, we knew a little work on our own would pay off now.

"Some people say we haven't played nobody, but we beat two teams in the top five. Things like that are things we have put up with all year. It has just made us work harder. We're going up against a team like Nebraska, and we have an opportunity to change all the opinions. That's the extra bit we got from going undefeated. We get to play a team that is big time, a team that is always in the top 20 in the nation. What an opportunity!

"I hope we can give the ACC recognition with this game. Teams will start to respect us more if we win. What will do it more is for us to win the national championship. We felt coming down here early and staying here was in the best interest of the team. The seniors wanted it this way. We talked to the underclassmen a little bit, but the final decision was

175

Linebacker Johnny Rembert (90) makes the final hit on a Nebraska runner.

left up to us. If we had started practice and broken up to go home for Christmas, we could have lost the groove once we got in it. I feel we can keep on clicking now, and there will be plenty of Christmases for all of us to celebrate after this game is over. We'll be ready for Nebraska."

The players did indeed work hard. Ford had devised morning and afternoon workouts. Nevertheless, the players responded with spir-

ited drills. Their attitude pleased Ford. He decided to reward them by giving the team a private party on Christmas Eve, the night before the squad would leave the following morning by bus on the final leg of their journey to Miami and their date with destiny.

"Everybody had a good time," said Ford. "We made it as much like Christmas for them as possible. Of course, riding a bus on Christmas day isn't exactly the way you want to cele-

preparing for Nebraska. When the two-bus caravan arrived at the Dupont Plaza Hotel in downtown Miami, Ford quickly made arrangements with the manager to have a belly dancer entertain following the team dinner. When dessert was being served that evening, a scantily clad belly dancer made her appearance to the whistles and applause of the surprised players. Supported by a band, she danced around the room, stopping every so often at a table, then jumping on top to the cheers of the group, and continuing dancing. A well-schooled professional, she then began to pull a number of players off their chairs to accompany her in the aisle between the tables.

The subtle Ford had a surprise of his own. He walked over to where his freshman 300-pound nose guard William Perry was sitting. Within seconds, he was escorting his behemoth lineman, called GE by his teammates because he resembles a refrigerator, to the stage. He turned him over to the belly dancer. Perry, not shy as freshmen go, took it from there. Light on his feet despite his bulk, Perry improvised quite a few moves of his own and loosened up the audience. When he was finished, he got a rousing, standing ovation. It was a fun-filled night.

"I think we helped take a little bit of the sting out of the kids' being away from home," said Ford. "We've had one workout since we got here, and we'll get down to some serious work on Sunday afternoon. We won't go two times a day like we did in New Smyrna, but we'll try to get it in tone for Friday."

Ford depended on Perry, although he was only a freshman. He fulfilled his coach's faith in him by accounting for a number of big plays during the season, while splitting playing time with William Devane. The 48 tackles he was credited with set a record for rookies. Perry didn't lose sight of what was expected of him despite the merriment of the night.

"We had fun at the party, but I didn't come down here just to play around," said Perry. "I know the Nebraska center, Dave Rimington, from looking at film. Once you get him down, he just keeps coming back at you. But I like going against big-time people. He's been honored by winning the Outland Trophy, and he's got a name, but he's going to have to prove to

brate, but we had no choice."

Ford did a lot of thinking as the bus headed south to Miami. Several times he stared out the window, alone with his thoughts. He was convinced that it would be a good idea to throw the team another party on Christmas night, only with something a little more than the round of Christmas carols the players sang the night before. He really wanted to relax his players before the final week of hard work in me that he's good.

"It's been a pretty good year. I'm new; and yet, I knew we were going to have a good season this year. It will be a great year if two more things happen—if we don't lose to Nebraska and if I don't try to get in a Volkswagen between now and time for the game."

Back in Six Mile, South Carolina, Addie Dillard was having a celebration of her own, far from the bright lights of Miami. She is, perhaps, Clemson's oldest fan and marked the occasion with her 99th birthday. Affectionately called "Miss Addie," she had a special birthday wish, a victory for her Tigers in the Orange Bowl, as she blew out the candle on her birthday cake with several friends at Harvey's Love and Care Home.

"I'm very anxious to see it," said Miss Addie. "I feel awfully shaky about it, but I feel like Clemson will win. They haven't lost a game this year. The game will be very close, and I believe it will be decided at the very end of the game."

Miss Addie had been born in 1882, seven years before Clemson was founded. She grew up following Clemson football from the first year Clemson competed in 1896 and has remained loyal to the Tigers ever since. She attended Clemson's opening game of the season against Wofford and was visited by Ford before the kickoff. She carried a whistle with her and blew it whenever Clemson scored. She called it her good luck piece. All during the season she either listened to the Clemson games on radio or watched them on television.

"I was a little scared right at the first when Wofford scored," said Miss Addie. "I was also a little scared of Carolina and Maryland. I was surprised in the last game against South Carolina by the 29-13 score. I thought it would be a little closer. I think Danny Ford is wonderful. He's a nice fellow and he's a good coach, a very good coach."

She remembers being at the laying of the cornerstone for the Clemson campus landmark, Tillman Hall, in 1889. "I was small, but I can remember it," she says proudly. Later, she worked as a telephone operator and an office manager at Clemson for 25 years. Her husband, Joseph, who died in 1954, worked in the textiles department of the college.

"My husband and I used to go to every one of those games," Miss Addie said. "He was as much of a Clemson lover as I was. I really love the place and the people. You can't keep from loving Clemson."

Ford didn't forget Miss Addie's birthday. Although he was heavily involved with practice, he took time to send Miss Addie a birthday card. Ford wrote:

"Happy 99th Birthday! We are all down here in Miami, but we wanted to take a minute to let you know how proud we are to have you pulling for us in the Orange Bowl. Wish you could be here, too. Again, Happy Birthday to a real Tiger!"

There were about 25,000 Tiger fans in Miami for the game, but B. C. Inabinet was not one of them. He was conspicuous by his absence; he means that much to Clemson football. Clemson officials had requests for as many as 40,000 tickets but were only allocated 20,000 by the Orange Bowl committee. Although Clemson officials managed to secure an additional 3,000 tickets, they were still well short of the demand of rabid Tiger fans.

Inabinet, who never misses a Clemson game, was forced to miss the biggest one of his life. A week before the Orange Bowl, he suffered a heavy nose bleed. It might not have been serious to the average person, but to the jovial 400-pound Inabinet there was concern. He was taken to a hospital in Columbia with the fear that he might be near a stroke. His doctors told him that he would be hospitalized for a week of extensive tests. He was released on New Year's Day, too weak to even think about flying to Miami. Instead he went to his home in Myrtle Beach, where he and his wife, Kitty, would watch the game alone. It was not his style. He had planned a big celebration in Miami, where he had reserved 40 rooms in the Dupont Plaza Hotel for his managers at Defender Industries and his friends, all loyal Clemson supporters. He looked at his misfortune philosophically.

"It was a warning," said Inabinet. "I had been working hard for several weeks, and the good Lord told me to slow down. I was so weak from all the tests and the tubes stuck in my arm, and I just wanted to rest. As much as I love Clemson, I couldn't have made it to the

Kicker Donald Igwebuike opens Clemson's scoring with a 41-yard field goal in opening period.

Orange Bowl. Dr. Atchley called me every day in the hospital and so did Bill McLellan and all those good Clemson people so that I felt wonderful knowing so many people cared. That's what Clemson is all about, people caring. I just wished I could have been there with them."

Naturally, Frank Howard was there. It wouldn't have been the same without him in Miami. He had led Clemson to the Orange Bowl for the first time in 1951 and took them back in 1957. He was sought after by a great many visiting sportswriters and more often than not couldn't walk through the lobby of the hotel without being stopped for an hour or two. As long as he had his chewing tobacco with him, Howard didn't mind talking.

"First time we come down here, one of these Miami sportswriters wrote, 'What IS a Clemson? Is it a vegetable or a fruit?'" said Howard one morning. "Shoot, we done outgrew that now, least I hope; but what still irritates me is that a lot of people think Clemson never has been no dang where. Why, Clemson has been

to the Cotton Bowl, two Orange Bowls, and a bunch of Gator Bowls.

"You know, the first time we came down here, we stayed at the Flamingo, over yonder on the beach. It's been torn down since. I took my boys in that hotel and let them have anything in the world they wanted to eat, all that banana bread and stuff. Then, I took them out and worked them so hard they threw it all up.

"Well, then I told them to be in their rooms by about 10:30 every night. I told them I wasn't going to spot-check them. I checked one night; and three were missing, my three best ones. I waited up on them. About 1:30 they came in, and I ate them up, told them they were too sorry to play with my good boys. I told them I was going to send them home on the Greyhound the next morning.

"Well, then I got to thinking to myself that maybe I'd got into this too deep; so I told them I'd let the rest of the team vote on whether they could play or not. Just before the team met to vote, I told one of the assistant coaches

179

The signs say it all.

to go around and talk to the boys. I told him, 'You make dern sure they all vote to let those three play.' The University of Miami had a Smith, and I had a Smith. Miami was leading us 14-13 late in the game. My Smith tackled their Smith for a safety; and we won, 15-14.

"In that other Orange Bowl game in 1957, we were behind 20-0 at halftime. I went in the dressing room and raised hell. We came back and got them, 21-20. But then, after we scored that last time, my quarterback called an onside kick, why I'll never know, and Colorado recovered it and scored and beat us, 26-21.

"Now when I first came to Clemson, all they were saying was that they *hoped* to win the state championship. That meant beating South Carolina, The Citadel, Erskine, Wofford, Presbyterian, Newberry. That's quite a difference from now, ain't it? Being number one is a lot higher than I ever got them. This is the greatest thing that's ever happened here. I had

hoped someday to see us there, but it was a little doubtful. Teams like Alabama, Texas, Notre Dame, Michigan, Ohio Sate, Penn State, those are the ones who are usually there. Reputation and tradition have a lot to do with it. It's very good to be in that class. Clemson's overcome a whole lot to finally get there. I thought it could happen, but I never thought I'd live to see it."

Still, despite its number one rating, Clemson still found a lack of respect, not only with the oddsmakers but with several Nebraska players. Three days before the game, a couple of Nebraska players poked fun at the Tigers.

"Clemson, that's in North Carolina," snapped Nebraska defensive end Jimmy Williams.

"Isn't it in South Carolina?" asked Nebraska quarterback Mark Mauer.

Perry Tuttle jokingly countered back. He wasn't about to get upset.

"Well, it's somewhere close to South Bend,"

180

he remarked. "Everybody wants to know where Clemson is."

Actually, the slight worked to Clemson's advantage. The players approached the game seemingly comfortable in their role as underdogs. They weren't the least bit tense and were quite anxious to prove to a nationwide television audience that they were truly the nation's top team.

"We're underdogs, and we're expected to get beat," said Perry Tuttle, the Tigers' top receiver with 47 catches for 827 yards and seven touchdowns. "You have to be lucky to go through the season undefeated, but I guess I'm not surprised we're underdogs. I think that because a lot of people expect us to lose, there isn't as much pressure on us. I know I feel loose, and I anticipate a great game. We've wanted to be number one for a long time, and now we want to prove to everyone we belong there.

"Thanks to Homer, I've had a great season. The thing about Homer is he's quiet. But understand, when Homer talks, people listen—like E. F. Hutton. One time, late in the first half of the Georgia game, it was 0-0, and everybody was panicking, going crazy. Homer walked into the huddle and yelled, 'Shut the hell up!' Oh, man! Everybody went whaa! Nobody ever heard Homer cuss before, and then everybody cracked up. I said, 'Homer, what? That's not you, man.'" Jordan gave Tuttle a cold look. Then, a few minutes later, he hit Tuttle with an eight-yard touchdown pass to key Clemson's victory.

"We kid around an awful lot now," said Tuttle. "Like one day before a game I said, 'Now, Homer, I'll give you one hundred dollars if you give me six passes.' And he said, 'I'll give you fifty back if you catch them all.' Against Maryland, we were on their 14-yard line. Homer got under the center. He looked at Jerry Gaillard, the other receiver. He was thinking about checking off, but he wasn't real sure of himself. Then he looked at me, and I made a tiny nod with my head. Homer called out, 'Purple,' and once he said that I knew what the deal was. I took off down the sidelines; Homer lobbed the ball toward the right flag, and I caught it for a touchdown."

Jordan fulfilled his role as the leader of the

offense his junior season. It was personally gratifying to him; yet, the team had to prove themselves every week. They had to do it one more time. They were anxious to face Nebraska.

"We still think we've got something to prove," said senior center Tony Berryhill. "We've still got some respect to gain. I don't know if we'd be able to keep our respect if we lost. We've got to win this game. All of us are itching to play. We're tired of practicing; we're tired of Miami, and we're tired of looking at Nebraska on film."

Ford, too, saw enough of Nebraska. What he saw didn't make him feel any better. He didn't hide the fact, either. His concern this time was justified.

"Nebraska will be the toughest opponent a Clemson football team has ever played, bar none," said Ford the day before the game. "We know that much from watching the film. For

Just in case anyone needs reminding who is number one.

every running play they've got, they have a pass play off of it; and for half of their plays, they've got trick plays off of them. On top of that, they are a misdirection football team. They've got more of that kind of stuff than any football team I've ever seen."

Statistically, the teams were about even. Nebraska averaged 5.7 yards a play and Clemson 5.3. Nebraska outscored their opponents by 246 points, Clemson by 216. Nebraska averaged 31 points a game and Clemson 26. Defensively, it was even closer. Each team gave up an average of 3.6 yards a play and about nine points a game. There was nothing left but the game itself. The scoreboard would be the final determination.

The Orange Bowl was a wave of orange on a warm, humid night. About half of the 72,748 fans in attendance sported some clothing of orange. Then, too, Clemson decided to wear its orange pants for the third time of the season. They had done so against Georgia and Maryland and had won both times. They also had worn the pants in the final game of the 1980 season when they defeated South Carolina. The orange britches held a special meaning to the players. It created an air of excitement for Clemson fans in the moments before the game began.

Nebraska was anxious to receive the opening kickoff. Mike Rozier took Igwebuike's kick on the seven and brought it back to the 25. Quickly, the Cornhuskers broke the huddle; and I-back Roger Craig ran inside for six yards. Fullback Phil Bates also went over right guard but only got two yards. On third down, Nebraska malfunctioned. Quarterback Mark Mauer tried to pitch out to Craig but fumbled. An alert William Devane pounced on the ball on the Nebraska 28, which elicited a loud response by the Clemson fans. The Tigers had the first big break of the game.

Jordan came out throwing and hit tight end Bubba Diggs with a snappy three-yard pass on the 25. Tailback Cliff Austin broke through on the next play and picked up a first down on the 18. After fullback Kevin Mack was stopped for no gain, Jordan went to the air. He missed wide receiver Frank Magwood in the end zone. When he tried to pass for a second straight time on third down, he slipped

and fell back on the 27-yard line. Nevertheless, Igwebuike sent Clemson into an early 3-0 lead when he booted a 41-yard field goal.

Rozier brought the crowd to its feet when he took Igwebuike's kickoff on the goal line and raced to the 31-yard line before he was caught. Rozier then carried the ball four consecutive times and picked up a total of 13 yards. On second down from the 44-yard line, Mauer hit split end Todd Brown with a 13-yard pass on the Clemson 43. An illegal procedure penalty on Clemson brought the ball to the 38. After Rozier got three yards, Bates ran for five yards and a first down on the 30. Another illegal procedure penalty cost the Tigers five more yards. Nebraska was threatening on the Clemson 25 with a first and five. Mauer decided to go for all of it. He sent wing back Anthony Steels deep into the end zone and pitched back to Rozier who then delivered a 25-yard touchdown pass that fooled the Tigers. Kevin Seibel added the extra point to send Nebraska into a 7-3 lead.

Clemson couldn't do anything following a nifty 38-yard kickoff return by Perry Tuttle. Austin gained three yards; and after overthrowing wide receiver Jerry Gaillard, Jordan came back to him with a short two-yard pass that was well short of a first down. Freshman Dale Hatcher didn't show any signs of nervousness when he kicked a high, 43-yard punt that had to be fair caught on the Nebraska 13-yard line.

A holding penalty on the first play put Nebraska into deeper trouble on the seven-yard line. After two plays got the Cornhuskers to the 16, strong safety Tim Childers left Clemson fans cheering when he sacked Mauer for an 11-yard loss on the five-yard line. The Tigers were certain to get excellent field position from that point. They did, too, when Billy Davis signaled for a fair catch of Grant Campbell's punt on the Cornhuskers' 47-yard line.

Jordan wanted to strike quickly. He sent Tuttle on a fly pattern into the end zone, but the pass was broken up at the last second by safety Jeff Krezci. However, on his next pass to Jeff Stockstill, the junior wide receiver was interfered with on the 25-yard line. On first down, Chuck McSwain was stopped for no gain. Jordan then got four yards on a keeper;

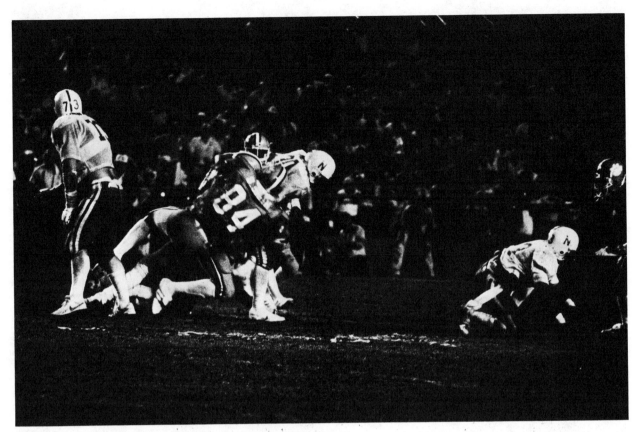

Defensive end Bill Smith brings down a Cornhusker.

but when he tried it again, he couldn't gain anything. Igwebuike was sent in to try a 37-yard field goal. He was accurate in bringing Clemson closer, 7-6, with just over a minute left in the first period.

On the first play after the kickoff, a holding penalty sent Nebraska to its 10-yard line. Rozier managed to get five yards, then the Cornhuskers were caught clipping on the next play and were penalized back to the six-yard line where the quarter ended. The Cornhuskers were in trouble again. After two plays produced 18 yards, they got out of danger when Campbell boomed a 66-yard punt that Davis managed to catch on the 14-yard line and brought back 10 yards to the Clemson 24.

Jordan started from there with an eight-yard pass to Tuttle. McSwain ran to the 37 for a first down. After Jordan got six yards and McCall three, the big fullback got two more for a first down on the 48. After a pass failed and McSwain lost two yards, the Tigers had a third and long. Jordan went deep. He threw far downfield to Magwood. Safety Sammy Sims tipped the ball; but Magwood, who never

stopped concentrating on the ball, grabbed it and fell on the Nebraska 12-yard line. Tiger fans were anticipating a touchdown. Jordan moved for two yards. However, on second down, Tiger fans moaned. Jordan tried to connect with Tuttle in the end zone, but his pass was intercepted by cornerback Ric Lindquist. Clemson was repelled.

The ball was moved out to the 20-yard line. After a ground play picked up two yards, the Cornhuskers were penalized 10 yards for clipping. They were in the hole again on the 12-yard line. Mauer got them some breathing room with an 11-yard pass to Rozier to bring up a third and seven. The Clemson defense came through once more. On a draw play up the middle, Bates fumbled; and Jeff Davis recovered on the 27.

Clemson had a golden opportunity to take over the lead with 7:11 left in the half. Jordan passed seven yards to Tuttle. Austin then cracked over center for five yards and a first down on the 15. Mack got five more. He carried again, and Clemson hearts sank. Mack fumbled, but he managed to recover the ball

Tailback Chuck McSwain tries for first down yardage.

for a one-yard gain to the nine where Clemson called for a time out with 5:05 showing on the clock. Jordan huddled with Ford on the sidelines. The young coach wanted to remind Jordan not to rush into any mistakes because there was ample time remaining. He told him to try a quarterback draw. Jordan did, gained four yards and a big first down on the five-yard line. He ran again and got three more. Then he pitched to Austin, and the tailback raced across the goal line from two yards away to give the Tigers a 12-7 lead. With 3:56 to go, Clemson decided to try a two-point conversion. Jordan tried to deliver the pass to Tuttle but was pressured into underthrowing it.

Nebraska got to midfield after the kickoff. However, on fourth and 15 the Cornhuskers tried to catch Clemson relaxed with a fake punt. The Tiger defense was waiting and turned back the play after a yard gain. Clem-

son got the ball on its 49-yard line with 1:21 to play. Austin ran for three yards, and Jordan scrambled for four. After an incompleted pass, Jordan ran wide for six yards and a first down on the Nebraska 38. Another pass went incomplete. Jordan was then dropped for a four-yard loss before the Tigers desperately called time out with two seconds remaining. Igwebuike was sent in to try a 58-yard field goal but was short. Nevertheless, the Tigers trotted off the field to the cheers of their supporters with a 12-7 advantage.

Although they received the second half kickoff, the Tigers couldn't do anything to keep their fans cheering. Starting from the 20, McCall got three yards. McSwain then broke loose around left end and gained 10 yards to the 33. Clemson was then stymied. First, Jordan overthrew Tuttle. On the next play, Clemson was caught holding and was assessed a 10-

five. Jordan kept the drive going with a 16-yard pass to Tuttle on the Nebraska 42. McCall went for six yards and then four more for another first down on the 32. Jordan then hit Diggs with a quick seven-yard pass. McSwain found an opening in the center of the line and moved for nine yards and another first down on the 16. The Tigers were in field goal territory now. On the next play McCall got everyone thinking touchdown. He burst through the middle for 12 yards and still another first down on the four-yard line. Then disaster almost struck. After McSwain got a yard, he was dropped for a 10-yard loss to the 13-yard line. On third down, Jordan called Tuttle's number in the huddle. Tuttle sped to the end zone, made a quick move on cornerback Allen Lyday that spun him around, leaped, and pulled down Jordan's touchdown pass that gave the Tigers more room to roar, 18-7. Bob Paulling made it 19-7 with his conversion that capped the 75-yard, 12-play drive.

Following the kickoff, the fired-up Clemson defense shut down Nebraska. It enabled Clemson to get the ball back with 5:07 lit on the clock, and charged from a 47-yard punt return by Davis that electrified the crowd before he was caught from behind on the Nebraska 22. Austin got to the 19, but a second down holding penalty pushed the Tigers back to the 31. Jordan came back with a 16-yard pass to Gaillard on the 15. However, on a third and three play, he was nailed with a five-yard loss on the 20. It was now left to Igwebuike. He came through with a 36-yard field goal that stretched Clemson's lead to 22-7.

There was only 2:36 left in the period when Nebraska took over on its 15-yard line. After an incompleted pass, Craig ran for nine yards and then four and a first down on the 24. Staying on the ground, Bates added five yards, Mauer four, and then Craig again for three and another first down on the 40 when play subsided in the third period.

Mauer opened the final quarter with an 11-yard pass to Jamie Williams on the Clemson 49. After Craig got six more yards, the Tiger defense stiffened; and Nebraska was forced to punt, the ball being downed on the Clemson 19-yard line. A five-yard run by Jordan and a six-yard one by Mack quickly got Clemson a

yard penalty. After McCall gained four yards, the Tigers were flagged for clipping, which resulted in a 15-yard penalty that set them back to the 20-yard line. On third and 23, Jordan could only collect eight yards on a pass to Gaillard. However, Hatcher got them out of any danger by booting a 51-yard punt.

From the Nebraska 33, Bates got a yard. Mauer missed with a pass; and Rozier managed to gain four yards up the middle, which meant that Nebraska had to punt. When Campbell did so, Clemson began its second offensive series of the third period from its own 20-yard line. Ford talked to Jordan before the quarterback took the field. They both realized that a five-point lead wasn't enough and that Clemson needed more points.

Jordan opened with a 12-yard pass to Tuttle on the 37. McSwain could get only five yards on two carries, which brought up a third and first down on the 30. However, that was as far as they got. Jordan missed on two pass attempts, and Austin was halted for no gain. Clemson had to kick. Irving Fryar made a fair catch of Hatcher's punt on the Nebraska 31-yard line.

When Mauer led the offense on the field, 12:05 remained. Nebraska had to score at that point in order to have a chance to overtake Clemson. Mauer missed with a pass, then ran for six yards. Rozier shook loose on the outside for eight yards and a first down on the 45. Carrying up the middle this time, Rozier found enough daylight for a nine-yard advance. After Mauer failed on a pass, Rozier came through again. Faking a pass, he bolted up the middle for eight yards and another first down on the Clemson 38. Mauer gave the ball to Rozier again. This time he produced 12 yards and still another first down on the 26. Nebraska was on the move. While the Tiger defense was keying on Rozier, Craig broke loose around left end on the longest run of the night and scored standing up. Nebraska then went for the two-point conversion and made it. With 9:15 left, they now trailed 22-15, a touchdown away.

Clemson couldn't generate any offense after the kickoff, and Nebraska got the ball right back again on its 37-yard line with 7:49 remaining to play. They had ample time to score. It was a big series for the Tiger defense. Rozier shook Tiger backers with an apparent 13-yard run to midfield. However, Nebraska was called for holding on the play and penalized to the 33. Rozier came back with runs of four and six yards. But on third and four, Mauer was stopped for a three-yard loss when he attempted to pitch out to Craig. Nebraska had to punt, and Campbell's booming 60-yard punt landed in the end zone.

There was 5:24 remaining when Clemson put the ball in play on its 20-yard line. They had to produce some first downs in order to keep possession while running out the clock at the same time. Ford and Jordan decided to accomplish the objective on the ground. McCall carried three straight times and accounted for 11 yards and a first down on the 31. McSwain then tried and got four yards. When McCall could only get two yards, Jordan faced a cru-

cial third down. He needed four yards to keep control of the ball and quite possibly the game. Jordan called his own number in the huddle, a misdirection run. He started wide to his right, then cut back to the middle, and turned on the speed. He raced for 23 yards before he was brought down on the Nebraska 40-yard line. With just over two minutes left in the game, it was a big first down, the biggest of the struggle.

The Clemson faithful could sense the victory now. It was up there on the scoreboard and the clock, which was Clemson's ally with each passing second. A delay of game cost the Tigers five yards. Only 1:53 showed on the clock. McCall got a yard. Nebraska used its final time out. Just 1:43 was left. Using up the clock as much as possible, Jordan ran wide to his left for four yards. McSwain took a pitch-out for a yard. Clemson delayed on fourth down and was penalized five yards. They were working the clock to the maximum. There was only 0:17 seconds to tick off. Jordan kept the ball himself. He scrambled around from one side to the other before he was dropped for a two-yard loss.

Clemson was only six seconds away from an unbelievable unbeaten season and a national championship. Nebraska had time for only one play. Clemson knew they had to prevent a desperation long pass from being completed in its secondary. Mauer dropped back and threw deep. The frenzied fans in the Orange Bowl rose from their seats. Defensive end Andy Headen met the challenge to Clemson's championship. On the 15-yard line, he knocked down the one pass that could have spoiled Clemson's dream. It was all over. Clemson did it. The field was a sea of orange.

The celebration swept into the dressing room. It was a struggle to get inside. Outside, a mass of delirious Clemson fans were chanting, "We're number one...We're number one," as they blocked the tunnel leading to the locker room. Once inside, the players hugged one another, flicked victory cigars, and shouted, "ACC...ACC...ACC." It was a scene like no other. They deserved to bask in the glory of the biggest night in Clemson football history.

"We're awfully proud of our boys," ex-

Wide receiver Perry Tuttle (22) and wide receiver Jerry Gaillard (41) go up in the air wit after Tuttle caught a 13-yard touchdown pass in the third qu

Happiness at the end of the game overcame the exhaustion.

claimed an exhausted but happy Ford. "We finally proved that there's more to the ACC than basketball. They didn't believe this team in Las Vegas. Nebraska was favored. They didn't believe this team in Nebraska. Out there the newspapers were asking if we belonged in the big time. Well, you can't brag until you've proved your facts. We've proved it. Now, we can brag.

"No matter what they all say, nobody else in America has done what we've done this year. We beat the No. 2 team (Georgia); we beat the No. 4 team (Nebraska), and we beat the No. 8 team (North Carolina). We've beaten three teams in the Top 10, and nobody else has beaten even two. We played 11 and whipped 11 to get to be No. 1. Now, we've played 12 and whipped 12.

"Shoot, before the game I saw us getting behind by a lot of points early. When it started, I saw us staying close all the way and them blowing us out in the fourth quarter. Then, when the fourth quarter came, I saw them winning by one point with a two-point conversion in the last minute. I saw everything. From what I had been hearing and reading, I figured there were more ways for us to prove we didn't belong on the field with Nebraska than to prove that they didn't belong on the field with us."

Ford then broke away from a cordon of writers to talk on the telephone. B. C. Inabinet was on the other end. Tears were in Ford's eyes as he spoke. The emotionally spent Inabinet cried, too; but the tears between the two were tears of joy. Inabinet had suffered through 25 years of Clemson's frustrations, and in just three years Ford had removed it all. The only empty feeling Inabinet had at this very moment was that he was too ill to be in Miami to celebrate with everyone.

Like Inabinet, Jordan couldn't do any celebrating, either. He lay on his back in the trainer's room completely exhausted. Fred Hoover, the team's trainer, was attending to Jordan, who was so fatigued he needed intravenous injections of glucose and water in both arms to prevent his body from dehydrating. He later had to be helped to take a shower and then was sent directly to the hotel and put to bed by a couple of aides. There would be no celebrating for Jordan later that night at the team's victory party. Although he was voted the game's most valuable player, Jordan couldn't even participate in any interviews requested by the press. Yet, he really didn't mind at all. The game, the triumph, had meant too much to him. Besides, Jordan is a quiet person to begin with.

"The doctors put me right to bed and wouldn't let me out all night," said Jordan the next morning. "I tried to sit down in front of my locker after the game, and I got real shaky, I couldn't sleep, though. I just lay there thinking about the game. I just feel sore all over. Nebraska is a hard-hitting team. They didn't show us anything we didn't prepare for. We didn't have to change a thing at halftime. I hurt on the outside, but I feel great on the inside. It will take time for it to sink in just what has happened. Once it does, I will cherish it for the rest of my life."

Nobody realized it at the time, except for Dr. Bryan Harder, one of the team's physicians; but Jordan, indeed, suffered severe exhaustion. It just wasn't a case of being drawn and tired from the heat. Harder explained it that night after attending to the exhausted quarterback.

188

"It's a little bit more severe than most cases of heat exhaustion," said Dr. Harder. "If the game had lasted any longer, Homer wouldn't have made it."

More than anyone, Tuttle missed Jordan. He had caught five passes for 56 yards and a touchdown, despite being challenged by Nebraska's zone coverage, which can so often confuse a quarterback and a receiver. Tuttle and Jordan had been close friends throughout the season. The senior wide receiver, more than any other player, helped Jordan experience his best season.

"You know, at 7:30 this morning Homer came into my room and woke me up and said, 'I'm so nervous I can't sleep,'" said Tuttle. "I said, 'Homer, those big farmboys are going to kill you.' But in the game he was so confident. We called 50 different plays, and Homer carried on 25 of them. Actually, he was reading their defense well and checking off at the line of scrimmage. He's the guy who makes us click.

"I came into the huddle before the touchdown; and Homer said to me, 'If they're in Coverage One (inside zone), run to the corner. If they're in Coverage Five (outside zone), hope that it doesn't get intercepted.' They were in One, I think, so I went to corner; and there was the ball."

Clemson actually beat Nebraska at its own game-strength, which made George Dostal happy. Dostal had said before the season started that this was the strongest Clemson team he had seen in the seven years he'd been the strength coach. Physically, Clemson wore Nebraska down. The Tigers also reverted to another Nebraska trademark, depth, to achieve their triumph, matching the Cornhuskers' employment of four running backs. Austin, one of the four used by Clemson, had the scare of his life hours before the game when he was trapped in an elevator at the hotel for several hours.

"I was there from 2 to 4:30," revealed Austin. "I didn't know if I was going to be able to get out. The longer I was in there, the more I thought I might miss the game. I meditated a lot and told myself that if I got out I was going to give it all I had against Nebraska. This is the greatest feeling in the world. We proved we were the better team. Toward the end of the game we kept driving on them, and you could see in their eyes how tired they were."

Back in Clemson, they weren't the least bit tired. A crowd of about 300 people had made its way out of the bars and homes near downtown and gathered in the center of town. Cars from neighboring towns began arriving with their horns blaring. No one could remember the last time Clemson had experienced a traffic jam. Yet, the town police didn't seem to mind this particular night.

"They were blocking the street, stopping traffic, standing on the roadway, drinking and hollering, and just being happy," said Sgt. Jerry Crenshaw. "Quite a number of fans or young people got a little overenthused from drinking and beating down on passing cars with their open fists."

The celebration lasted long into the night. Before it was over, the city police had arrested seven persons and the Pickens County sheriff's deputies three others, which really wasn't all that bad considering the occasion. Nobody could deny the happy fans the greatest night in Clemson's football history. They had waited a long time to become number one.

"It's a once-in-a-lifetime thing for some people," said Jim Mayben, the manager of a spot named Under The Table.

Indeed it was for everyone who loves Clemson, but that's what Clemson is all about.

1981 ORANGE BOWL

January 1, 1982
Miami, FL

CLEMSON	6	6	10	0	–	22
NEBRASKA	7	0	0	8	–	15

CU—Igwebuike 41 FG
UN—Steels 25 pass from Rozier (Seibel kick)
CU—Igwebuike 37 FG
CU—Austin 2 run (Pass failed)
CU—Tuttle 13 pass from Jordan (Paulling kick)
CU—Igwebuike 36 FG
UN—Craig 26 run (Craig run)
Attendance: 72,748

EPILOGUE

"I TURNED DANNY IN"
South Carolina Bumper Sticker

**"I'D RATHER BE ON PROBATION
THAN GET BEAT BY FURMAN"**
Clemson Bumper Sticker

Several weeks before the South Carolina game, B. C. Inabinet was driving on one of the major thoroughfares in downtown Columbia. Anyone who is even remotely involved with Clemson knows about Inabinet's involvement with his *alma mater*, because he is one of Clemson's biggest supporters. On this particular warm, fall day in early November of 1982, Inabinet was glaring at a bumper sticker on a car in front of him. He was so obsessed by it that he bumped into the car when it stopped for a traffic light. Upset by the slight jolt, the driver stormed out of his car, but seeing Inabinet's size, he wisely refrained his vocabulary. Inabinet courteously apologized, saying he was so taken back by the bumper sticker that he wasn't aware that the traffic light was red. The bumper sticker, which bore the message, "I Turned Danny Ford In," was prophetic.

Several weeks later, while Inabinet was entertaining some 20 people in his private box at Clemson Memorial Stadium during the South Carolina game, Inabinet appeared somewhat subdued. He had reason to be, although no one fully understood why. Only a day before the game against Clemson's biggest rival, Inabinet had learned from school president Dr. William Atchley that Clemson was going to be placed on probation for a period of two years, starting in 1983, by both the NCAA and the Atlantic Coast Conference. It would mean that Clemson would not be eligible for the conference championship, which it had won in 1981, and could not appear on national or regional television during that period of time.

It was a bitter end to Clemson's 1982 season. After a loss and a tie in its first two games, the Tigers had roared on to nine consecutive victories and won the ACC title for the second straight year. Weeks before the NCAA and ACC penalties were made known, Dr. Atchley announced

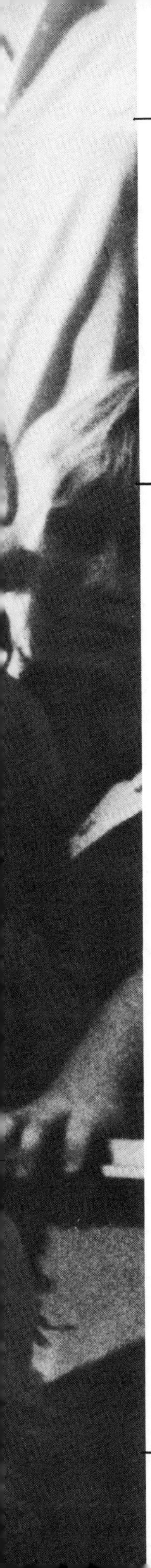

The spirit that is Clemson.

that Clemson would not participate in any bowl game after the 1982 season. It was only a prelude of what was to come. Three days after the South Carolina game, Clemson's probationary status was revealed. The school was being severely penalized for recruiting violations which had taken place several years earlier. Some of the violations had occurred as far back as 1977, before Danny Ford had assumed the position of head coach.

A somber Atchley read from a well-prepared text in announcing the NCAA sanctions:

"The events of this day, and the probation we now face, represent an adversity for Clemson.

"But there's a group of young people who have shown us time and time again how to deal with adversity and disappointment. In fact, they're the ones most affected by the penalties we must bear. Of course, I'm talking about the young men on our football team.

"Their great victory last Saturday was proof again that they can deal with adversity, as they have dealt with adversity every week this entire season. They have shown us how to be champions in victory, champions in defeat, and champions in times of bitter disappointment. By their actions and attitudes they've reminded us of our heritage.

"Clemson University and Clemson people are known for their courage, their high standards of achievement, and their contributions of talent and thought to the affairs of our state and this nation.

"Our first order of business is education, and we pride ourselves on the fact that 75 percent of our students who come here on athletic scholarships end up getting their degrees.

"We also pride ourselves on the fact that we keep our student-athletes on scholarship even after their eligibility is used up, as long as they continue to make satisfactory progress toward graduation.

"Clemson people everywhere have a great tradition to uphold—a tradition of pride, integrity, courage, and the ability to overcome adversity.

"As Clemson people—a special people—we will turn this adversity into opportunity. We will stand tall. We will have greater unity than ever. We will support each other.

"Because no matter what the NCAA, or the ACC, or anyone else does, nothing can defeat the desire and determination of the Clemson family. People are always going to know who we are because we're going to fight to be national champions in everything we choose to do."

Despite the probation, there are positive aspects to it that should be emphasized. One is that nothing can demean the national championship, the first in the school's history, which Clemson won in 1981. The other is that the harshness of the NCAA edict will serve as a rallying cry to bring the Clemson family even closer.